UNDERSTANDING THE SOMME 1916

AN ILLUMINATING BATTLEFIELD GUIDE

Thomas Scotland & Steven Heys

Helion & Company

Helion & Company Limited
26 Willow Road
Solihull
West Midlands
B91 1UE
England
Tel. 0121 705 3393
Fax 0121 711 4075
Email: info@helion.co.uk
Website: www.helion.co.uk
Twitter: @helionbooks
Visit our blog http://blog.helion.co.uk/

Published by Helion & Company 2014
Designed and typeset by Bookcraft Ltd, Stroud, Gloucestershire
Cover designed by Farr out Publications, Wokingham, Berkshire
Printed by Henry Ling Limited, Dorchester, Dorset

Text, images and maps © Thomas Scotland and Steven Heys 2014
Front cover: 51st (Highland) Division Memorial gazing towards Beaumont-Hamel.
Rear cover: View from Serre No 3 Cemetery.

ISBN 978 1 909384 42 2

British Library Cataloguing-in-Publication Data.
A catalogue record for this book is available from the British Library.

For details of other military history titles published by Helion & Company Limited contact the above address, or visit our website: http://www.helion.co.uk.

We always welcome receiving book proposals from prospective authors.

To all those soldiers of the Great War
with no known resting place.

Contents

Main Maps

The main maps are based on the following four maps in the Carte Topographique, Serie Bleue: 2407O, 2407E, 2408O, 2408E

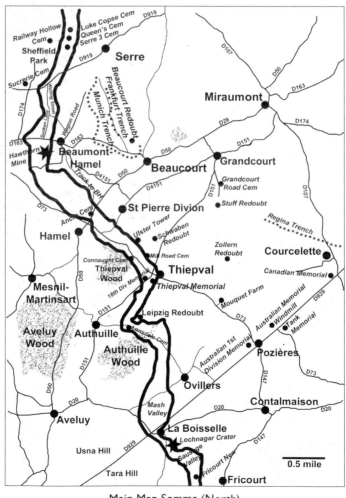

Main Map Somme (North)

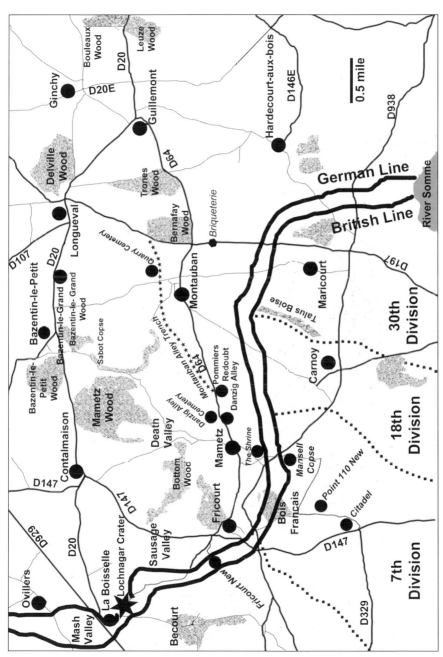

Main Map Somme (South I)

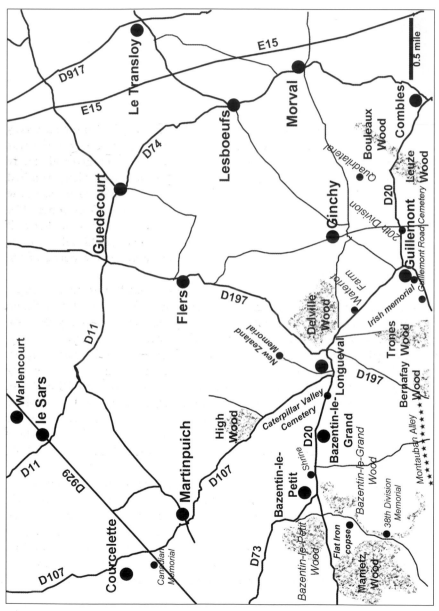

Main Map Somme (South 2)

Chapter 1

Setting the Scene

At the outbreak of the Great War in 1914, Herbert Kitchener, Secretary of State for War, was one of a small minority who thought that the war would not be over by Christmas and that it would be a prolonged and bloody affair. Great Britain had always relied heavily on the Royal Navy and had a very small Regular Army. Kitchener called for volunteers to enlist in the army to form New Army or Service Divisions. By the end of September 1914 half a million men had enlisted, and by the end of the year a further half million had joined the army. While some of these men would fight at Loos in September 1915, the majority would first see action at the Battle of the Somme in July 1916.

At the outbreak of hostilities in August 1914, Great Britain sent an expeditionary force to France under the command of Sir John French to fight on the left flank of the French 5th Army which was positioned near Charleroi on the River Sambre. The British Expeditionary Force (BEF) consisted of four infantry divisions and a cavalry division. With all the appropriate support troops between the channel ports and the front line to ensure that the fighting divisions were supplied with food and munitions, approximately 90,000 men went to France. They made their way to the Belgian town of Mons, where they first saw action on Sunday 23 August 1914. This small British force was referred to by Kaiser Wilhelm II as a "contemptible little army", and those men who survived the battles of 1914 proudly called themselves the "Old Contemptibles."

The 'Old Contemptibles' sustained very heavy casualties, so that by the end of 1914 it was estimated that of the original number of approximately 1,000 officers and men who made up each battalion, only 1 officer and 30 men remained. All the others had been killed, wounded, were missing, or some had become prisoners of war. Battalions of regular infantry soldiers, which had been overseas in different parts of the empire at the outbreak of the Great War, were rushed to France to replace the greatly depleted ranks of the original BEF.

As well as the BEF, which was created to go overseas to wherever it was needed in the British Empire, Great Britain also had a Territorial Army. This had been created to have a defensive role, which was to protect the shores of Great Britain while the BEF went elsewhere. Both the Expeditionary Force and the Territorial Army had been established as part of the Haldane Army Reforms in 1906-07. So great were the losses of men in the opening weeks of the Great War, however, that soldiers of the Territorial Army were invited to sign up for overseas service. Entire divisions were mobilised and by 1915 there were six territorial divisions fighting in France. These included the 46th (North Midland), 47th (London), 48th (South Midland), 49th (West Riding), 50th (Northumbrian) and 51st (Highland). Such was the urgent need for men that some Territorial Army battalions were even separated from their parent divisions, and were sent to fight with Regular Army Divisions which had become critically short of men. For example, the 4th Gordon Highlanders of the 51st Division were sent to fight with the much-depleted 3rd Division near the Belgian city of Ypres. The 3rd Division had suffered very heavy casualties during the First Battle of Ypres during October and November 1914. The first Territorial Army battalion to fight overseas was the 14th Battalion, County of London Regiment (London Scottish), which fought at Messines Ridge (south of Ypres) on 31 October 1914. The compositions of the different units in the British Army are shown in Table 1.1.

By way of contrast, both France and Germany had huge armies comprised of conscripted men. In August 1914, the French armies had a total of 1,300,000 men, and the German armies had 850,000. Moreover, the Germans could mobilise 4,300,000 trained men within a matter of days. In the opening months of the war, the brunt of the allied fighting was borne by France.

Because France and Russia had signed an alliance in 1892, Germany knew that if there was going to be a war it would have to be fought on two fronts. The

Table 1.1 BEF formations and units.

Formation/Unit	Command Rank	Strength
Army	General	Approximately 150,000
Corps	Lieutenant-General	50,000 but depends on number of divisions allocated to the Corps
Division	Major-General	12,000
Brigade	Brigadier	4,000
Battalion	Lieutenant-Colonel	1,000
Company	Captain	250
Platoon	Lieutenant	60
Section	Corporal	15

Schlieffen Plan was developed to deal with this problem. Its success depended on defeating France quickly in the west before tackling the Russians in the east. This entailed the use of seven armies against the French five. The three northern German armies would sweep through Belgium and attack the French from the north. In the centre they would attack through Luxembourg and push the French back through the Ardennes, while the two German armies in the south in Alsace and Lorraine would soak up pressure from the French.

The Germans knew that the French would be desperate to retake Alsace and Lorraine after forfeiting them in the Franco-Prussian War of 1870-71 and that they would be sure to attack the two German armies in Alsace and Lorraine with utmost strength. Meanwhile the other German armies would push the French forces back and the First German Army would sweep behind the French and would trap them by driving the French armies towards Alsace and Lorraine. The Germans had planned that this could all be achieved within six weeks, which was the time they thought it would take Russia to mobilise and then the Germans could turn their attention and military forces to Russia in the east.

The French implemented their own plan at the outbreak of hostilities, which was called 'Plan 17'. The Germans would be attacked vigorously on every front with every available resource and would be removed from French territory. French losses in the opening days of the war in these initial battles (known as

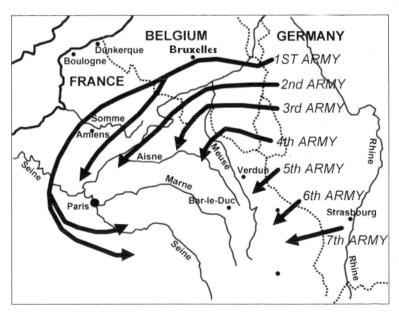

Figure 1.1 Schlieffen Plan.

"The Battle of the Frontiers") were enormous. As a result, the French retreated from their frontiers with Belgium, Luxembourg and Germany, and crossed the River Marne where they stopped. The BEF during this time was on the left flank of the French 5th Army, where it kept its position, withdrawing 120 miles from Mons to the east of Paris between 23 August and 5 September 1914.

However, the Schlieffen Plan did not go as was intended and soon began to unravel. The allied armies were in full retreat, and sensing victory, the German pursuit of them was relentless. Von Kluck, commander of the First German Army made a critical mistake. Instead of sweeping to the rear of any

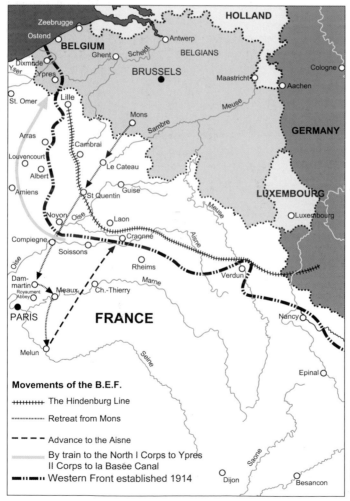

Movements of the B.E.F.

╫╫╫╫╫╫ The Hindenburg Line

⋯⋯⋯⋯⋯ Retreat from Mons

━ ━ ━ ━ Advance to the Aisne

▬▬▬ By train to the North I Corps to Ypres
     II Corps to la Basée Canal
▬╍▬╍▬ Western Front established 1914

Figure 1.2
Western Front
1914-18.

French forces, which would have meant going to the west of Paris, and then herding them into the trap in Alsace and Lorraine, he marched to the east of Paris, exposing the flank of the First German Army to a new French 6th Army, formed for the defence of Paris.

The French struck hard into the side of the First German Army and turning to face the threat, a gap opened between the First and Second German Armies, which was exploited by the BEF and by the French 5th Army, while other French armies also went onto the offensive. What followed was the Battle of the Marne between 5 and 9 September 1914. This was a most decisive victory for the allies. The Germans withdrew to north of the River Aisne, where they stopped and began to dig defensive trenches to hold the allies at bay.

Fierce fighting ensued, in what became known as the Battle of the Aisne, but neither side made progress and stalemate became established. To the north, there followed a series of attempted outflanking manoeuvres, extending to the Belgian coast, the so called "race to the sea" when each side tried to gain

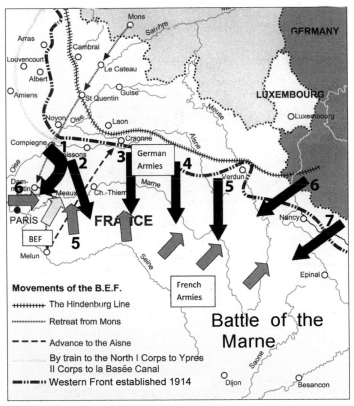

Figure 1.3 Battle of the Marne.

the upper hand, but each failed. As they moved, men dug trenches and the Western Front was formed. As part of the outflanking process, the BEF took up positions from La Bassée to Ypres in French Flanders and Belgium respectively to be closer to their supply lines. A fierce battle was fought at Ypres during October and November 1914 during which the notorious Ypres Salient was formed. To the south, the lines extended to the Swiss border.

Great Britain was under considerable pressure from her French ally to take over more of the Western Front and to play a more active role. By September 1915, the British section of the Western Front extended from Ypres in the north to Loos-en-Gohelle, just north of Vimy Ridge, in the south.

In April and May 1915, the British Second Army fought a defensive battle in Belgium at Ypres during the Second Battle of Ypres (Figure 1.4), while the British First Army commanded by General Sir Douglas Haig launched attacks in northern France at Neuve Chapelle, Aubers Ridge, Givenchy and Festubert between March and May 1915 to support its French ally. These were relatively small-scale battles compared with subsequent engagements and the British learnt from each of these. These attacks invariably originated in response to French requests for support while they, the French, launched larger-scale offensives further south.

These requests from the French were partly to give support, but partly to draw the British into committing themselves to playing a greater role, which they did in September 1915 at the Battle of Loos. Once again, General Haig commanded the British First Army.

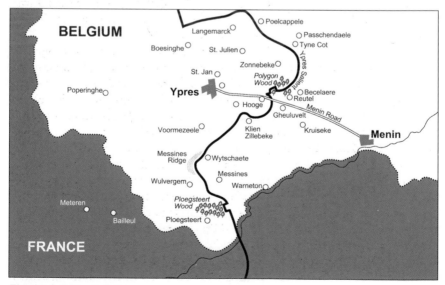

Figure 1.4 Ypres Salient.

Figure 1.5
British Offensives French
Flanders 1915.

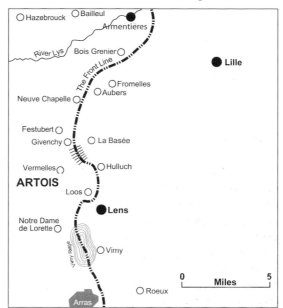

Loos was characterised by a major shortage of shells, because the industrial might of Great Britain had not yet been fully harnessed to the war effort. For the first and last time, the British high command placed reliance on chlorine gas to secure a successful outcome, which failed. In places the wind was blowing in the wrong direction, so that British soldiers were asphyxiated by their own gas.

In the wake of Loos, there were important developments. It was recognised that Sir John French did not have the necessary qualities to be Commander-in-Chief of the British armies in France and Flanders, and he was removed from office. General Haig was appointed Commander-in-Chief in his place. It is against this background of failure at Loos that Haig would undergo his first major test at the Battle of the Somme in 1916. Two British armies fought under Haig's direction on the Somme. These were the Fourth Army commanded by General Sir Henry Rawlinson and the Reserve Army (later renamed Fifth Army) under General Sir Hubert Gough. Both of these men had been promoted to command armies having been corps commanders at the Battle of Loos in 1915. All three men were new to their promoted positions and therefore lacked much experience on taking command.

Meanwhile at home in Great Britain, the shell shortage of 1915 was addressed by the appointment of David Lloyd George as Minister of Munitions in May of that year. The new minister immediately set about mobilising British industry and increasing shell production. Germany had made preparations for war and had accumulated huge stores of shells, and Great Britain was a long way behind. By June 1916, British production of heavy guns had greatly increased to 150 a month and shell production had increased to allow an expenditure of 300,000 shells every week.

On 23 December 1915, Haig agreed that the British would take over more of the Western Front from the French, so that by January 1916, the British section extended as far south as the River Somme. By then, Great Britain had additional divisions available including two Canadian Divisions. The Indian Corps, including two infantry divisions and a cavalry brigade had arrived in 1914, but suffered greatly because of the climatic conditions in the winter months of 1915 and so their infantry was re-deployed to Mesopotamia. However, the Indian Cavalry remained in France as part of the overall cavalry force. This was maintained in readiness should there be a British breakthrough and would be used to exploit any such penetration of the German defences. By mid-1915, with increasing numbers of men being deployed on the Western Front, a British Third Army was formed in France. Initially, this was commanded by General Sir Charles Monro and was deployed astride the River Somme. General Rawlinson then briefly held command when Monro went elsewhere.

A further Canadian Division arrived and so a Canadian Corps containing three divisions was formed. The Australian and New Zealand forces (Anzacs) arrived in France in early 1916, so that with many more troops at his disposal, Haig was able to expand his armies. General Rawlinson was given command of the newly formed Fourth Army on 5 February 1916, while Sir Edmund Allenby took over the command of the Third Army from Rawlinson.

Upon his appointment as Commander-in-Chief, Haig was instructed by Secretary of State for War, Lord Kitchener, to cooperate closely with his French ally. General Joffre, commander of French forces was very anxious indeed to pursue a joint venture, with the British playing a major role in carrying it out. In fact, French losses in 1915 had been so great that without a major British offensive to increasingly shoulder the burden, France might lose the war. Since the start of the war, the French had suffered almost 2 million casualties killed, wounded and missing.

Chantilly Conference

On 29 December 1915, an inter-allied conference was held in Chantilly. Joffre proposed a combined offensive by both French and British armies astride the River Somme in the mid-summer of 1916. Joffre wanted Haig to take responsibility for joining the offensive on a 12 mile front north of the River Somme. All plans were thrown into disarray when the Germans seized the initiative in February 1916 and attacked the French at Verdun. As a result, the French had to divert a great many soldiers unexpectedly to fight the Germans at Verdun and the Somme became a predominantly British battle, with a revised goal to relieve the pressure on the French at Verdun. Rawlinson's Fourth Army was given the responsibility of conducting the British offensive at the Battle of the Somme, while Allenby would support Rawlinson with the Third Army.

BRITISH FORCES ON THE SOMME IN 1916

Fourth Army

Rawlinson's Fourth Army played a leading role in the Battle of the Somme. The northern limit of his section of the Western Front was level with the German held village of Serre, while the southern limit was opposite Maricourt. Of eleven divisions employed on the Fourth Army's front on 1 July 1916, seven were New Army Divisions. The way in which the British forces were lined up against the Germans on the first day of the battle is shown in Figure 1.6.

Table 1.2 summarises corps and divisional commanding officers in the Fourth Army and is provided as a historical record rather than essential reading!

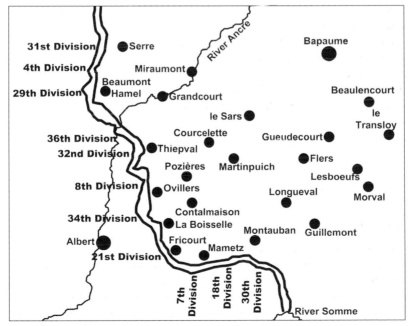

Figure 1.6 Fourth Army Divisions 1 July 1916.

Third Army (Diversionary)

In addition, the VII Corps of Allenby's Third Army which was commanded by Lieutenant-General Sir Thomas D'Oyly Snow, planned to create a diversion at Gommecourt, which was a couple of miles north of Serre. It was hoped that this would relieve the pressure on the Fourth Army by diverting German artillery and men to deal with the British attack at Gommecourt. However, the diversion did not succeed. Two territorial divisions in the VII Corps, the 56th (London) and 46th (North Midland), suffered 4,314 and 2,455 casualties, respectively. There were no gains made. Moreover, this diversion did not result in the movement of a single piece of German artillery to Gommecourt from the Fourth Army area as had been hoped; unfortunately the Germans already had formidable defences in place in Gommecourt to deal with the diversionary attack. The attack at Gommecourt will not be discussed further since its brief role had no further bearing on events on the Somme battlefield.

Reserve Army

The newly-formed Reserve Army was commanded by General Gough. Gough was allocated the three British cavalry divisions and two infantry divisions (the 19th and 49th). After the Fourth Army had broken through German positions the expectation was that the Reserve Army cavalry would attack Bapaume, a large town at the northern end of the battlefield area and prevent the arrival of German reinforcements. The cavalry would prevent the escape of retreating enemy infantry, and the Reserve Army would then be able to pave the way for the Fourth Army to break out behind the German forces and roll up their defences.

Table 1.2 Corps and Divisional Commanders in the British Fourth Army, 1 July 1916.

Corps	Corps Commander	Division	Division Commander
VIII	Hunter-Weston	31	O'Gowan
		4	Lambton
		29	de Lisle
X	Morland	36	Nugent
		32	Rycroft
III	Pulteney	8	Hudson
		34	Ingouville-Williams
XV	Horne	21	Campbell
		7	Watts
XIII	Congreve	18	Maxse
		30	Shea

Australian Imperial Force (AIF)

Four Australian Divisions fought in France in 1916, the 1st, 2nd, 4th and 5th. The 1st and 2nd Divisions had fought at Gallipoli in 1915, before being sent to Egypt where they re-grouped following their losses at Gallipoli. Reinforcements were sent from Australia which allowed the formation of two further divisions, the 4th and 5th.

The Australian Divisions first started to arrive in France in March 1916. The 1st and 2nd Divisions were particularly involved in the fighting at Pozières (part of the Reserve Army), while the 4th Division fought at Mouquet Farm after the capture of Pozières. The 5th Division was involved in an action at Fromelles in Northern France on the night of 19/20 July 1916, which was a diversion instigated to draw enemy resources away from the Somme area. However, it failed completely with substantial loss of life and 5,500 casualties were sustained by the Australian 5th Division. The 3rd Australian Division was raised in Australia and then went directly to Great Britain for final training and did not see action during the Battle of the Somme. It arrived in France in December 1916 after the battle was over.

New Zealand Division

The New Zealand Expeditionary Force (NZEF) was closely tied to the AIF for much of the war. When the Gallipoli campaign began, the New Zealand contingent was insufficient to complete a division of its own, so it was combined with the 4th Australian Infantry Brigade. This resulted in formation of the New Zealand and Australian Division. This division, along with the Australian 1st Division, formed the Australian and New Zealand Army Corps (ANZAC).

After the Gallipoli campaign had ended, the NZEF formed its own infantry division, which served on the Western Front for the rest of the war. From 1916 until the formation of the Australian Corps in 1918 (made up of the five Australian Divisions) there were always two 'ANZAC' Corps (I Anzac Corps and II Anzac Corps) despite the fact that there was only one New Zealand Division. During the Battle of the Somme, the New Zealand Division fought with the Fourth Army.

Canadian Divisions

Three Canadian Divisions, the 1st, 2nd and 3rd, fought on the Somme. They arrived in September and relieved the Australian Divisions. They were involved in heavy fighting near Pozières at Mouquet Farm, at Courcelette and at Regina Trench with the Reserve Army.

The 1st Newfoundland Battalion also fought on the Somme, but Newfoundland was not part of Canada in 1916. It was an independent dominion in the early 20th century and only joined Canada in 1949. The Newfoundlanders fought with the regular 29th Division on the opening day of the Battle of the Somme.

The South African Brigade

The South African Brigade sailed from Alexandria in Egypt to France between 13 and 15 April 1916. By 23 April 1916, the leading units had arrived at Steenwerck in Flanders. The entire brigade came under orders of the 9th (Scottish) Division, in which it replaced the 28th Brigade since the 9th (Scottish) Division had sustained such heavy losses at the Battle of Loos.

Indian Army

In 1914, Indian Expeditionary Force A was sent to reinforce the British Expeditionary Force. In France it formed the Indian Cavalry Corps and Indian Army Corps composed of, the 3rd (Lahore) and 7th (Meerut) Divisions. (In France, these formations were simply known as the 'Lahore' and 'Meerut' Divisions, to distinguish them from the 3rd and 7th British Divisions.) The Indian Army Corps fought in Flanders and France in 1914 and 1915, but barely endured the harsh winter before subsequent transfer to Mesopotamia. The Indian Cavalry remained, some of whom were involved in the 14 July 1916 attack at High Wood.

Number of British Divisions on the Somme 1916

By the time the Battle of the Somme petered out in mid-November 1916, 44 British Divisions had rotated through the Somme and seen action. There were 10 Regular Army Divisions, 8 Territorial, 1 Naval and 25 New Army Divisions. The New Army Divisions made up 58% of the total British presence on the Somme.

GERMAN ARMY ON THE SOMME 1916

Prussian military forces had progressively increased in number following the accession to the throne of Wilhelm I in 1860. The war of 1866 made Prussia head of the North German Federation, which meant that Hesse-Darmstadt, Württemberg, Bavaria and Baden were bound to place their forces at the disposal of Prussia in time of war. The formation of the German Empire in 1871 made expansion of armed forces easier still, for by the Constitution, one percent of the population could be in training under arms.[1]

German forces that the British encountered on the Somme were much more experienced than the British New Army Divisions. Germany had operated a conscript system before the Great War and 50% of her men between 20 and 22 years of age had spent time in the army. After leaving the army their names were retained on a reserve list and they underwent regular training with the reserve until the age of 27. Even then they underwent further training up to age 39 with the Landwehr. The Landwehr in Prussia was first formed in March 1813, which called up all men capable of bearing arms between the ages of eighteen and forty-five, and not serving in the regular army, for the defence of the country. After 1815 this force was made an integral part of the Prussian Army, each brigade being composed of one line and one Landwehr regiment. In 1859 the Landwehr troops were relegated to the position of reserves to be recalled in times of national emergency. Finally, after the men had been in the Landwehr, they were then part of the Landsturm until the age of 45, during which time they could be called into military service to act as a 'home guard'.

General Erich von Falkenhayn was Chief of General Staff and General Fritz von Below commanded the German Second Army on the Somme. Von Below was sufficiently concerned by the build up of British forces during the early part of 1916 that he considered launching an attack. He requested more forces to carry this out, but a Russian offensive in the East required resources to be deployed there and so prevented this from happening. The German Second Army then had to bear the brunt of the allied attack. On 1 July 1916, von Below had six divisions in the front line (121st, 12th, 28th Reserve, 26th Reserve, 52nd and 2nd Guards Reserve). There were a further four and a half divisions in reserve and also additional heavy artillery at von Below's disposal.

Falkenhayn was replaced as commander of German forces at the end of August 1916 by Field Marshal Paul von Hindenburg. General Erich Ludendorff was made First Quartermaster General, and was Hindenburg's deputy. These two men would come to dominate German military policy on the Western Front for the remainder of the war. Falkenhayn was replaced because of his Verdun policy; the battle of Verdun was a battle which began in February 1916 and lasted until the following December. He opted to attack the fortified city of Verdun where circumstances favoured a successful German offensive.

---

1 Edmonds, J.E., *Military Operations France and Belgium*, 1914 (London: Imperial War Museum Department of Printed Books, in association with Battery Press, Nashville, 1996), pp.20-22.

Verdun was isolated on three sides and railway communications to the French rear were restricted. Falkenhayn believed that the French would cling fanatically to what would become a death trap. He believed that the French General Staff would be compelled to throw in every man they had to protect Verdun and that 'France would bleed to death'. However, Falkenhayn's policy also resulted in very heavy German casualties.

German strategy changed under the new regime of Hindenburg and Ludendorff. The concept of a "defensive" battle was introduced, the idea being to move away from the belief that men must line up shoulder to shoulder in trenches, and that any lost ground must be immediately retaken by a counter-attack. The new German thinking was that their enemy should wear himself out against a more thinly held front, but which was well supplied with machine guns and with *minenwerfers* (trench mortars). Defence became more elastic with reserves being held further behind the front line, and only going forward in a counter-attack to recapture lost ground. While this policy was introduced to a certain extent on the Somme, it would only become established practice by 1917.

THE ROLE OF ARTILLERY AT THE BATTLE OF THE SOMME

The shortage of shells in 1915 and the appointment of Lloyd George as Minister of Munitions in May, led to a mobilisation of British industry as part of a concerted war effort. In addition, the new ministry included a "Trench Warfare Department" and a "Munitions Invention Department", which between them were responsible for most of the research into air defence and chemical warfare, as well as development of grenades and mortars. Shell production between the months of March 1916 and January 1917 is summarised in Table 1.3.

The Great War was, first and foremost, an artillery war. The aims of British artillery on the Somme may be summarised as having three clear functions:

- Destruction of barbed wire;
- Destruction of dugouts;
- Destruction of hostile batteries (counter-battery work).

Table 1.3 British shell production per month.

Date	Shrapnel	High Explosive, Smoke, Chemical
March 1916	952,708	818,932
September 1916	1,885,234	3,279,776
January 1917	2,868,234	4,129,945

The British bombardment commenced on 24 June. Initially planned for five days, it was extended to seven due to inclement weather. Nothing like it had been experienced before as a total of 1.7 million shells were fired over this short period of time. Yet, it achieved much less than expected. There was a shortage of high explosive shells, and a significant number failed to explode, because manufacture had been faulty. The evidence is still there for you to see, since many unexploded shells are still being found, particularly when fields are ploughed to reveal an iron harvest of ordnance that is set aside by local farmers for removal and safe disposal.

As a result of faulty high explosive shells, much of the barbed wire was still intact after the bombardment. It would require considerably more experience with shell manufacture and the later development, and use, of the so called "106 fuzes" which detonated the shell on impact very effectively before British shells could reliably destroy German barbed wire. However, these would not come into regular use until 1917. German soldiers had not been killed as they were protected by their deep dugouts. The Germans had been on the Somme for two years already and had had the time to construct some of the best defensive systems of the day. Counter-battery work was in a very early and primitive state in 1916 and, in fact, very little attention was given to it by the British artillery.

Figure 1.7 Iron harvest on the Somme.

There was a further very important contributory factor to the failure of the British artillery barrage in the days leading up to 1 July 1916. Generals Rawlinson and Haig disagreed about the goals they were aiming for when the battle began. Rawlinson favoured a limited type of offensive action called "bite and hold". By this it was meant that there would be a steady but limited advance, capturing a small amount of enemy territory and consolidating this gain before attacking the enemy again in a similar fashion. Haig had a tendency to be over optimistic about what could be achieved and this put men at risk. He anticipated that the coming offensive action would result in a successful breakthrough of the enemy lines. Haig instructed Rawlinson to double the depth of artillery fire on German positions, to help bring this about. However, he did not have extra artillery to do this, and consequently there was a 50% reduction in the density of fire. As a result, in the centre and north of the battlefield particularly, counter-battery work was almost non-existent, although in the south, artillery arrangements were significantly better, and the positive impact of this will be explained later.

As 0730 on 1 July approached, the constant artillery barrage lulled men into a false sense of security. Nothing like it had ever been encountered before. Surely no one could survive such a sustained bombardment. Nevertheless, the failure of artillery on 1 July was the single most important cause of the disaster that will be remembered forever as the worst single day in British military history. The following chapters will examine what actually happened on that day and over the subsequent days, weeks and months. We will endeavour to explain why things happened the way they did.

Chapter 2

Montauban and Pommiers Redoubt, 1 July 1916

It is generally assumed that 1 July 1916 was a complete disaster, but this is not entirely true. There were two relative successes here in the southern part of the battlefield, at Montauban and Mametz. Of course, the key word here is 'relative'. Our journey around the Somme Battlefield will start here in Montauban and Mametz and to orientate yourself check Main Map Somme (South1) at the beginning of this book.

The village of Carnoy, a good starting point when thinking about the attack in the south, was just behind the British line on 1 July. The divisions which attacked from near Carnoy were the 18th and 30th Divisions. The 30th Division was one of Kitchener's New Army Divisions, made of mostly volunteers from 1914, and comprised the battalions shown in Table 2.1.

Each BEF Division was allotted a pioneer battalion which would be devoted to various types of labouring work. These men were experienced in the various construction industry trades and general labouring. They underwent basic military training including firearms, but were also supplied with the necessary additional tools required for the work they were assigned to do in the field as pioneers.

Table 2.1 30th Division infantry orders of battle 1 July 1916.

21st Brigade	89th Brigade	90th Brigade
18th King's (2nd Liverpool Pals)	17th King's (1st Liverpool Pals)	2nd Royal Scots Fusiliers
19th Manchesters (4th Manchester Pals)	19th King's (3rd Liverpool Pals)	16th Manchesters (1st Manchester Pals)
2nd Wilts	20th King's (4th Liverpool Pals)	17th Manchesters (2nd Manchester Pals)
2nd Green Howards	2nd Bedfords	18th Manchesters (3rd Manchester Pals)

Pioneers 11th South Lancs

It was not unusual to include occasional Regular Army battalions in any New Army Division to add experience, although even in Regular Army battalions there were few soldiers who had been involved in the start of the war in 1914. Most had been killed or wounded. The aim of the 30th Division's attack was to capture the village of Montauban that was due north of its position. The right flank of the 30th Division marked the southern limit of the part of the Western Front held by the British. The boundary with the adjacent French troops was the village of Maricourt. Here, British men fought alongside French soldiers who were fighting on the north bank of the River Somme.

The 18th (Eastern) Division was also a New Army Division, and its battalions were recruited from London and the southeast of England. It was made up of the battalions shown in Table 2.2. The 18th Division attacked German positions between Montauban itself and approximately two thirds of the way towards the adjacent village of Mametz where the 7th Division was attacking. The attacking formations of the 30th and 18th Divisions at 0730, 1 July 1916 are shown in Figure 2.1.

The men of the 18th Division had to attack up a significant slope to reach the German positions. Over the summit of this slope, adjacent to the road between Montauban and Mametz, was a German strongpoint called Pommiers Redoubt, which was just over half a mile from the British front line. Pommiers Redoubt was a formidable circular trench fortress, bristling with machine guns and protected by belts of barbed wire.

From Carnoy follow the road, the "Grande Rue", up the hill as it goes towards the village of Montauban. Carnoy is tucked in a valley and as you leave it you will see Montauban appearing on the skyline ahead of you. The easiest way to identify many of the villages on the Somme is to look at the church steeples because they are usually different, and can be distinctive, in their appearance. The church steeple in Montauban has an unmistakably bulbous appearance. In 1916 it was the largest village on the Somme having some 274 houses. It is considerably smaller today, like all the surrounding villages. This area never seemed to fully recover from the events which took place here during the Great War.

Table 2.2 18th Division infantry orders of battle 1 July 1916.

53rd Brigade	54th Brigade	55th Brigade
8th Norfolks	11th Royal Fusiliers	7th Queen's
6th Royal Berks	7th Bedfords	7th Buffs
10th Essex	6th Northamptons	8th East Surreys
8th Suffolks	12th Middlesex	7th Royal West Kents

Pioneers 8th Royal Sussex

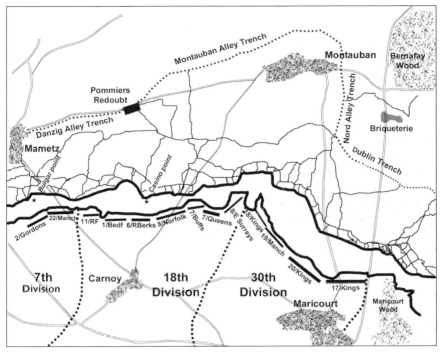

Figure 2.1 18th and 30th Divisions 1 July 1916.

As you look to the right of Montauban, you will see Bernafay Wood. Before the Great War, a local railway branch line ran provided a service connecting the villages with each other and also to neighboring larger towns. Montauban Station was located within Bernafay Wood, but was completely destroyed during the war although it was rebuilt later. When the trains finally stopped running in the 1950s, the station building was initially maintained but then was converted to a bed and breakfast which certainly now is very atmospheric! It is ideally suited to groups of travelling Scotsmen on bicycles who like to play the bagpipes without being asked to do so and so disturbing the neighbours – as we do frequently! Photographs of the station both before the Great War, and now are shown in Figures 2.2. and 2.3.

As you continue on your journey towards Montauban, look to your immediate right and you will see a long, thin, finger of a wood becoming visible a few hundred yards away. This projects up from the eastern margin of Carnoy, and points towards Montauban. This is Talus Boise, and the British front line ran around the tip of this slender wood running from your left to right. The tip of the wood was also a divisional boundary between the 30th and 18th Divisions. Figure 2.4 shows Talus Boise from a distance. This

Figure 2.2 Montauban Station within Bernafay Wood before the Great War; the station was re-built after the war and closed in the 1950's.

Figure 2.3 Montauban Station today is a very atmospheric bed and breakfast accommodation; situated in a now tranquil setting within Bernafay Wood, one can only imagine what it must have been like here in July 1916.

photograph was taken from approximately two miles away, from a position just behind the British front line of the 7th Division before 1 July which is called the Bois Français sector. You can see a few of the houses in Carnoy and the two or three isolated trees in a line over a few hundred yards to give you the line of the road between Carnoy and Montauban. Talus Boise can be seen to the right of the houses. On the skyline you can see Bernafay Wood, which is mostly overlapping the adjacent Trônes Wood, which you will be visiting later.

Keeping Talus Boise in view, stop when you become level with the tip of it. You are now on the approximate location of the British front line where it crossed the road. The German front line was parallel to your position and a couple of hundred yards to the north. The village of Montauban, which was heavily fortified, was about three quarters of a mile behind the German front line. The cyclist coming towards you is actually right in the middle of No Man's Land.

If you look to the left of the road as you face towards Montauban, you will see a steady upward incline. You cannot see the summit from your position. Men from the 18th Division went up this slope through the fields towards

Figure 2.4 Talus Boise from the heights behind the British positions of the 7th Division at Bois Français; Talus Boise projecting to the north beyond the village of Carnoy, its tip marked the position of 18th and 30th Divisional boundaries. Bernafay Wood, overlapped by Trônes Wood, can be seen beyond and Leuze Wood is seen on the horizon.

Figure 2.5 The cyclist coming towards the camera is in No Man's Land. The village of Montauban is behind the cyclist. To the right of the village is Bernafay Wood. The tip of Trônes Wood can also be seen, although it is mostly concealed behind Bernafay Wood.

Pommiers Redoubt, the fortified German position near the summit of the hill, and close to the road between Montauban and Mametz already referred to. You cannot see where it was from your present position.

Turn round to face back towards Carnoy, and look towards a wooded area situated on a hillside a couple of miles away in the 2 o'clock position. This is the Bois Français, from where the photograph in Figure 2.4 was taken. The front lines swept away from where you are standing, and went up and around that hillside, before descending towards the village of Fricourt (not visible from your present position). The Bois Français section of the line was held by the 7th Division and will be visited shortly.

Turning back to face Montauban, the 30th Division attack began from the tip of Talus Boise to your right and extended further over to the right (the east), towards Maricourt, where British soldiers advancing on the far right were in contact with attacking French forces. The 18th Division attacked from the tip of the wood, across towards your present position on the road in front of you and over the fields to the left of the road. It attacked the ground from the left margin of Montauban as you look from your position to two thirds of the way along the road towards the next village of Mametz. It is generally assumed that none of the objectives were captured during the opening day of the Somme offensive. However, this is not strictly true, because here in the

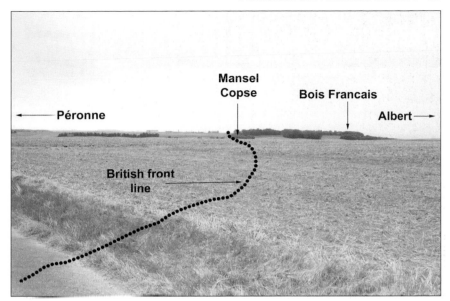

Figure 2.6 Looking in the opposite direction from the same position on the road between Montauban and Carnoy towards high ground where 7th Division had its front line prior to 1 July. One of the few advantageous positions held by the British on the Somme, British observers on the higher ground could easily register on the enemy guns.

south, the 18th and 30th Divisions achieved their goals. As you will appreciate from Figure 2.4, there is a wonderful view of Moutauban and its surroundings from the Bois Français sector. This provided clear views over German positions around Montauban and beyond.

British artillery spotters were ideally placed to observe German gun positions and trench systems. A concentration of British artillery fire during the seven days before the start of the Battle of the Somme (as explained before) inflicted heavy casualties on defending German troops around Montauban. Adjacent French artillery also helped to bombard German positions here and tried to destroy as much of the German defences as they could in the days before the attack began on 1 July. The batteries of the defending 12th and 28th Reserve Divisions were badly disrupted because British artillery here took full advantage of the position to pour heavy fire onto hostile artillery positions. Generally speaking, counter-battery fire was sorely neglected and lacked effectiveness during the battle, but this was not so here in the south, where the importance of good artillery support was appreciated. It also happened that there were relatively few German artillery pieces around Montauban, most of them being concentrated against the British to the north at the villages of Serre, Beaumont-Hamel and Thiepval and towards the centre of the battlefield at La Boisselle. The barbed wire protecting the German front line was almost completely destroyed around Montauban and enemy front line trenches here were also badly disrupted.

The British used the first primitive creeping barrage against positions around Mametz and Montauban. In a creeping barrage, artillery fired on a given target, then moved further on at a predetermined time and over a designated distance in front of the attacking troops. The advancing infantry moved behind the creeping barrage and were protected by it, because German defenders had to protect themselves from the barrage until it passed over them. Elsewhere British artillery fire moved directly from bombarding the German front line to targeting positions further to the rear.

Sounds by Night

I hear the dull low thunder of the guns
Beyond the hills that doze uneasily
A sullen doomful growl that ever runs
From end to end of the heavy freighted sky:
A friend of mine writes squatted on the floor,
And scrapes by yellow spluttering candle light.
Ah, hush! He breathes, and gazes at the door,
That creaks on rusty hinge, in pale afright!
No words spoke he, nor I for well we knew
What rueful things these sounds did tell.
A pause-I hear the trees sway sighing thro’
The gloom like dismal moan of hollow knell,
Then out across the dark, and startling me
Burst forth a laugh, a shout of drunken glee.
                    Roderick Watson Kerr MC 1893-1960.

With grateful thanks to Neil Kerr for permission to reproduce his father’s poem

There was less strength in depth to German defences here compared with their positions at Serre, Beaumont-Hamel, Thiepval and La Boisselle. German troops at Montauban were more concentrated within the front line trench system, which meant they were particularly vulnerable to the effects of shelling if it was delivered accurately. Once the German front lines had been overrun by the British in the southern part, the way was open to Montauban beyond because of their less well developed lines of defence behind the front line system. In this area of attack, the British employed "mopping up" troops, who followed on after the soldiers carrying out the initial attack had taken the front line. These men were ready to stop German soldiers emerging from dugouts behind the attacking British troops and firing on them from the rear.

On the 18th Division front, a series of small mines was detonated under the German front line close to the road where you are standing. Huge newly developed flame projectors were also employed. These were very primitive weapons of mass destruction. They took many hours of work to install below ground in covered saps where they were prepared to discharge an oily flaming stream until of no further use.

Thus having overwhelmed the front line trench system, the way was open for the 18th Division to advance up the slope towards Pommiers Redoubt. Here, the barbed wire was not cut and each man carried his own wire cutters that were painstakingly employed against the remaining barbed wire obstacles. 18th Division's rigorous pre-battle training familiarised its attacking units with the enemy by considered use of specially prepared scale models. Pommiers Redoubt was attacked on both sides and by 0930 was in British hands.

The 18th Division sustained 3,115 casualties killed, wounded and missing. One of their casualties was Captain W.P. Nevill, of the 8th East Surreys who began his attack near the tip of Talus Boise on the right flank of the 18th Division. After consultation with his commanding officer, Nevill had issued four footballs, one to each of the four platoons of men in the company he commanded. The plan was to kick them across No Man's Land as they advanced to help keep the men going. However, heavy German machine gun fire resulted in many casualties including Nevill himself, who was killed and is buried in Carnoy Military Cemetery (Grave reference E 28). Advance troops from the 18th Division went beyond Pommiers Redoubt and even ventured down the incline on the other side, before returning to consolidate their position in Montauban Alley Trench (see below).

On the far right of the 30th Division attack, men from the 17th and 20th King's (1st and 4th Liverpool Pals) supported by the 19th King's (3rd Liverpool Pals) and 2nd Bedfords found the wire well cut and the German front line was quickly taken with very few casualties. The advance continued quickly up the slope towards Montauban and to a trench called Dublin Trench which was to the south of Montauban. To the left, men of the 18th King's (2nd Liverpool Pals) and 19th Manchesters (4th Manchester Pals) met stiffer opposition, coming under the same machine gun fire that Nevill and the East Surreys were also experiencing with the 18th Division. Nevertheless, progress was made and the men on the left of the attack met up with those on the right. A fortified briqueterie (see Figure 2.1) in front of Montauban was captured by the British, and shortly after 1030 the barrage moved into Montauban itself and a smoke screen protected advancing British soldiers. The reserves then moved through from the rear to overcome the remaining German resistance in Montauban. The 2nd Royal Scots Fusiliers, 16th Manchesters (1st Manchester Pals) and 17th Manchesters (2nd Manchester Pals) occupied the village.

Men from the 30th Division pushed on and captured Montauban Alley, which was a trench on the reverse slope north of the village and which linked with Pommiers Redoubt towards the left. It was a job well done. As they occupied this position, surviving German defenders could be seen running away through the fields towards the second main defensive line which ran through the village of Longueval, about a mile to the north. The 30th Division sustained 3,011 casualties killed, wounded and missing on 1 July 1916.

Keep going till you reach the top of the road where it meets the D64, turn right and go into Montauban and go past the church. Shortly before you leave the village, stop at the memorial on your right-hand side which was erected to commemorate the Liverpool and Manchester Pals who captured the village on 1 July.

It is hard to imagine what it must have been like standing on this spot on 1 July in the shattered ruins of the village, one of the very few captured on the first day of the Battle of the Somme. As you will see, the 7th and 21st Divisions fighting around the villages of Mametz and Fricourt respectively,

Figure 2.7 Manchester and Liverpool Pals Memorial.

also experienced some success, but there was nothing to be optimistic about elsewhere.

Take the road opposite the Liverpool and Manchester Pals Memorial, and follow it out of the village (to the north), now going out of Montauban. There is a quite a steep downward slope as you leave the village down into a valley where you will see Quarry Cemetery, Montauban. Stop and look back up the hill you have just descended. Montauban Alley Trench, which was captured by the 30th Division, was approximately half-way between where you are standing and the village beyond. It extended from Pommiers Redoubt to your right and then passed to the top (northern) end of Bernafay Wood to your left. You will appreciate that Montauban Alley was on a downward slope behind the village, unseen by British eyes from ground level, and therefore relatively safely positioned from shellfire. The Germans commonly employed every contour and geographical feature of the land to their advantage when they sited their trenches.

Now retrace your steps to Montauban and return to the Manchester and Liverpool Pals Memorial. After 1 July, General Rawlinson who was in command of the British Fourth Army favoured another attack on those

Figure 2.8 At certain times of the year, notably after the fields have been ploughed, it is possible to see the outline of trench systems weaving their way through the fields as wispy lines of chalk. This is thought to be Montauban Alley Trench, situated on a reverse slope behind the village of Montauban, and therefore protected from British artillery spotting and attack.

objectives which were not taken on the first day of the battle. These were in the more northerly parts of the battlefield between Serre and La Boisselle, where what happened will be explained later. However, he was overruled by Haig, who decided to exploit the gains made around Montauban and Mametz (Chapter 3).

The British Fourth Army would now confine its fighting to the south of the main road running between Albert and Bapaume (see Main Maps Somme (North) and Somme (South 1)), while the Reserve Army (later to be called the Fifth Army) under General Gough would be introduced and would take over the front north of that road.

To begin to get a glimpse of the next major proposed offensive, which took place on 14 July 1916, continue along the main road running through Montauban travelling towards Bernafay Wood (this is an easterly direction) until you leave the village boundary. Bernafay Wood is directly in front of you, just beyond the junction of the D64 with the D197.

Bernafay Wood was still occupied by the German after 1 July. As you proceed towards the wood, look through the fence on your left-hand side and you will see the village of Longueval, which is approximately 1 mile away. Scanning the horizon from left to right you will observe several woods which played a very important part in the southern portion of the battlefield:

Figure 2.9 Going from Montauban towards Bernafay Wood, captured 3 July 1916 by 9th (Scottish) Division.

- Mametz Wood and Bazentin-le-Grand Wood on the far left
- High Wood in the centre distance
- Delville Wood and Longueval at the centre right
- To the immediate right is Bernafay Wood.

The attack on 14 July occurred straight in front of you between these woods on the left and Bernafay Wood on the right, then moving up to Longueval and Delville Wood and finally continuing on towards High Wood which you can see on the skyline. You will return to this spot in a subsequent chapter when the attack on 14 July is explained in detail.

However, before any such attack could proceed, it was first essential to capture Bernafay Wood and the adjacent Trônes Wood so as to protect their right side from enemy machine gun fire as they moved forwards. The 9th (Scottish) Division, not employed on 1 July was given the job of capturing Bernafay Wood, which it duly did on 3 July. The 9th (Scottish) Division was one of Kitchener's New Army Divisions, but unlike most divisions fighting on the Somme, it had seen action at the Battle of Loos. Heavy casualties sustained during the Battle of Loos resulted in a major reorganisation (See Table 2.3). The battalions of 28th Brigade (one of the three component brigades of the

Figure 2.10 Looking north: rectangular area of ground attacked 14 July. High Wood is on the centre skyline; to the right is the village of Longueval and Delville Wood; the corner of Bernafay Wood is in the foreground; to the left, Bazentin-le-Grand Wood can just be seen with a very small part of Mametz Wood beyond.

Table 2.3 9th (Scottish) Division showing major reorganisation of constituent battalions.

26th (Highland) Brigade	27th (Lowland) Brigade	28th Brigade
8th Black Watch	11th Royal Scots	6th KOSB (transferred to 27 Brigade 6/5/16)
7th Seaforths	12th Royal Scots	9th Scottish Rifles (transferred to 27th Brigade 6/5/16)
8th Gordon Highlanders (transferred to 15th Division 7/5/16)	6th Royal Scots Fusiliers (transferred to 15th Division 3/5/16)	10th Highland Light Infantry (transferred to 15th Division 14/5/16)
5th Queen's Own Cameron Highlanders	10th Argyll and Sutherland Highlanders (transferred to 26th Brigade 3/5/16	11th Highland Light Infantry (transferred to 15th Division 14/5/16)
10th Argyll and Sutherland Highlanders	6th KOSB (transferred from 28th Brigade 6/5/16)	
	9th Scottish Rifles (transferred from 28th Brigade 6/5/16)	

9th Division) were replaced by the South African Brigade, which remained with the division for the rest of the war.

It proved to be relatively easy to capture Bernafay Wood, but it was very difficult for the 9th Division to hold because once the Germans had been forced out of the wood, they poured dense shellfire back into the wood to inflict many casualties on the men who were now occupying this position.

We will now leave Montauban and explain what happened to the men of the 18th Division who were attacking between Montauban and Mametz. Proceed along the main road through Montauban in the opposite direction from Bernafay Wood (this is a westerly direction) towards Mametz. You are now on ground taken by the 18th Division. As you go, you will notice that you cannot see to your left to Carnoy because you are below the summit of the hill. You will get views to your right as you proceed and will notice that as you approach Danzig Alley Cemetery and Mametz that the terrain falls away from you on your right. Pommiers Redoubt was close to the left side of the road and Montauban Alley was on the hillside below you to the right as you travel towards Mametz. Montauban Alley ran almost parallel to the road before it linked with Pommiers Redoubt.

The attacking troops of the 30th Division in Montauban reached the part of Montauban Alley near the village, while the 18th Division captured the Pommiers Redoubt before entering the part of Montauban Alley close to the redoubt. Remaining segments of Montauban Alley were still in German hands and these were secured by bombing parties from both the 18th and 30th Divisions who were moving towards one another. Germans who had been here could be seen running north across the fields towards Mametz Wood. By the close of the day all objectives had been secured and 1 July had been a success for the 18th and 30th Divisions.

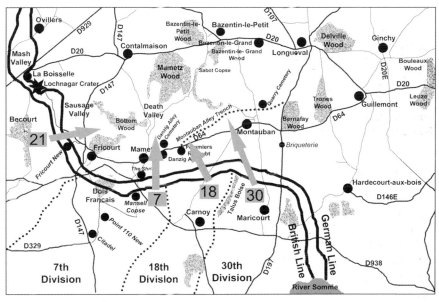

Figure 2.11 21st, 7th, 18th and 30th Divisions 1 July 1916.

Chapter 3

Mametz, 1 July 1916

Your journey looking at what happened to the 18th Division has just taken you along the D64 towards Mametz in a westerly direction. As you reach Danzig Alley Cemetery, you are heading into the area which was attacked by the 7th Division on 1 July 1916. The attack on the village of Mametz, (the village can be seen from Danzig Alley Cemetery), was carried out by the 7th Division. This was a Regular Army Division, although by 1916 there were few original soldiers of its constituent battalions left from the start of the war as they had mostly been killed, wounded or were missing. Some New Army battalions were attached to the 7th Division to help restore its numbers of men. On 1 July, the battalions making up the Division are shown in Table 3.1, and how the battalions lined up to face the enemy is illustrated in Figure 3.1. Nowhere over the length of the British Fourth Army's front did they have such an advantageous position. They had excellent views from behind their own front line here towards Montauban, Bernafay Wood and beyond.

On the left of the 7th Division was the 21st Division, which was to attack the Germans to the north side of the village of Fricourt, around which the front line changed from an east to west to a south to north direction (see Figure 3.1) from where you are looking. This allowed British artillery fire

Table 3.1 7th Division infantry orders of battle 1 July 1916.

20th Brigade	22nd Brigade	91st Brigade
8th Devons	2nd Royal Warwicks	2nd Queen's
9th Devons	20th Manchesters (5th Manchester Pals)	1st South Staffs
2nd Border	1st Royal Welch Fusiliers	21st Manchesters (6th Manchester Pals)
2nd Gordon Highlanders	2nd Royal Irish	22nd Manchesters (7th Manchester Pals)

Pioneers 24th Manchesters (Oldham Pals)

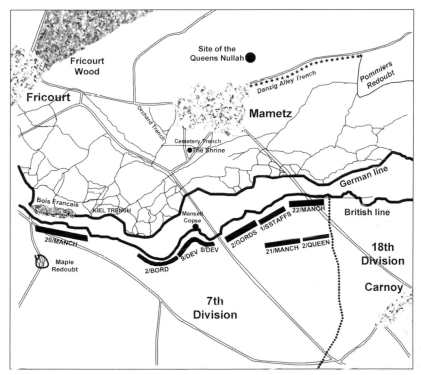

Figure 3.1 7th Division 1 July 1916.

from the heights behind their own lines to pour shellfire along the length of the German front line around Fricourt, providing a much more effective bombardment against the German defenders.

A creeping barrage was also employed in this section as had been used at Montauban. However, the barrage moved too fast to provide sufficient protective cover for the men advancing behind it. The infantry were left behind as the creeping barrage targeted the enemy too far in front of the following soldiers. Also, it did not have the density of shell fire which would come to characterise creeping barrages employed in later years of the war and which would increase their efficiency greatly. The barrage fell exclusively on the German front line, and only lifted at 0730 when the attack started and moved onto further German positions at a rate of 100 yards per minute. When the creeping barrage technique had been refined and used in later years it would bombard over a much greater depth of enemy territory, allowing for lethal variations of a well-orchestrated barrage to reverse direction from time to time and thus catch the enemy unawares. This would leave him in two minds about the imminence of attack. The 9th (Scottish) Division was particularly innovative in the development of the creeping barrage. At first, on 1 July 1916, only shrapnel was fired by the artillery. Thanks to a particularly enthusiastic General Officer Commanding Royal Artillery [GOCRA] 9th Division, Brigadier-General W.T. Furse, high explosive was subsequently used and became universally adopted over time. This resulted in a much more effective barrage than with shrapnel alone. Furse was promoted to the position of Master General of Ordnance at the end of 1916 and continued to develop his innovative techniques for delivering barrages for the remainder of the war.

Although in general British artillery did not effectively subdue the German artillery during this battle, the 18th and 30th Divisions placed great importance on the destruction of hostile batteries as did the French who were positioned and fighting to the right side of the 30th Division. The French were concerned that German guns in the sector where you are now would inflict considerable damage on the French infantry as they advanced and they therefore took steps to deal with the threat by shelling this sector. Once again, as they had done in front of Montauban, the Germans had concentrated greater numbers of men in forward areas and had less strength in depth behind their front line, so making their front line more vulnerable to attack. With the assistance of the creeping barrage, most British troops were in the German front line within a couple of minutes of the barrage lifting, although not all battalions were successful, as we shall see.

Spend a little time to begin with at Danzig Alley Cemetery. Pommiers Redoubt was between this position and Montauban, and defenders within it could look towards Mametz, as well as cover the ground with fire over which the 18th Division would advance. Danzig Alley Cemetery, on the right side of the road as you look towards Mametz is named after a German trench that communicated with Pommiers Redoubt. Danzig Alley ran from the village of Mametz and was within the field to your left (south) side of the road that you are on as you travel towards Mametz. It was captured by men of the 7th Division. Go into the cemetery, walk straight ahead and look at Mametz village from the wall which is towards your left. Beyond Mametz, you can just see the northern part of the next village which is Fricourt. You will see Fricourt Wood to the right hand side of the village which projects some distance beyond the village.

Go to the far corner of Danzig Alley Cemetery and look to the right of Fricourt Wood. You will see Mametz Wood which is on the far side of a valley which runs through between Mametz and Bazentin-le-Petit and which became the main route up to High Wood later in July 1916. This valley became known as "Death Valley" after it had been captured, because the Germans knew it was a major thoroughfare to the front line and they frequently shelled it. You will have the opportunity to visit "Death Valley" shortly.

Figure 3.2 View from Danzig Alley Cemetery towards Mametz. Fricourt Wood extends a considerable distance beyond Fricourt. 21st Division attacked on the other side of the village.

Figure 3.3 Mametz Wood from Danzig Alley Cemetery; the former was captured by the 38th (Welsh) Division on 11 July 1916.

Down the slope below the far wall of Danzig Alley Cemetery was the Queens Nullah, a natural depression in the ground which was a place in which troops could congregate on the forward slope in reasonable safety. On 22 July, Major-General Ingouville Williams (GOC 34th Division) (see Chapter 5) was struck and killed here by an exploding shell. He had walked from the nearby village of Contalmaison so that he could get an idea of the terrain his men would have to fight over during the ensuing days. He was on his way back to his staff car which was awaiting him and parked on the outskirts of Montauban when the shell exploded and he was killed.

The 7th Division captured Mametz and threatened Fricourt and Fricourt Wood by outflanking them from this side. The 21st Division advanced from the far side of Fricourt to a position which also pressurized the Germans within the village. As result, German defenders spontaneously evacuated Fricourt on the night of 1 July. As a result of this German withdrawal, the way was now open to attack Mametz Wood which would have to be captured before any further attack could be carried out to push further into German territory here in the south. See Main Map Somme (South 1) to appreciate this. Before proceeding with your tour of the front line on 1 July, now is a good time to take the opportunity to break off and take a small diversion to consider what developments took place at Mametz following the successful attack and prior to the great night assault on the 14 July (Chapter 7).

MAMETZ WOOD

Proceed from Danzig Alley Cemetery into Mametz and turn right onto the C4 towards Contalmaison, and then keep to the right when the road forks, following signposts for the 38th (Welsh) Divisional Memorial. When you reach the memorial, which is on a small hill opposite Mametz Wood, you will appreciate that you are in a valley. It was referred to as "Death Valley", although Robert Graves called it "Happy Valley" in his irreverent biographical work *Goodbye To All That* which describes his auto-biographical account on the Somme.[1]

As explained above, before the British could launch any further attack into German territory, Mametz Wood had to be captured to prevent the left side of the attacking force coming under machine gun fire from this wood. The 38th (Welsh) Division took over from the 7th Division and launched several attacks on Mametz Wood between 7 and 11 July 1916. It did so without any support from adjacent divisions that would have given some protection to the advance of the 38th Division in the centre of the attack. Only brief

---

1   Graves, R., *Goodbye to all That* (Harmondsworth: Penguin Group, 1960), p.182.

artillery bombardments were employed which were insufficient to overcome the strong German defences in the wood. The 38th Divisional Commander, Major-General Ivor Philips was responsible for sending men to attack the wood without providing them with adequate artillery protection. As a result of his shortcomings, he was relieved of his duties, and Major-General Herbert Watts, (who had been with the 7th Division), took command. Watts ensured that there was a more effective creeping barrage in subsequent attacks. The 38th Division finally captured Mametz Wood on 11 July. Having sustained some 4,000 casualties killed, wounded and missing, it took no further part in the offensive.

Return to Mametz to continue your tour of the front line. When you reach the village, turn right on the D64 through Mametz and just before you leave the village there is a small road to your left which is called Rue Saint Martin. Follow this narrow road for about 100 yards and it takes you to the communal cemetery of Mametz. Stop on the road at the corner of the cemetery wall. You are standing on a position which was known as the Shrine. There was a German machine gun position located here just a short distance behind the German front line on 1 July. The German front line was a few yards in front of you. The German front line came down parallel to the far side of Fricourt which is the next village to your right, crossed the road and then went up and over the hillside ahead of you. Then it came back down the hill and crossed

Figure 3.4 38th (Welsh) Division Memorial near Mametz Wood.

back across the road again to the side you are on to the right of the small wooded area you see in front of you. The wooded area is called Mansel Copse. The British line ran parallel to the German line, and actually came through Mansel Copse and crossed the road at that point.

Mansel Copse is from where men from the 8th and 9th Devonshires attacked German positions on 1 July. There is a particularly poignant story relating to this position in the front line. Men of the 9th Devonshires had occupied their trench in Mansel Copse for a considerable time before 1 July; Captain Duncan Martin was worried about what he saw when he looked through a trench periscope. He could see across to the communal cemetery at Mametz, where you are standing now and realised that the Shrine would be an ideal place to position a machine gun. He knew that if there was one, and unless it was put out of action, it would take a heavy toll of the men of the 9th Devonshires when they went over the top to attack the German front line at the start of the battle. Martin made plasticine models of the route he and his men would take in the forthcoming attack and realised that they would pass through the field of fire of any machine gun at the Shrine as they moved forwards. He expressed his concerns to his superior officers but they appear to have ignored him. When Martin led out A Company of the 9th Devonshires his worst fears must have been confirmed since he and many of his comrades were killed and others wounded as they passed into the zone of fire of this machine gun.

Figure 3.5 Looking across to Mansel Copse from the Shrine, a German machine gun position adjacent to the communal cemetery; the entrance to the Devonshire Cemetery is at the tip of the arrow. The British front line was within Mansel Copse and crossed the road just beyond it.

To the right side of the Devonshires (to the left from your position as you look over to Mansel Copse), the 2nd Battalion of the Gordon Highlanders advanced across the road over to your left. When the day was over, the dead of the 8th and 9th Devonshires lay scattered all over the field in front of the Shrine, while beyond them to your left lay the dead of the 2nd Gordon Highlanders. After Mametz had been captured the battlefield was cleared of the dead and the bodies of the Devonshires were buried in their trench from where they had started their attack in Mansel Copse. They lie here to this day. Dead Gordon Highlanders were buried in their own cemetery which you will see down the hill and to your left on this side of the main road (in Figure 3.5 you will see Gordon Cemetery).

If you now cross the busy road running between Albert and Péronne and turn left onto the road, within a couple of hundred yards is a small road to the right which leads you to the entrance of the Devonshire Cemetery. At the entrance you will find a stone memorial bearing the words:

The Devonshires held this trench. The Devonshires hold it still.

Within the cemetery, you will find the gravestone commemorating Captain Martin which is located at Row A1.

Another of the men of the Devonshires who lies buried here is William Noel Hodgson (Row A3). He volunteered for service in 1914 in the wave of patriotic fervour which swept the land. Born in 1893 at Thornbury in Oxfordshire, the

Figure 3.6a Devonshire Cemetery.

Figure 3.6b Devonshire Cemetery Commemorative Marker.

Figure 3.7 Lieutenant Noel Hodgson's grave; his poem, written shortly before he was killed, anticipated his own death.

son of the Bishop of Edmundsbury and Ipswich, he was educated at Durham School and Christ Church College in Oxford. He had already won a Military Cross at the Battle of Loos in 1915. He was a poet and published under the pen name of Edward Melbourne. A few days before his death he penned the following lines anticipating his imminent death.

> I, that on my familiar hill,
> Saw with uncomprehending eyes
> A hundred of thy sunsets spill
> Their fresh and sanguine sacrifice.
> Ere the sun swings his noonday sword
> Must say goodbye to all of this.
> By all delights that I shall miss
> Help me to die, O Lord.

Hodgson was indeed killed, shot through the neck by a bullet in the area right in front of you as he was carrying grenades to his men.

Go to the far wall of the cemetery, where the trees in Mansel Copse lead away from the cemetery, and you can still see remnants of the original trench system meandering through the trees.

The next section of the journey leads you to an area just behind the British line on the front of the 1st Battalion of the Royal Welch Fusiliers, and offers you a glimpse of what it was like in the weeks and months leading up to the first day of battle. It is quite suitable for cycling or walking, but can be rough in places if you are in a car. After leaving the cemetery turn right, and go up the road beside Mansel Copse. It soon becomes a rough track, with a steep climb to the top of the hill, where there is a fork in the track. Take the right fork, and continue along this road (a westerly direction) until you reach a wooded area that is ahead of you and to the right. This is the Bois Français which you have already seen in the distance from the road between Carnoy and Montauban. Take the opportunity to have a good look round. There is a splendid view to be had.

In the distance is the village of Montauban which was captured by the 30th Division on 1 July, while the ground to the left of the village was captured by the 18th Division. It is also possible to see Bernafay Wood on the skyline to the right of Montauban. If you look in the distance, just to the left of Montauban you will see Delville Wood. From the vantage point here, depending on the time of year, it may be possible to see traces of the trench lines as they wind away through the ploughed fields below you, and skirt round the end of the village of Carnoy. Wispy chalk marks show where the trenches were. These faint chalk lines were caused by the fracture of the chalk stratum when the trenches were dug, but they are only visible when the fields have been ploughed and before the crops start to grow.

The 1st Battalion of the Royal Welch Fusiliers spent the few months in the line before 1 July, opposite the Bois Français. In this battalion were Robert

Figure 3.8 Panoramic view from the hill behind Mansel Copse; Montauban is in the distance. Delville Wood to the left of the village; Bernafay and Trônes Woods are on the right. Trônes Wood is hidden by overlapping woods.

Figure 3.9 Vague chalk outlines through the fields show the British and German front lines. The village in the distance is Carnoy, which was just behind 18th and 30th Divisions.

Graves, Siegfried Sassoon and Bernard Adams, three noteworthy men of literature. The first two are well known, but the latter less so. John Bernard Pye Adams was born in November 1890. Educated at Malvern College and St John's College Cambridge, he was a quiet, intellectual man and excelled in Greek. He had strong religious convictions and had it not been for the war, he would probably have become a missionary in India. He volunteered to join the army in November 1914. After being wounded in June 1916 he was sent home to Great Britain, during which time he wrote a book entitled *Nothing of Importance*. This is a vivid account of life in the front line at a time when nothing of consequence occurred and yet death, in many guises, was never far away. Adams vividly described the mining and counter-mining, mortar attacks and sniping that took place constantly.

In his book, he sketched a map of the area trench system, which will help you to visualise the general layout in what are now, for the most part, ordinary fields without any distinguishing features. There are still some mine craters to be seen and their position is shown in Figure 3.10. The track you are travelling along and which is outlined in the sketch map was present in 1916. The British front line ran along the margin of the craters which you can still see. There were 'saps' which were small trenches dug from the front line at right angles and pointing towards the enemy front line so as to get that little bit closer without being detected. These ran at right angles to a trench called Rue Albert on the left side of the track you are travelling along.

For part of his time spent here, Adams was the sniping officer. He drew diagrams in his book to illustrate how sniping positions were used.

Note the sniper positions, marked on Adams' sketch in Figure 3.10, one on either side of the craters. The snipers would fire diagonally and not straight across. The sniper to the right covered the German line obliquely to the left, and vice versa. Snipers were protected by a metal plate in front of them, which was camouflaged by sandbags. The plate had an obliquely placed slit, allowing the snipers to see their target, but preventing them being seen by

Figure 3.10 Sketch of front line trenches at Bois Français; the Snipers' Post and Aeroplane Trench have been identified on the map. (Adams, B., *Nothing of Importance*. Reprinted by Methuen & Co Ltd, London. First published 1917, p.102).

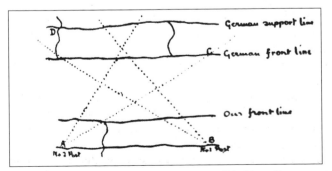

Figure 3.11 Diagram of sniping positions (*Nothing of Importance*).

the enemy from directly in front. Bernard Adams described how one of his snipers had sat for a whole day, waiting for his chance to shoot a German sniper in Aeroplane Trench (see Figure 3.10, and also Figure 4.8) who had killed a number of men in Adams' battalion. After sitting patiently from early morning until evening, it began to get dark, but the Welsh sniper still sat and waited for his chance. He eventually reported to Adams and gave an animated account of what happened:

> There had been another long wait, and the outline of the sunken road began to get faint. Then slowly, very slowly, a pink forehead had appeared over the top, and as slowly disappeared. I had to wait another minute, sir; then it appeared again, the whole head this time. He thought it was too dark to be seen....Oh, he won't worry us any more, sir.[2]

The Sniper

Two hundred yards away he saw his head;
He raised his rifle, took quick aim and shot him.
Two hundred yards away the man dropped dead;
With bright exulting eye he turned and said,
'By Jove, I got him!'
And he was jubilant; had he not won
The meed of praise his comrades haste to pay?
He smiled; he could not see what he had done;
The dead man lay two hundred yards away.
He could not see the dead, reproachful eyes,
The youthful face which Death had not defiled
But had transfigured when he claimed his prize.
Had he seen this perhaps he had not smiled.
He could not see the woman as she wept
To hear the news two hundred miles away,
Or through his every dream she would have crept.
And into all his thoughts by night and day.
Two hundred yards away, and, bending o'er
A body in a trench, rough men proclaim
Sadly, that Fritz, the merry is no more.
(Or shall we call him Jack? It's all the same.)

W.D. Cocker

Reproduced by kind permission from Messrs Brown, Son & Ferguson, Ltd.

---

2   Adams, B., *Nothing of Importance* (London: Methuen & Co Ltd, 1917), pp.133-153.

Adams died on 27 February 1917, after being badly wounded whilst fighting in the Serre area, which is to the northern limit of the battlefield and will be visited later.

Second Lieutenant David Thomas was a popular young officer in the 1st Battalion Royal Welch Fusiliers. Shot through the neck during a working party on 18 March 1916, he seemed to be alright at first, because there were accounts of him walking back to an advanced dressing station called the 'Citadel', less than a mile behind the front line. There was a sense of relief expressed by his fellow officers, who thought that Thomas had a "blighty" wound (a term used to describe a wound which would enable the wounded soldier to get back home!). He would be safely out of the action for a while. Figure 3.12 was taken from just behind the British front line, and looks back towards the Citadel. The track down which Thomas made his way to the advanced dressing station is clearly seen.

But all was not well, and by the time Thomas reached the advanced dressing station at the Citadel he was struggling for breath and choked to death. This was presumably because the tissues in his neck had become swollen as a result of the wound and the damage to the tissues, and the swelling blocked his airway so he couldn't breathe. He died before a operation which involves making a small opening (called a tracheotomy) into his windpipe could be carried out, which may have saved his life.

Figure 3.12 From behind Bois Français. Point 110 New Military Cemetery is indicated and the road along which the wounded were taken to the Citadel Advanced Dressing Station is shown. Its approximate position was in the slight hollow offering some protection.

Thomas was a particular friend of Siegfried Sassoon, who was affected very badly by his death. Sassoon and Robert Graves went to Thomas's burial in what can be clearly identified now as a typical "pal's cemetery", called Point 110 New. It is less than half a mile behind the British front line, and was used as a burial ground in 1916. Thomas still lies where he was buried in the presence of his friends nearly one hundred years ago. Buried beside Thomas are Captain M.S. Richardson and Second Lieutenant Pritchard, who were also close friends.

Richardson was killed by a shell exploding nearby. He had no obvious wound visible on his body, and presumably the shock wave from the exploding shell caused lethal damage to his internal organs; the lungs, the gastrointestinal tract (containing gas) and the brain being most susceptible to severe and fatal damage. Pritchard was the Stokes Mortar officer for the battalion, and he was killed by a direct hit from what the soldiers called a "Whiz-bang", which was a high explosive shell, fired from close range. The "whiz" from the shock wave of the passing shell was heard a brief moment before the report of that shell being fired. Hence the grim irony of the song *Hush! Here comes a Whizz bang!*

Point 110 New Military Cemetery can be reached by turning to the left after passing across in front of the Bois Français, going past an embankment where once upon a time battalion HQ in Maple Redoubt had been (see Figure 3.10). The first cemetery passed on the right is Point 110 Old, where fatalities were also buried by their comrades. However, it was dangerously close to the front line and burials here were stopped. Point 110 New Military Cemetery was opened a few hundred yards further away. It was here where Graves and Sassoon stood over the open graves of their three friends, who were being buried at the same time.

In his semi-autobiographical work, *The Complete Memoirs of George Sherston*, Sassoon described the death and burial of David Thomas (known as Dick Tiltwood in *The Complete Memoirs*):

> Dick had been killed. He had been hit in the throat by a rifle bullet while out with the wiring-party and had died at the dressing station a few hours afterwards. The battalion doctor had been a throat specialist before the war, but this had not been enough. The sky was angry with a red smoky sunset when we rode up with the rations. Later on, when it was dark, we stood on the bare slope just above the ration dump while the Brigade chaplain went through his words; a flag covering all that we were there for; only the white stripes on the flag made any impression on the dimness of the night. Once the chaplain's words were obliterated by a prolonged burst of machine-gun fire; when he

Figure 3.13 The graves of Thomas (far left of the photograph), Richardson and Pritchard in Point 110 New Military Cemetery.

had finished, a trench-mortar canister fell a few hundred yards away, spouting the earth up with a crash....A sack was lowered into the ground. The sack was Dick. I knew death then.[3]

Leave Point 110 New Military cemetery and turn left; a journey of approximately 800 yards leads you to Citadel New Military Cemetery. This was the site of the advanced dressing station. The organisation of medical services has been discussed in a previous book, *War Surgery 1914-1918)* and so will not be covered at length here.

You can imagine the scene here at the Citadel on 1 July, where the tents of the advanced dressing station, which was part of what was called the Field Ambulance, were located. Men would have been brought here by stretcher from the Regimental Aid Post where simple treatments such as stopping bleeding etc would have been administered. The Regimental Aid Post was always close to the front line and for this area would probably have been located close to battalion HQ at Maple Redoubt near the front line.

---

3   Sassoon, S., *The Complete Memoirs of George Sherston* (London: Faber & Faber, 1986), pp.273-74.

At the Citadel, medical officers would have been busy triaging the wounded into three groups:

- "Lightly wounded", whose problem was not life or limb threatening and who could be kept in the forward area before returning to the front line or transferred back to the main dressing station;
- Those with "severe but survivable" wounds would be sent back to the appropriate casualty clearing station which was the main operating facility (the MASH equivalent of today);
- Those with "non-survivable" wounds would be given pain relief and set aside to die. It was considered there was no point expending valuable time on those with perceived fatal injuries.

It required skill and experience when dealing with large numbers of casualties to make the right decision. An error of judgement might well have had fatal consequences for the casualty concerned. Here at the Citadel, after administering what treatment they could, medical personnel would have organised for the evacuation of the wounded by transferring them to a convoy of motor ambulance wagons which would have been standing in a queue on what is now the D147 between Fricourt and Bray Sur Somme. This convoy would have taken the casualties back to casualty clearing stations for further treatment.

Look back towards Point 110 New Military Cemetery; field ambulance stretcher-bearers would have made their way backwards and forwards over the very same track, bringing wounded from the Regimental Aid Post near Maple Redoubt. Walking wounded made their way in your direction. This is the very path Second Lieutenant David Thomas traversed before succumbing to his wound. The 7th Division sustained 3,410 casualties killed, wounded and missing on 1 July. Leave the Citadel for D147 and turn right. You can, if you wish, cycle down to Fricourt where 21st Division went over the top on 1 July.

Figure 3.14 From within the Citadel New Military Cemetery which was the position of the advanced dressing station, the road, which is now the main avenue between Bray Sur Somme and Fricourt (to the right), is visible along with Fricourt on the immediate right. In 1916 this road would have contained motorised ambulance wagons waiting to take casualties back to a casualty clearing station where complex surgery would have been undertaken.

Chapter 4

Fricourt, I July 1916

When you come out of Citadel New Military Cemetery, turn right and continue until you reach a roundabout. Turn right onto the D147 which is the main road that runs between Bray Sur Somme and Fricourt. It is an easy downhill journey on a bicycle and quickly brings you to a junction with the D938 (a busy road running between Albert and Péronne). The front lines crossed the road near here, the British very close to where you have stopped and the German line was further to your right as you face towards Fricourt.

The lines then swept up onto the hillside behind and to your right before coming down the hillside again at Mansel Copse opposite Mametz (see Chapter 3), before going towards a position nearly midway between Carnoy and Montauban and then continuing beyond the end of Talus Boise pointing towards Montauban. In the other direction, the respective lines went up the left side of Fricourt as you stand facing the village at the road junction. (Main Map Somme (South 1)).

Cross over the road, and go up the main street into Fricourt. Perhaps it is important to say that places to stop for a coffee are few and far between and there is one here in Fricourt, on the right-hand side of the road as you ascend through the village, so make the most of it! From the centre of the village, follow signposts for Fricourt New Military Cemetery. When you get to the track that leads down to the cemetery, look round towards the village. You will see the village nestling in a hollow. There is a line of trees and scrubland between your position and the village which marks the location of the Tambour Mines (see below). On the hillside beyond the village to the right of the church steeple is the Bois Français, from which you have just come (Chapter 3).

There is a track about 50 yards long down to the gate of Fricourt New Military Cemetery. Follow this track and stop when you reach the cemetery gate. You are now standing in the middle of what was No Man's Land on 1 July 1916. In Figure 4.2 the British front line was beyond the cemetery. The German front line was behind the camera and parallel to the British line.

Figure 4.1 View of Fricourt, Tambour Mine sector and the hillside with Bois Français beyond.

Figure 4.2 Fricourt New Military Cemetery is in the middle of what was No Man's Land on 1 July 1916.

Stand at the gate and face towards Fricourt. The German line ran along close to the margin of the rough scrubland ahead of you. This rough scrubland is where three Tambour Mines were laid prior to the attack on 1 July. The Tambour was originally a projection of the British line into the German line close to where the cemetery is today. There had been a great deal of mining both by the British and Germans in the months leading up to the Battle of the Somme and by 1 July, the entire Tambour area was a warren of impassable shell craters. Now while still at the cemetery gate, turn through 180 degrees and look beyond the far end of the cemetery. There is slight upwards incline running from left to right. The British line was to your left and the German line up to your right. You are looking along the length of No Man's Land in the general direction of La Boisselle, which is the next village along the front line and in a northerly direction. Soldiers of the 21st Division attacked up this slope for as far as you can see. In fact, the 21st Divisional boundary was further on near Becourt Wood, which you will pass by in Chapter 5.

You are of course looking away from the village of Fricourt when you are facing in this direction. The further away from the village attacking troops of the 21st Division were, the better were their chances of succeeding in their objective. This was because they were further away from the German machine guns in Fricourt and a German machine gun close to the northern

Figure 4.3 From this position just outside Fricourt New Military Cemetery, looking straight ahead, La Boisselle is just over the horizon. The British line was to the left and the German line to the right; the nearer to Fricourt (behind you), the heavier the losses.

end of the Tambour Mine area that was firing on them. In contrast, the closer advancing soldiers were to the village, the greater were the numbers of casualties inflicted. This was particularly the case for the 10th West Yorkshires who advanced across No Man's Land where, just to the north of the mine area, the cemetery stands today (see below).

Fricourt itself was not attacked directly on 1 July by the 21st Division because it was felt it was too strongly defended by the Germans for the British to make a frontal attack straight away. Whilst the 7th Division attacked Mametz (as you look at the village of Fricourt from your position at Fricourt New Military Cemetery Gate, Mametz is directly beyond Fricourt and cannot be seen), the 21st Division attacked at Fricourt in a manoeuvre designed to gain the ground adjacent to the side of the village and Fricourt Wood beyond it. In the same way, the 7th Division (Chapter 3) would capture the ground adjacent to the other side of Fricourt and therefore the village would be threatened from both sides. After completing their outflanking manoeuvres, the plan called for the 7th and 21st Divisions to link up beyond the village. The order of battle for the infantry of 21st Division is shown in Table 4.1.

It was intended that after the outflanking manoeuvres had been carried out, an attack would be launched by battalions from the 17th Division on the village of Fricourt later in the day. A brigade of the 17th Division had been seconded to fight as part of the 21st Division. It had been given the specific task of taking Fricourt while the 21st Division carried out the outflanking manoeuvre. The battalions of the 17th Division are shown in Table 4.2 and the way in which they lined up on the morning of 1 July is shown in Figure 4.4.

The Tambour Mines had been prepared by the British with the aim of destroying a part of the German front line and diverting German enfilade machine gun fire away from the attacking troops of the 21st Division. The three mines were detonated at 0728 just two minutes before zero hour at 0730. They increased in size from north to south with 9,000, 15,000 and 25,000 lbs of ammonal respectively. The largest mine failed to detonate. The plan

Table 4.1 21st Division infantry orders of battle 1 July 1916.

62nd Brigade	63rd Brigade	64th Brigade
12th Northumberland Fusiliers	8th Lincolns	9th King's Own Yorkshire Light Infantry
13th Northumberland Fusiliers	8th Somerset Light Infantry	10th King's Own Yorkshire Light Infantry
1st Lincolns	4th Middlesex	1st East Yorks
10th Green Howards	10th Yorks and Lancs	15th Durham Light Infantry

Pioneers 14th Northumberland Fusiliers

Table 4.2 17th Division (attached 21st Division) infantry orders of battle 1 July 1916.

10th West Yorks
7th East Yorks
7th Green Howards
6th Dorsets

Pioneers 7th Yorks and Lancs

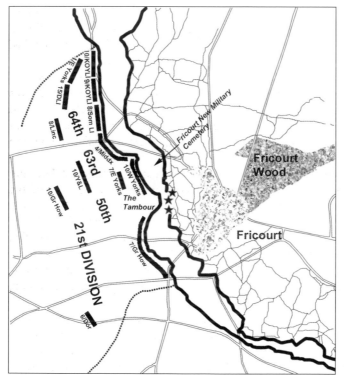

Figure 4.4 21st Division 1 July 1916.

was to destroy the German front line and for the debris thrown up to prevent German machine gunners from directing fire against assaulting battalions to the north of the Tambour position.

Those battalions of the 21st Division which attacked furthest away from Fricourt, to the north, made reasonably good progress. These were the 9th and 10th King's Own Yorkshire Light Infantry, the 1st East Yorks and the 15th Durham Light Infantry. They advanced for a distance of approximately three quarters of a mile. They were on the right side of the 15th and 16th Royal Scots of the 34th Division (See Chapter 5). Although they were far enough away from Fricourt to avoid fire from the village, they did come under heavy machine gun fire from German positions closer at hand and suffered heavy casualties. This came about because unfortunately there was little support from the 34th Division that was attacking around La Boisselle to the north of Fricourt. Its attack failed completely. It suffered, as you will discover in Chapter 5, the heaviest casualties of any division on 1 July.

Returning to the attack on the flank of Fricourt, and closer to the village itself and therefore passing closer to the northern end of Fricourt New Military Cemetery, the battalions here made less progress. These were the 10th Green Howards, the 12th and 13th Northumberland Fusiliers and the 1st Lincolns. Their objective was Fricourt Farm beyond the end of Fricourt Wood. They did not reach this goal because of heavy machine gun fire from Fricourt. However, they did manage to make some progress and reached a sunken road which was occupied and a counter-attack by German defenders was thrown back. As you look at the slope running from left to right (with your back to the village of Fricourt) these men were moving from left to right across the field (shown in Figure 4.3).

As already explained, some men had been attached to the 21st Division (from the 17th Division) specifically for the attack on 1 July. One of the battalions was the 10th West Yorkshires, which launched one of the most disastrous attacks of the day. If you now look towards Fricourt and into the fenced off scrub area, this is the site of the Tambour Mines. The 10th West Yorkshires attacked to the left of the Tambour position, which was too scarred with craters to allow easy passage. It was thought that the detonation of the mines under the German Tambour would protect the advancing Yorkshiremen.

After the detonation of the mines, the 10th West Yorkshires attacked across your position at the cemetery gate. Their role was to provide support for the soldiers of the 21st Division to their left and also to help with a planned attack on Fricourt later in the day by the 7th Green Howards. However, the Germans turned their fire on them from a machine gun nearly opposite the cemetery gate just beyond the mines and the 10th West Yorkshires sustained very heavy casualties. By the end of the day only 21 men from the 10th West Yorkshires returned to the front line. The Battalion lost 23 of its 24 officers and 717 of its 750 men.

Fricourt New Military Cemetery was begun by survivors of the 10th West Yorkshires to bury their dead. Of the 210 burials here, no fewer than 159 are men from the 10th West Yorkshires, and most of the others are from the 7th East Yorkshires who followed up the attack of the West Yorkshires one hour later. They too suffered heavy casualties.

Figure 4.5 Looking towards the village of Fricourt from Fricourt New Military Cemetery; the three Tambour Mines were located in the field where the cows are grazing. Men from the 10th West Yorkshires attacked through here and suffered terrible casualties from a nearby machine-gun.

Figure 4.6 Fricourt New Military Cemetery: gravesite of a member of 7th East Yorks; a poignant message from the granddaughter he never knew lies in the foreground. The ripples of a single tragic death travel through years to the present!

Figure 4.7 Looking to Fricourt and beyond to Bois Français. Siegfried Sassoon watched events unfold from his 'opera box' on the adjacent hillside.

Look beyond the Tambour Mine area towards Fricourt and then scan the hillside beyond. You will see Bois Français which you have visited in Chapter 3. The 1st Battalion Royal Welch Fusiliers spent several months there before the Battle of the Somme. It was in reserve on 1 July and did not fight.

Look to the open ground to the right of·the Bois Français in Figure 4.7. The poet Siegfried Sassoon watched events unfold at Fricourt from this hillside. His battalion, the 1st Royal Welch Fusiliers, was in reserve on 1 July. He was unable to watch his colleagues in the 7th Division advance because the contour of the hillside blocked Mametz from his view. Instead, he watched the men of the 21st Division moving forwards towards Fricourt:

> 7.45am: the barrage is now working to the right of Fricourt and beyond. I can see the 21st Division advancing about three-quarters of a mile away on the left and a few Germans coming to meet them, apparently surrendering. Our men in small parties (not extended in line) go steadily on to the German front line. Brilliant sunshine and a haze of smoke drifting along the landscape; Some Yorkshiremen a little way below on the left watching the show and cheering as if at a football match; the noise almost as bad as ever.[1]

Sassoon continued to watch intermittently from his position, which he described as his "opera box".

---

1   Sassoon, S., *The Complete Memoirs of George Sherston* (London: Faber & Faber Limited, 1937. Reprinted London: Faber & Faber, 1986), pp. 331-33.

2.30pm: There were about forty casualties on the left (from a machine gun in Fricourt). Through my glasses I could see one man moving his left arm up and down as he lay on his side; his face was a crimson patch. Others lay still in the sunlight while the swarm of figures disappeared over the hill. Fricourt was a cloud of pinkish smoke. Lively machine gun fire on the far side of the hill; at 2.50, no one to be seen in No Man's Land – except the casualties.[2]

What Sassoon was witnessing, at approximately 1430, was an ill-advised attack launched at the insistence of XV Corps headquarters, which was responsible for both the 21st and 7th Divisions. There had been reports that 21st and 7th Divisions had taken all their objectives, and that German artillery was withdrawing further back towards Pozières. However, these were wildly optimistic reports and were without foundation as battlefield communications were very poor in 1916. As the 7th Green Howards advanced across No Man's Land, they were cut to pieces by machine gun fire from Fricourt. The 21st Division sustained 4,256 casualties killed, wounded and missing, while the three battalions of 50 Brigade sustained 1,115 casualties.

The 7th Division, as you have already seen in Chapter 2, achieved its objectives. It captured Mametz and formed a flank extending beyond the far side of Fricourt from your position at Fricourt New Military Cemetery. The success achieved by the 21st Division was more limited although its gains resulted in it being able to flank Fricourt from the near side of the village as you stand at the cemetery. The soldiers furthest from the machine guns in the village advanced the greatest distance, while those closer to the village were less successful. Men from the 17th Division were wiped out as they either attempted to establish a position immediately adjacent to the village (10th West Yorkshires and 7th East Yorkshires) or attacked the village at 1430 in the afternoon of 1 July (7th Green Howards).

Nevertheless the gains of 1 July meant that the defending Germans in Fricourt were in danger of being cut off by any further advance on both sides of the village. On 2 July, a patrol from the 7th Division found that the Germans had spontaneously evacuated Fricourt during the night of 1/2 July. As a result, the 7th, 17th and 21st Divisions linked up behind the village. From his so-called "opera box" on 2 July, Sassoon observed:

Fricourt occupied this morning without resistance; I am now lying in front of our trench in the long grass, basking in the sunshine, where yesterday there were bullets. Our new front line on the hill is being shelled. Fricourt is full of troops wandering about in search of souvenirs. The village was

---

2   Ibid.

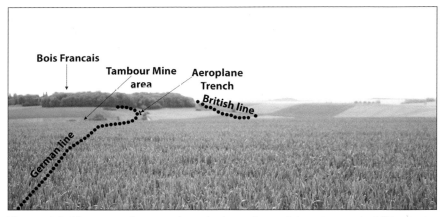

Figure 4.8 This image illustrates how the lines changed direction around Fricourt by marking the approximate position of the British and German front lines. Bois Français and the track leading from there to Fricourt were just in front of the German line; the position of Aeroplane Trench is also marked; the Tambour Mine sector is just visible from the position from where this photograph was taken. Fricourt New Military Cemetery is below the crest of the hill ahead and is not visible. The British front line curved below the crest of the hill ahead and was on the far side of Fricourt New Military Cemetery.

a ruin and is now a dust heap. A gunner has just been along here with a German helmet in his hand. Said Fricourt is full of dead; he saw one officer lying across a smashed machine gun with his head bashed in-"a fine looking chap", he said, which rather surprised me.[3]

You have now completed the trip around the southern part of the battlefield. Some objectives were achieved and a limited amount of territory captured. This was, however, achieved at a huge cost in terms of numbers of killed, wounded and missing. Moving farther north, you will appreciate there were no more significant gains on 1 July.

Leave Fricourt New British Cemetery and retrace your steps up the grass pathway. Proceed approximately 100 yards until you arrive at a T-Junction with a bulldozed track. If you have driven and wish to proceed to La Boisselle return to your car. If on foot or bicycle, turn to your left and proceed along the track. Figure 4.8 was taken after going approximately 100 yards along this track. It will allow you comprehend the way the line changed direction as it passed around Fricourt west to the east and then from south northwards to the 34th Division sector (See Chapter 5)

---

3   Ibid, p. 334.

Chapter 5

La Boisselle and Ovillers, 1 July 1916

The next destination is La Boisselle, so if travelling by car make your way back to Fricourt village and from there proceed to La Boisselle, following signposts for *La Grande Mine* to the Lochnagar Mine Crater to begin. If you are on foot or on a bicycle, then there is an interesting track which takes you to the Lochnagar Mine Crater. To get there, leave the New British Military Cemetery at Fricourt and retrace your steps up the grass pathway which led you to the entrance of the cemetery. Turn right at the top of the pathway and go approximately 100 yards, when you will come to a T Junction with a bulldozed track. Turn left onto the track. This will lead you first over the ground gained by the 21st Division on 1 July 1916 and then onwards towards the area covered by adjacent battalions on the right side right of the 34th Division, which was attacking the area we will be visiting.

Another New Army Division, the 34th Division was commanded by Major-General Ingouville Williams, known to his men as "Inky Bill". The division's task was to capture the village of La Boisselle and to advance to Contalmaison, a full mile behind the German front line (see Main Map Somme (South 1)). The 34th Division was also to support the adjacent 8th Division as it attacked Pozières (see Main Map Somme (North)). By capturing Contalmaison, the 34th Division would provide protection for the 8th Division against any German counter-attack coming from the direction of Mametz Wood. Table 5.1 shows the order of battle for the 34th Division and Figure 5.1 how the battalions lined up on 1 July.

The village of La Boisselle is on the main road between Albert and Bapaume (the D929). It was of great strategic significance because it was in the centre of the battlefield. As explained in Chapter 1, it was very important for the British Fourth Army to gain control in the centre between the villages of La Boisselle and Pozières. This would enable General Gough's Reserve Army to exploit the gain by using the cavalry to ride on to Bapaume and prevent deployment of German reinforcements. Bapaume was a large town and was a key position because it was a centre of German communications. The cavalry would also

Table 5.1 34th Division infantry orders of battle 1 July 1916.

101st Brigade	102nd Brigade	103rd Brigade
15th Royal Scots	20th Northumberland Fusiliers, 1st Tyneside Scots	24th Northumberland Fusiliers, 1st Tyneside Irish
16th Royal Scots	21st Northumberland Fusiliers, 2nd Tyneside Scots	25th Northumberland Fusiliers, 2nd Tyneside Irish
10th Lincolns (Grimsby Chums)	22nd Northumberland Fusiliers, 3rd Tyneside Scots	26th Northumberland Fusiliers, 3rd Tyneside Irish
11th Suffolks (Cambridge)	23rd Northumberland Fusiliers, 4th Tyneside Scots	27th Northumberland Fusiliers, 4th Tyneside Irish

Pioneers 18th Northumberland Fusiliers

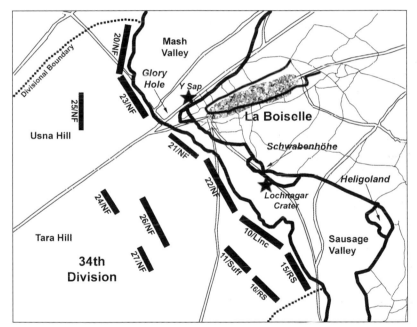

Figure 5.1 34th Division 1 July 1916.

help the British Fourth Army infantry to advance to Bapaume and then to break out beyond the German positions there.

La Boisselle stands at the foot of the Pozières Ridge. Pozières itself is near the highest point of this ridge and dominates the surrounding terrain. The capture of this central area of ground would give the British a commanding position over the battlefield in all directions. However, British artillery was less effective around La Boisselle than it was at Montauban and Mametz. It failed to destroy the barbed wire around La Boisselle. The Germans were secure in deep dugouts and had much greater strength in depth here in the central part of the battlefield than at Mametz and Montauban. La Boisselle was very heavily fortified, with commanding views over the battlefield on either side of the village.

There was another very important factor. There was a disagreement between General Rawlinson and his Commander-in-Chief General Haig about British objectives on 1 July. Rawlinson favoured a "bite and hold" approach, using available artillery to bombard a manageable area of German held territory before capturing and retaining control of it. Any German counterattack would be repulsed before making preparations for the next limited attack. Haig thought that Rawlinson was being too cautious, and instructed him to double the area of his artillery barrage, so that when the British broke through they would encounter less German resistance. This was a mistake, because by doubling the area his artillery was now expected to cover, the density of fire would be cut by a half. This was particularly important at La Boisselle which was very strongly defended. Rawlinson complied with Haig's orders without raising any serious objection to his plan. As a result, La Boisselle was inadequately bombarded and the Germans' own artillery remained intact as it had hardly been damaged.

To make matters worse, the British heavy artillery at La Boisselle stopped firing on German front line positions at 0700 on 1 July and directed fire on Pozières, some two miles behind the German front line. This meant that only field guns with little destructive power against solidly constructed German trenches were used for the 30 minutes leading up to the start of the infantry attack.

For those of you who are walking or cycling, you should now begin your journey along the track towards La Boisselle. As you do so, look at the open terrain surrounding the track and think just how exposed the men attacking across here would have been to enemy machine gun fire. The British line was to your left as you make your way along the track. The German line was on the higher ground to your right. No Man's Land was approximately 500 yards at its widest part, which you will reach presently. You will come to a section of the track where there is a wood at the bottom of a fairly steep slope down to your left. This is Becourt Wood. Stop when you are level with it.

Becourt Wood was a short distance behind the British front line and marked the boundary between the 21st and 34th Divisions. Men from the 21st Division advanced between the Tambour Mines and your present position. The 34th Division attacked between where you are standing and over to the north side of La Boisselle ahead of you. Just beyond the far border

Figure 5.2 This photograph is taken going from Fricourt towards La Boisselle. Becourt Wood is down to the left and the British front line was (running from right to left) half-way between the wood and where this photograph was taken. Becourt Wood was the divisional boundary between the 21st and 34th Divisions.

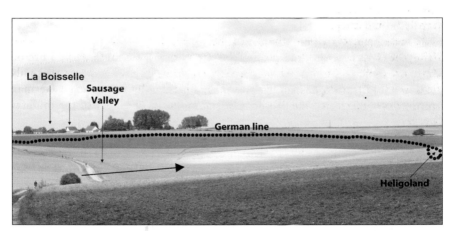

Figure 5.3 The cyclists are travelling across Sausage Valley towards La Boisselle which can be seen beyond the valley. The German front line skirted round Sausage Valley. No Man's Land is wide here and it was all uphill! Where the 16th Royal Scots attacked is marked with an arrow. Note the major disruption of the chalk layer in the field to the right. Several large shells must have detonated to cause this. This may have been caused by concentrated artillery fire directed against advancing British soldiers in Sausage Valley on 1 July, or perhaps intermittent fire against British soldiers who congregated here before going up the line in the days after the capture of La Boisselle.

of Becourt Wood (Figure 5.2) was a trench called Bon Accord Street, where the commanding officer of the 16th Royal Scots, Lieutenant-Colonel George McRae had his Battalion headquarters (see also Chapter 6). The battalions attacking ahead of you beyond Becourt Wood were the 15th and 16th Royal Scots. They advanced across the widest part of No Man's Land to the German front line 500 yards away to your right. Now look straight ahead of you. There is a steep hill which goes down into a valley before ascending as it approaches La Boisselle straight ahead. The British called this Sausage Valley.

Two German front line trenches swept round the higher ground along the margin of Sausage Valley, called Bloater Trench to the left, and Kipper Trench to the right. They were connected by a stronghold named Heligoland which can be seen in Figure 5.4. The German front line dominated the British front line while La Boisselle also held commanding views over British positions.

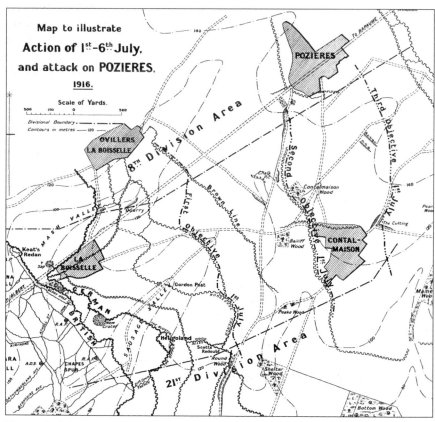

Figure 5.4 Sketch map La Boisselle defences (Shakespear, J. *The Thirty-fourth Division 1915-1919*. London: H.F. & G. Witherby, 1921).

The 34th Division's goal was to capture the village of Contalmaison. The many trench systems which had to be overcome to reach Contalmaison are shown in Figure 5.4. The 15th and 16th Royal Scots came under very heavy machine gun fire from Heligoland and failed to reach Contalmaison. They only succeeded in occupying a position called the Scots Redoubt after skirting round Heligoland. By nightfall on 1 July, the Germans were still in possession of Heligoland. The approximate position of Heligoland will be pointed out shortly as you proceed towards the Lochnagar Crater.

As you travel through Sausage Valley, the 15th and 16th Royal Scots would have been crossing in front of you from left to right on their way to the German front line. Murderous fire rained down on these men as they advanced. It came from Kipper and Bloater Trenches, from Heligoland and from La Boisselle. When you have gone half-way between Becourt Wood and La Boisselle and are in the lowest point of Sausage Valley, stop and turn 90 degrees to your right. Scan round the hillside approximately 400 yards away. Bloater trench was on the hillside to your left, and Kipper trench to your right. Heligoland was almost straight ahead and was opposite the widest part of No Man's Land (see Figure 5.4).

Here is what one soldier of the 16th Royal Scots had to say about the attack. His name was Jim Miller and he came from Kirkcaldy in Fife.

> It was cruel. We had no chance. You remember Jimmy Dods that we used to pal about with? I saw him fall beside me. We were going over when he was hit in the chest. I do not think he knew anything. That was when I got mine, only I was lucky for it was just my leg. I crawled into a shell-hole with poor Jimmy just behind me, where I could see the bullets still tearing into him. It was just awful to see. I think it was deliberate on the part of the Hun, for they were potting at the wounded all day long. Thank God he was dead by then. Others were not so lucky, and I cannot rid myself of the sound of their cries. I saw Jock Marshall go down, just cut in two by machine gun bullets. He is dead for certain. And Willie Hadden. Stevie, the drummer, was hit while trying to help the wounded, him and Willie Robb, who was already hit when he got another in the chest. The bullets were like hailstones.[1]

The 15th and 16th Royal Scots gained a few hundred yards. They fought their way through Kipper Trench (Figure 5.4) and moved onto the second line and Scots Redoubt. The Germans still held Heligoland, temporarily trapping

---

1   Alexander, J., *McCrae's Battalion; The story of the 16th Royal Scots* (Edinburgh. Mainstream Publishing, 2003), p.164.

the few men who had made it into the German second line. That was the closest they got to Contalmaison.

As you proceed through 'Sausage Valley' you will see a knoll of trees ahead of you at the end of the track. This marks the position of the Lochnagar Mine Crater. Stop where you can get a good view of the crater outline.

MINING ON THE WESTERN FRONT

By autumn 1914, opposing trenches ran from the Swiss border to the Flanders coast. An impasse had been reached and both sides employed every means to try to overcome this deadlock. There were developments in artillery, chemical and aerial warfare; there was also an unseen and ever expanding underground war, as men dug beneath the enemy and planted mines under strong points to blow them up in their efforts to try to make a breakthrough.

At Festubert on 20 December 1914, the Germans struck by planting and exploding 10 mines positioned under an Indian Brigade. As a result, almost 1,000 yards of trench systems were destroyed which also damaged British morale, since there was uncertainty as to where and when the next mine would be detonated.

In February 1915 the British MP for Wednesbury, Major John Norton Griffiths, approached Kitchener with plans to develop British mining

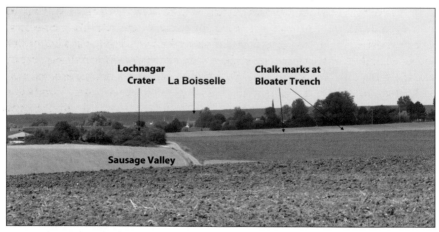

Figure 5.5 The site of Lochnagar Crater can be identified from the rough area of bushes and trees as the track rises out of Sausage Valley towards La Boisselle. This photograph was taken from the high ground above Sausage Valley. The Grimsby Chums and Cambridge Battalion advanced on the near side of the crater towards the German front line. The chalk visible in the field probably represents the German front line at the beginning of Bloater Trench as it swept away from the village around Sausage Valley.

operations and the War Office approved a Royal Engineers tunneling scheme. Eight tunneling companies were formed (each one comprising 600 or more miners), with a further 12 companies formed during 1915, and one more in 1916. In total, there were 33 mining companies by mid-1916 from Great Britain, New Zealand, Canada and Australia.

Griffiths was appointed to recruit suitably skilled miners, who would be essential for such operations. Pay was six shillings a day, which was more than the daily wage of an infantryman. Mining engineers and geologists joined the mining companies to lead them. Training in military matters was short and miners were quite independent, which sometimes led to conflict with other soldiers. The 'Controller of Mines', a senior officer of the Royal Engineers was in overall command. The 'Inspector of Mines', stationed at the HQ of the British Expeditionary Force, had overall responsibility for deciding on the appropriate disposition of the mining companies.

Clay kickers were recruited to dig tunnels; these men specialised in digging underground sewers and railway tunnels in London and Manchester. 'Clay kicking' required them to lie on their backs, on a board, and dislodge the face of the tunnel using a special shovel with both feet as they worked. Other important men in the mining team were "baggers" who put the spoil in bags and "trammers" who pushed the spoil along the mine in rubber-wheeled carriages on narrow gauge railways before it was removed and disposed of without being noticed.

The first aim in the underground war was to create defensive systems to protect trenches and to reduce the impact of enemy offensive mining activities. The next objective was to dig tunnels and sow mines under identified important locations and blow them up. Such mines were usually employed in support of major offensives. They had to avoid detection by the enemy defensive networks.

A lateral or transversal gallery was built for defensive purposes. This was a tunnel dug straight out into No Man's Land and then turned through a right angle to run parallel to the front line trench. If it happened that Germans were tunneling towards the British line they would reach this lateral gallery. It was constructed at a sufficient distance from the front line, so that if the lateral gallery was breached and a charge detonated to destroy it, it was at a safe distance away and little damage was done.

'Listening posts' were built every 20 yards along the length of the lateral gallery. To begin with men would detect enemy mining activity by putting water into tins. If the water vibrated, it might be an indication of enemy tunneling activity close by. Techniques became more sophisticated with provision of "geophones" which were mercury-filled wooden devices with two nipples attached to a stethoscope. Enemy digging could be more easily detected and localised by using two compass bearings of the sound and using geometric triangulation techniques.

Miners on both sides dug deeper, trying to gain an advantage, so deeper transversal tunnels were dug to counteract these efforts. At La Boisselle, just a few hundred yards away from Lochnagar Crater near the southern end of the village, a warren of underground tunnels and chambers called the 'Glory Hole', resulted in a series of galleries at depths of 30 feet, 60 feet and finally 120 feet. Whilst attempts to prevent mines being detected by the enemy resulted in digging ever deeper, this had the disadvantage that a bigger explosive charge would be necessary to break through to the surface when the mine was eventually detonated.

Enemy offensive mining operations were sought out and destroyed, which involved blowing them up by entering them using small tunnels, then introducing an explosive charge called a camouflet. These charges were employed to cave in the enemy tunnel. Sometimes an enemy tunnel would be broken into, either deliberately or accidentally and fierce hand-to-hand fighting would ensue using any suitable weapon in the confined space.

Ground conditions along the Western Front varied depending on where you were. While mining in Flanders was in blue clay with very wet ground conditions bringing frequent serious problems with flooding and collapse of tunnels, here on the Somme tunnellers had to deal principally with chalk, which was harder to dig and made more noise when cutting it at the tunnel face. Sometimes seams of flint were encountered which made matters even more difficult. Tunnels in the Somme area were less likely to collapse and consequently few timber supports were required.

The work was hard and miners worked up to 12-hour shifts in wet, cold and dark conditions. They worked in silence, often wore soft shoes and floored the tunnels with rugs and carpets to absorb the sound and to minimize the risk of detection. Naked flames could not be used since there was a risk of explosions so civilian miners' lights or electrical lighting was used if available. Ventilation was assisted by the use of bellows type pumps to keep the tunnels supplied with fresh air. It was possible in good conditions to dig up to 20 feet of mine length daily.

There was ever-present risk of death from underground enemy action, from collapse of the underground working and from asphyxiation from carbon monoxide poisoning. Canaries and mice accompanied the miners and were used to indicate the presence of carbon monoxide. Rescue teams who had undergone safety training and had mine rescue equipment available for immediate use helped to support the miners. No mine shaft was further than 200 yards from a mine rescue station. In 1916 the British had dug and exploded more than 700 mines and the Germans more than 650. The busiest month was June when up to four mines each day were detonated.

Lochnagar Mine and Y Sap Mine

Two mines had been dug, one on either side of La Boisselle. They were detonated at 0728 on 1 July 1916. Y Sap Mine was on the far side of the village. The Germans discovered it before it was detonated and moved men and machine guns away to safety. Y Sap Mine contained 40,000lb of the high explosive ammonal, a mixture of ammonium nitrate, trinitrotoluene, aluminum shavings and charcoal. This explosive was advantageous in that it was waterproof and very stable (even a bullet would not detonate it). It was stored in boxes which were stacked one top on top of the other when placed in the chamber. A small electrical charge was the method used to detonate. Ammonal was four times more powerful than gunpowder and had a detonation velocity of 9,842 miles per hour – capable of causing massive destruction.

The resultant crater caused by the explosion no longer exists today. The land was reclaimed as farming land and the crater filled in.

The second of these mines was the Lochnagar Mine (60,000lb of ammonal), positioned beneath a German strongpoint, the Schwabenhöhe. It had two adjacent chambers with 36,000lb and 24,000lb of ammonal, which would result in a single huge crater on detonation. Mining began in February 1916 about 100 yards behind the British lines. The tunnel was dug at a depth of 50 feet. Less than 200 yards separated the British and German front lines. Unfortunately the chambers stopped short of being directly under the Schwabenhöhe and only destroyed one relatively small part of it. Like all mines, while the effects were devastating, they were extremely localised, and may even have held up the progress of the infantry.

The explosion of the mine was observed by Cecil Lewis, famous for his classic memoir *Sagittarius Rising* (1936). Lewis was a notable postwar author and a co-founder of the BBC. Lewis was in the Royal Flying Corps and he was flying and observing what was happening below. He wrote:

> At La Boisselle the earth heaved and flashed, a tremendous and magnificent column rose up into the sky. There was an ear-splitting roar, drowning all the guns, flinging the machine sideways in the repercussing air. The earth column rose, higher and higher to almost four thousand feet. There it hung, or seemed to hang, for a moment in the air, like the silhouette of some great Cyprus tree, then fell away in a widening cone of dust and debris.[2]

---

2 Lewis, C., *Sagittarius Rising* (London: Peter Davies, 1936. Reprinted London: Corgi, 1969), p.78.

Lochnagar Crater was purchased on 1 July 1978 by Mr. Richard Dunning, and is maintained by 'Friends of Lochnagar'. This group of volunteers gives freely of its time and energy to maintain it and preserve it to commemorate the men of the 34th Division who fought and lost their lives here.

Men from the 11th Suffolks (Cambridge Battalion) and the 10th Lincolns (Grimsby Chums) moved past the near edge of Lochnagar Crater. As you climb out of Sausage Valley and get closer to the mine crater, these men would have crossed your path here from left to right on their way to the German front line. They too sustained heavy casualties from La Boisselle and from the strongpoint at Heligoland.

Standing at the margin of Lochnagar Crater you will appreciate just how big it is and what the scene must have been like as it exploded. As you are standing here at the edge of the crater, look over the commemorative cross which stands at the margin and near the entrance to the site. You will see traffic on the busy road between Bapaume and Albert. The road courses up a steep slope before disappearing over the brow of the hill to the town of Albert beyond. There is a hill to the left of the road called the Tara Hill, and another one to the right called the Usna Hill. These hills are important as you will see shortly.

German defenders in La Boisselle and in Bloater and Kipper trenches coursing around Sausage Valley had a clear view over the British lines and also to the Tara and Usna Hills beyond. As you look towards the Tara and Usna Hills, the German front line on 1 July came from the southern end of the village of La Boisselle across the field between you and the village, passing only a few yards away from the crater margin before going away from you to your right at 45 degrees to sweep round Sausage Valley as Bloater Trench (see Figure 5.4).

Imagine if you had been standing on this spot at 0730 on 1 July, you would have seen men from the four battalions of the Tyneside Irish coming over the brow of the two hills. The name "Tyneside Irish" was the "Pals Battalion" name given to these four battalions. They were New Army service battalions of Northumberland Fusiliers and their official designation can be found in Table 5.1. These men came from positions much further to the rear of the attacking soldiers in the front line. They began their advance from positions behind the brows of the Tara and Usna Hills. Major-General Ingouville Williams fully committed all his battalions on 1 July and had no reserves. The Tyneside Irish were brought into action as soon as the battle started. The immediate general aim of the British attack was to storm the German front line on either side of the village and then to turn inwards and destroy the Germans within the village before advancing to Contalmaison (See Main Map Somme (North)). Three battalions of Tyneside Irish came over the Tara Hill (to the left of the road), and one over the Usna Hill (to the right of the

Figure 5.6 Lochnagar Crater. The mine partly destroyed a German strongpoint called the Schwabenhöhe.

Figure 5.7 This shows the Tara and the Usna Hills, over which the Tyneside Irish came on 1 July. They were clearly visible on the skyline to German machine-gunners. Approximate front line positions are marked.

road). To the left were the 1st, 3rd and 4th Battalions Tyneside Irish. To the right was the 2nd Battalion Tyneside Irish. As the Tyneside Irish reached the brow of the hill they were visible above the horizon and they were hit by machine gun fire from La Boisselle. They sustained very heavy casualties long before they ever reached their own front line.

Two battalions of Tyneside Scots, the 2nd and 3rd Tyneside Scots attacked from the British front line between the village of La Boisselle and the Lochnagar Crater where you are standing, while two battalions, 1st and 4th Tyneside Scots attacked on the far side (north) of the village. Look along the line of the road that leads from the Lochnagar Crater to La Boisselle. As the 2nd and 3rd Tyneside Scots advanced, they were moving from your left to your right towards the German front line.

The German defenders were badly shaken but alive after the ineffective British bombardment and emerged from their dugouts to set up their machine guns. The Tyneside Scots were hit by devastating machine gun fire from the village and soon their dead and wounded lay strewn across the ground. The nearer that the men were to the lethal machine gun fire coming from La Boisselle, the more numerous were the casualties. Further away from the village, some men reached the still smoking cavity of the new Lochnagar Crater where you are standing and where they regrouped.

Walk round Lochnagar Crater to the far side of the crater. You will notice a wooden cross with the name Private George Nugent, who was a Tyneside Scot who went missing after the attack on 1 July. In 1998, a visitor to Lochnagar Crater noticed a boot sticking out of the ground. Excavations revealed an entire skeleton. The remains were identified by a straight razor with the victim's name on it. Nugent had finally been discovered after eighty-two years. He was buried with full military honours in Ovillers Military Cemetery.

There were no significant gains here on 1 July. Sausage Valley became strewn with the dead of the 34th Division. The attack had been a disaster. The open terrain on which the men were exposed to the Germans and the inadequate British artillery bombardment resulted in the heaviest losses sustained by any division on this day. The 34th Division lost no fewer than 6,380 killed, wounded and missing. There were so many casualties that the 34th Division was partly replaced on the evening of 1 July by the 19th Division.

Now leave Lochnagar Crater and go towards La Boisselle. You will reach the D20, where you should turn left. This road soon reaches a junction with the busy D929. There is an area of rough ground clearly visible over to your left just before you reach this junction. There are mine craters within this rough ground. This was called the Glory Hole, where mining and counter-mining went on during the war. Recently many tunnels have been excavated here in what is an on-going project. There was no attack launched at the Glory Hole because the ground here was so pitted with shell holes and craters of

Figure 5.8 Wooden cross marking the place where the remains of Private Nugent were discovered.

different sizes that it was impossible to attack across it. The respective front lines were only about 30 yards apart here.

Now make your way to the D20 junction with the D929. Cross the main road and follow the signpost for Authuille on the D20. As you leave the road junction behind, stop after approximately 150 yards and look back. Since there are no definite landmarks to use as a reference points, the following directions are approximate and subject to interpretation of position based on available maps. As you look back you will see La Boisselle straight ahead. To your left is a shallow valley, which was named Mash Valley by the British. Nothing remains of Y Sap Crater in the field immediately adjacent to the village on the left side of the road as this has been reclaimed as farming land. To your right you will see the Usna Hill and beyond it the main road which leads to Albert. Ahead of you the British front line came from the southern end of La Boisselle, at the bottom of the steep incline. It then ran along the field to your right close to and parallel to the road (see Main Map Somme (North)). The 4th Tyneside Scots attacked from this position. The 2nd Tyneside Irish attacked down the slope of the Usna Hill behind them. The 1st, 3rd and 4th Tyneside Irish came down the Tara Hill on the far side of the main road which leads to Albert.

Close to where you are standing, the British front line crossed to the field on the other side of the road (to your left as you face La Boisselle) before continuing in a northerly direction towards the next village of Thiepval. If you now turn round, the 1st Tyneside Scots attacked from the first 100 yards or so of this field (which is now to your right) at 0730 on 1 July. The attack on this northern side of the village fared no better than on the south, and heavy casualties were sustained from machine gun fire from La Boisselle.

To the left of the 1st Battalion Tyneside Scots was the 2nd Middlesex Battalion, part of the 8th Division. The ground covered by the 8th Division therefore extended from a position approximately 100 yards into the field towards which you are looking and extended as far as Authuille Wood which you will visit shortly.

The 8th Division was a Regular Army formation; its task was to take the village of Ovillers, before continuing to the shallow top of Mash Valley to attack and take Pozières, fighting alongside the adjacent 34th Division. The 8th Division was made up from predominantly regular army battalions, shown in Table 5.2. Their lineup is shown in Figure 5.9.

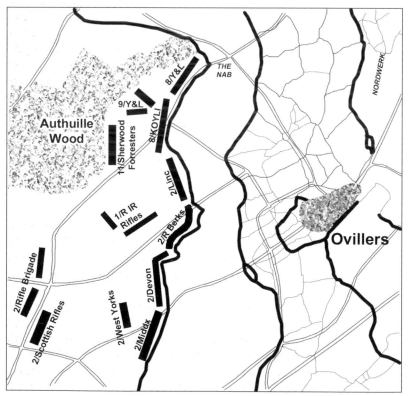

Figure 5.9 8th Division infantry.

Table 5.2 8th Division infantry orders of battle 1 July 1916.

23rd Brigade	25th Brigade	70th Brigade
2nd Devonshires	2nd Lincolns	11th Sherwood Foresters (attached from 23rd Division)
2nd Middlesex	2nd Royal Berks	8th King's Own Yorkshire Light Infantry (attached from 23rd Division)
2nd West Yorks	1st Royal Irish Rifles	8th Yorks and Lancs (attached from 23rd Division)
2nd Scottish Rifles	2nd Rifle Brigade	9th Yorks and Lancs (attached from 23rd Division)

Pioneers 22nd Durham Light Infantry

From your position here on the D20, look up Mash Valley. The German front line was very close to La Boisselle at the southern end of the village where the main road leaves to ascend between the Tara and Usna Hills. The German line remained close to La Boisselle as it skirted round the village, before leaving La Boisselle and crossing Mash Valley in front of Ovillers (Figures 5.1 and 5.9). You can see Ovillers near the top left of Mash Valley. At this point the German line was about 800 yards away from the British front line. It then went up onto the high ground to the left (Ovillers Spur) before passing to the tip of Authuille Wood. Mash Valley was a formidable obstacle. La Boisselle forms the boundary on the right side of this valley. Ovillers stands on the high ground towards the top of the valley. The left side of the valley is demarcated by the high ground of the Ovillers Spur, sloping down to Mash Valley. Fire could be directed into Mash Valley from three sides.

8TH DIVISION ATTACK, 1 JULY 1916

Part of the 8th Division attacked Ovillers directly up Mash Valley. These were men of the 2nd Middlesex and 2nd Devons, backed up by the 2nd West Yorks and the 2nd Scottish Rifles. As they went up Mash Valley they were exposed to the most devastating concentration of machine gun fire from all round the valley.

Success for the 8th Division depended on the operational success of neighbouring divisions – the 34th Division at La Boisselle on its right and the 32nd Division at Thiepval on its left (north). However, as you already know the 34th Division had failed and later, in Chapter 8, the failure of the 32nd Division will be explained. Consequently, the attack of the 8th Division was doomed because additional artillery and machine gun fire could be concentrated from adjacent positions.

Figure 5.10a Mash Valley up which 8th Division attacked towards Ovillers. La Boisselle is on the right; Ovillers is at the head of the valley. The Ovillers Spur forms the left side of the valley.

Figure 5.10b Looking up Mash Valley from the same position towards Ovillers and Ovillers Military Cemetery.

Lieutenant-Colonel Sandys was commanding officer of the 2nd Middlesex. He was wounded in the attack and was sent home to England. Only one officer and twenty eight men of his battalion answered roll call on the evening of I July. Sandys became very depressed as a result of this disastrous failure and committed suicide by shooting himself through the head in a room in the Cavendish Hotel in London. He was still alive when found, and was taken to St George's Hospital where he died on 13 September 1916.

You can now move on from your position at the bottom of Mash Valley. Proceed in the direction of Authuille. You will soon pass a minor road to your right that leads to Ovillers. Stop here for a moment and look up the road in the direction of Ovillers. The line of the 2nd Middlesex was mostly in the field to your right, but just extended across the road to the field on the left (see Figure 5.9).

Continue along the D20 towards the village of Authuille. You will pass a small roundabout where the D20 goes to the left through Aveluy and the road to Authuille, the D151, goes straight on. There is a crucifix set back in a copse of trees, so you must look hard to see this! British soldiers could congregate here in relative safety on their way up to the front line. Keep straight on to Authuille on the D151, and when you have nearly passed through the village, look for a signpost directing you to Lonsdale Cemetery. This is a minor road, with no designated number but follow it towards the cemetery. You will see the Thiepval Memorial to the Missing on the high ground to your left. Continue past the cemetery.

The road soon turns sharply to the right and goes through a wooded area with trees on both sides of the road. You are passing through the top end of Authuille Wood and are close to where the British front line passed on 1 July 1916. The British front line was in the trees to your right, whilst the German front line was to your left. Over the next 200 to300 yards you will be travelling along the middle of No Man's Land. (See Main Map Somme (North)). The soldiers of the 8th Division fought between here and Mash Valley, which is now approximately three quarters of a mile ahead of you.

Stop as soon as you get out of the wood into open ground. Look to your left. The German front line was approximately 100 yards away. The men who were involved in the attack here were the 11th Sherwood Foresters, 8th King's Own Yorkshire Light Infantry, 8th Yorks and Lancs and 9th Yorks and Lancs. They came under very heavy machine gun fire from a strongpoint behind the German front line called the Nordwerk. As you look in the direction of the German front line from your position the Nordwerk was approximately 200 yards behind the German front line and in your 1 o'clock position. No gains were made (Figure 5.9).

Keep going on the road that will take you to Ovillers. You will pass across ground where 2nd Lincolns, 2nd Royal Berkshires, 1st Royal Irish Rifles and

2nd Rifle Brigade attacked over very open ground. The approximate position of the front lines is shown in Main Map Somme (North). This attack too failed completely. Continue to Ovillers. You reach a T Junction within the village with another undesignated road. Turn right and go straight through the village. When you reach the end of the village, keep straight on. You will pass Ovillers Military Cemetery on your right where Private Nugent is buried. Continue until you join the D20. As you go, Mash Valley is to your immediate left. Turn left when you reach the D20 and return to La Boisselle. The 8th Division suffered 5,121 casualties for no gain whatsoever, and also had such terrible losses that it had to be replaced by the 12th Division, which was given the job of capturing Ovillers. This proved to be a very difficult task and will be discussed in Chapter 6.

Chapter 6

The Battle in the Centre: La Boisselle, Contalmaison and Pozières

FIGHTING AT LA BOISSELLE AFTER 1 JULY 1916

On 1 July 1916 the 34th Division failed to take any of its objectives. Instead of taking La Boisselle and going on to capture Contalmaison, the survivors of the division were back in their front line trenches. The 34th Division had sustained more casualties than any other division on 1 July and because of this they had to be replaced temporarily by the 19th Division.

General Rawlinson was of the opinion that he should make plans to capture those objectives which the British Fourth Army had failed to take on 1 July. Instead, he was told by General Haig that the Fourth Army would confine its activities to the south of the main road between Albert and Bapaume, which is the D929 today (See Main Map Somme (North)). Haig instructed Rawlinson to exploit the limited gains at Fricourt, Mametz and Montauban by making preparations for a major attack in that area. Rawlinson had to protect any such attack by securing the ground to either side. His first task in the present location to the left side was to remove the Germans from La Boisselle. Only then would the way be open to Contalmaison.

Haig planned to attack the German second line between Bazentin-le-Petit and Longueval. (See Main Map Somme (South 1)). Contalmaison was a key position on the left side. The capture of Contalmaison was important for another reason, which was unrelated to the proposed attack on the German second line between Bazentin-le-Petit and Longueval. Its capture would leave the way open to attack the village of Pozières, which was on the height of the Pozières Ridge. If the British could take Pozières, it would provide them with a commanding position in the centre of the battlefield. It would enable them to attack the German second line which ran through the very highest point of the ridge through a fortified windmill some 500 yards to the north of Pozières and it would provide the British with an alternative way of attacking Thiepval, from the rear, as will be explained in Chapter 9.

Start in the village of La Boisselle at the junction of the D20 with the D929 and make your way up the steep incline of the D20 going in the direction of Contalmaison. Stop when you reach the signpost indicating that you are leaving the village, and look back in the direction you have come from. If you are on foot or on a bicycle, it has been a long and hard climb! That part of the village near the junction of the D20 with the D929 was captured by soldiers of the 19th Division on 2 July. On 3 July, with inadequate and poorly co-ordinated artillery support, men from the same division attacked from both sides of the village, and then bombed their way through the shattered remnants of the buildings up the steep incline of the village to near where you are standing now. There were so many deep dugouts within the ruins of the village that the going was slow and difficult.

By this time, they were running out of bombs and a German counter-attack pushed them back almost to their starting point. Private G.T. Turrall of the 10th Worcesters won a Victoria Cross when he dragged his severely wounded officer, Lieutenant R. Jennings, back to a shell crater and protected him by fighting off numerous German bombing attacks. At nightfall, Turrall dragged Jennings back to the British front line. Jennings died, but not before telling others of Turrall's valour. After much further desperate close quarter fighting, the German defenders were pushed back again, close to where you are standing where they held on grimly until La Boisselle was finally captured on 4 July.

Now continue along the D20 in the direction of Contalmaison. Figure 6.1 is a photograph of La Boisselle with an arrow showing where you have been standing. The D20 is also marked with an arrow. Lochnagar Crater is just out of the picture to the bottom left at the end of the track. The German front line at Bloater Trench and Kipper Trench ran along round Sausage Valley below this road. As already explained the 15th and 16th Royal Scots attacked towards these trenches and suffered dreadful casualties (Chapter 5). They should have pressed on to capture Contalmaison had things had gone according to plan. In fact, the capture of Contalmaison turned out to be a prolonged and costly business which you will now appreciate as you go there. As already explained, General Rawlinson had been instructed by Haig to make preparations for a major attack in the area around Mametz and Montauban. Having captured La Boisselle, the next step was to secure the village of Contalmaison.

Multiple small attacks were launched by the 23rd Division in attempts to take Contalmaison. Between 5 and 10 July, eight attacks were carried out against the village and approximately 3,500 casualties were sustained but with no gains to show for this loss of life. Figure 6.2 shows the Divisions attacking towards Contalmaison.

As you travel on the D20, the 19th Division and the 34th Division (which had now rejoined the battle) launched attacks towards the left side of Contalmaison, while the 23rd Division to their right attacked the village.

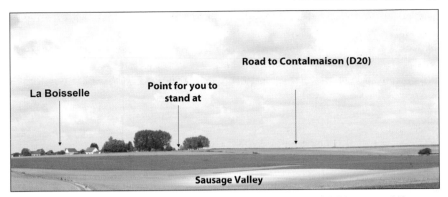

Figure 6.1 La Boisselle with the road to Contalmaison marked. Bloater and Kipper Trenches ran round the margin of Sausage Valley.

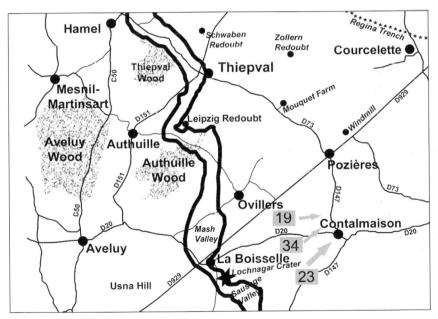

Figure 6.2 Contalmaison July 1916.

Contalmaison was finally taken by the 23rd Division on 10 July. As you travel along the D20 you can appreciate the general direction of attacks which were taking place. There was very little cooperation between adjacent divisions in coordinating artillery and infantry activity. Keep going to Contalmaison. When you reach the village the road divides with one part going to the left and the other turning to the right. If you follow the road to your right you will

Figure 6.3 Memorial to the 15th and 16th Royal Scots at Contalmaison.

see a church on the left-hand side of the road. Just in front of the church is a memorial to the 15th and 16th Royal Scots.

The 16th Royal Scots were known as McCrae's Battalion. Lieutenant-Colonel Sir George McCrae, their commanding officer, was a very popular figure in Edinburgh. Many soldiers in the 16th Royal Scots were players with Heart of Midlothian Football Club. At the outbreak of war in 1914, while many men volunteered to join the army, questions were being asked in the press and parliament as to why many men were still playing football and not joining the army. Sir George McCrae announced he would raise a battalion, the 16th Royal Scots, in seven days. Hearts players led the way and sixteen enlisted straight away. Players from other clubs enlisted as well as many supporters. Hearts manager John McCartney declared:

> Now then, young men, as you have followed the old club through adverse and pleasant times, through sunshine and rain, roll up in your hundreds for King and Country, for right for freedom. Don't let it be said that footballers are shirkers and cowards. As the club has borne an honoured name on the football field, let it also go down in history that it also won its spurs on the field of battle.[1]

---

1   Alexander, J., *McCrae's Battalion; The story of the 16th Royal Scots* (Edinburgh. Mainstream Publishing, 2003), p.82.

The battalion suffered 229 killed and 347 wounded on 1 July. Harry Wattie, acknowledged as the best inside-forward in Scotland at that time was amongst the dead. His body was never found.

Now that Contalmaison had been captured, the left side of the proposed attack on 14 July was protected. The way was also clear to advance and capture Pozières. This is where you will go next. Retrace your steps from your position at the memorial and turn left onto the D20 just past the church. After a short distance, turn right onto the D147, which is signposted to Pozières. It is about a mile and a half away. As you travel the short distance, you can reflect that things did not get any easier.

The 34th Division attacked towards Pozières on 14 July and on the following day without success. Men advancing in the direction you are going were exposed over the mile and a half of open ground. They came under heavy machine gun fire from Pozières as they approached the village. Two further failed attacks were made, the last on 17 July. The British front line was still 600 yards from Pozières. It was after returning from a reconnaissance trip to this area on 22 July that Major-General Ingouville Williams, Commanding Officer of the 34th Division, was killed at the Queens Nullah by an exploding shell (Chapter 2).

Since the British Fourth Army had failed to take Pozières, the Reserve Army under General Gough was now given the task of taking the village. The Australian 1st Division which had recently arrived on the Somme and had taken over the right flank of the Reserve Army was given the assignment. Although the Australian 1st Division was with the Reserve Army, the Australians would attack from either side of the road along which you are travelling (i.e. from the south side of the road between Albert and Bapaume). The Reserve Army's area of operation was normally on the far side of the Albert to Bapaume road. General Gough was very impulsive and wanted to proceed straight away. He planned to make the assault on Pozières on 19 July. However, Major-General Walker, commanding officer of the Australian 1st Division stated that there would not be an attack until his own artillery had been brought into position and all other available artillery had been put at his disposal. Therefore, the assault was delayed until the night of 22/23 July.

As you approach Pozières, stop when you are approximately 200 yards from the village. You can find a useful stopping reference point by looking to your right. You will see a large farm building and also the radio mast which can be seen from many parts of the battlefield. Stop when the radio mast is behind the building. The Australians had to deal with the problem that No Man's Land was around 600 yards wide, so they dug saps towards Pozières till they were 200 yards from the village, and level with your present position. The view you are getting from this observation point gives you an idea of how far the soldiers of the Australian 1st Division had to go before they reached the village.

Figure 6.4 Looking towards Pozières coming from Contalmaison; the southern end of the village is shown as is the 1st Australian Division Memorial.

An artillery bombardment opened on 19 July and on the evening of 22 July Australian soldiers crept forward to within 50 yards of their first objective, which was a German trench protecting the ruined remains of the village. The attack started at 0030 on 23 July. The men moved forward in the fields on either side of where you are into the ruined remains of the village. As they advanced, the Australians came under fire coming in from the right side from the German second line on the higher ground beyond the northern end of the village. It came predominantly from a German strongpoint called the Windmill, approximately 500 yards beyond the village. As you look to your right from your present position, the Windmill was just beside where the radio mast is today. As already indicated, you can just see the radio mast projecting beyond the top of the farm building.

Figure 6.6 was taken from an equivalent position on the other side of the village. The site of the Windmill is just to the left of the radio mast. This view gives you a better idea of where the German second line was and how far it was from the village. You will visit this position later in Chapter 9.

Now go into Pozières and stop when you reach the pavement at the junction of the D147 and D929. On the night of 22/23 July, there would have been Australian troops throughout the length of the village. As you stand here, it is worth reflecting on the following facts:

Figure 6.5 Looking to the north of Pozières in the direction of Bapaume, the radio mast is just visible above the farm building. The mast marks the position of the Windmill, which was a strongly fortified position on the German second line.

Figure 6.6 The site of the Windmill taken from an equivalent position the other side of Pozières; note the distance between this site and the trees which mark the northern limit of the village. This is the distance the 2nd Australian Division advanced to the Windmill after the 1st Australian Division captured Pozières.

- Australian success at Pozières was attributable to Walker's meticulous planning and his ability to resist attacking till the artillery was ready. The Australian artillery had had a devastating effect on the defending German troops in Pozières;
- Troops of the 1st Australian Division looked towards the northern end of the village in the direction of Bapaume and could see German reinforcements arriving to launch a counter-attack only to watch them disappear under a heavy artillery bombardment;
- After this failed German counter-attack, the 1st Australian Division sustained very heavy casualties. Since there was no German force in the village, enemy artillery could pour shellfire into the village without any fear of harming their hard-pressed infantry. The 1st Australian Division suffered 5,283 casualties primarily from heavy shellfire.

Now cross the road and take the D73 which leads to Thiepval. After about 100 yards there is a signpost directing you to the Australian 1st Division Memorial which you should follow.

The memorial is close to where there was a German blockhouse (a rarity on the Somme) which was called "Gibraltar". Given their heavy losses, this is a most appropriate place for the Australian 1st Divisional Memorial. There is an observation platform opposite the memorial. Go up the steps to the platform. If you look beyond the memorial you can see the Thiepval Memorial to the Missing in the distance. You may also see irregular chalk marks in the field beyond the memorial, provided there are no crops in the field. These are where trenches once were. In Chapter 9, the capture of a German strongpoint called Mouquet Farm will be discussed. Part of the force attacking Mouquet Farm did so through this field in the direction shown in Figure 6.7. Mouquet Farm is out of the photograph to the right. These chalk marks almost certainly represent what was a long and bitter struggle towards Mouquet Farm.

Now look 90 degrees to your left, or roughly the 9 o'clock position in relation to the Australian Memorial. You will see the village of Ovillers a mile away. Ovillers proved very difficult to take. The misfortunes of the 8th Division have been discussed in Chapter 5. On 2 July its capture became the responsibility of Gough's Reserve Army. The 8th Division was replaced by the 12th Division, which carried out a frontal assault on 3 July with predictable heavy casualties. After La Boisselle had been captured on 4 July, an attack was launched across the top of Mash Valley from the adjacent margin of La Boisselle, and a foothold gained in Ovillers. The 12th Division became exhausted and was relieved by the 32nd Division and many battalions from different divisions were used to try and take the village. It was eventually captured by the 11th Lancashire Fusiliers and the 2nd Royal Irish Rifles on the night of 15/16 July.

Figure 6.7 1st Australian Division Memorial at Pozières; the Thiepval Memorial is visible. British forces attacked across the fields in front of you coming from left to right towards Mouquet Farm. Mouquet Farm is not on the photograph, but you will see it if you look to the right in the distance. There are chalk marks in the field between that reflect the bitter fighting which took place.

Figure 6.8 From the observation tower looking towards Ovillers; the village of Ovillers is marked. It is to the right of Mash Valley as you look; the top of Mash Valley is also marked; La Boisselle is just out of the photograph to the left. After the capture of La Boisselle on 4 July 1916, a foothold was gained on Ovillers by launching an attack across Mash Valley from La Boisselle. After the capture of Ovillers, an unsuccessful attack was launched on Pozières by the 48th (South Midland) Division at the same time as the successful Australian 1st Division attack on the night of 22/23 July. The 48th Division was coming directly towards you.

Looking from the observation tower, you will appreciate that once Ovillers had been captured, a potential route directly from that village to your position on the observation tower had been made available to attack Pozières. On the night of 22/23 July, the 48th (South Midland) Division attacked from the shallow top of Mash Valley adjacent to Ovillers. It came under very heavy machine gun fire as it desperately tried to reach your position but the attack failed. In contrast to the excellent artillery support the Australians had benefited from, the 48th Division were given feeble support from artillery.

Having captured the village, the next major problem was to remove the Germans from their position at the fortified ruins of the Windmill beyond Pozières. Retrace your steps and return to the D929. Go to the northern end of the village in the direction of Bapaume and go a few hundred yards to the Windmill site where the Windmill fortifications once stood, and where the Australian flag flies. The remains of the fortifications of this site are across the road from a Tank Memorial and are very close to the radio mast. Look back in the direction of Pozières. You cannot see the village since your view is blocked by trees. You can remind yourself of the distance involved by glancing at Figure 6.6.

The Australian 1st Division was replaced by its 2nd Division on 25 July, which attacked towards the spot where you are standing because the German 2nd Line, called the OG Line, ran through the site of the fortified Windmill here. The line ran across the road towards the foot of the Bazentin Ridge to Longueval and Guillemont in one direction, where you will learn about it in Chapter 7 and through Mouquet Farm and to Grandcourt in the other, where you will again come across it in Chapter 9 (See Main Map Somme (North)). The Australian 2nd Division had to cross a wide and open No Man's Land from the northern end of Pozières to the Windmill site.

On 29 July the first attempt to take the position was a disaster because men advanced from Pozières to where you are standing with no covering fire. Trenches (saps) were then dug from Australian positions forward into No Man's Land towards where you are so that attacking troops would not have to advance so far in the open. After making due preparations, the 2nd Australian Division successfully attacked on 4 August while sustaining 6,846 casualties. The highest point on the battlefield was finally in British hands (See Figure 6.9).

The exhausted 2nd Australian Division was relieved by the 4th Australian Division on 6 August at the Windmill. A particularly intense German bombardment demonstrated the Germans were aware that a changeover was in progress. The newly-arrived battalions kept their heads down as they sheltered in sections of trench and dank dugouts. A determined German counterattack occurred at this spot on the early morning of 7 August. The Germans initially overwhelmed the Australian defenders in the dugouts and began to

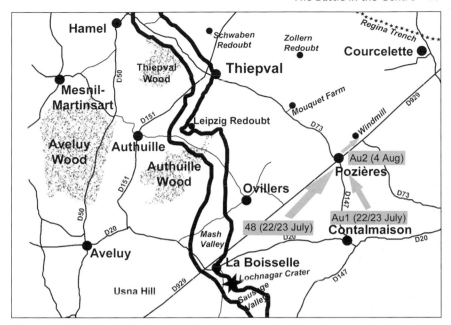

Figure 6.9 Pozières July-August 1916.

make their way towards Pozières, until a small party of Australians, led by Lieutenant Albert Jacka of the 14th Battalion, 4th Division, sprang out from a dugout near to where you stand and ferociously attacked the Germans. Jacka was wounded, but he saved the day. The lost ground was retaken. Had he not acted in this way, there is every possibility that the Germans could have retaken the heights above Pozières.

Albert Jacka had won a Victoria Cross at Gallipoli in 1915, the first Australian to do so. His act of bravery should perhaps have been worthy of a bar to his VC. Jacka was a controversial figure, however, who did not endear himself to military hierarchy. Furthermore, the Australians had been caught unawares in dugouts following the intense German bombardment, and should not have allowed themselves to be put in this position when the Germans launched their counter-attack. Nevertheless, Jacka was awarded a Military Cross for his heroism at Pozières.

Having captured Pozières, the next task the Australian forces was the seizure of Mouquet Farm (See Chapter 9).

Chapter 7

The Night Attack on 14 July 1916

High Wood to Waterlot Farm

There is a wood at the top of a hill,
If it's not shifted its standing there still;
There is a farm a short distance away,
But I'd not advise you to go there by day,
For the snipers abound, and the shells are not rare,
And a man's only chance is to run like a hare,
So take my advice if you're chancing your arm
From High Wood to Waterlot Farm.

Ewart Alan Mackintosh, (1893-1917)

In Chapters 2, 3 and 4, we explained the various actions in the southern part of the battlefield on 1 July 1916 which led to the limited successes experienced by the 7th and 21st Divisions at Mametz and Fricourt, and by the 18th and 30th Divisions at Pommiers Redoubt and Montauban. In Chapter 5, the difficulties and failures experienced by the 8th and 34th Divisions around the central part of the battlefield near La Boisselle and Ovillers were also explained.

After 1 July, General Rawlinson was of the opinion that he should attack those objectives which the British Fourth Army had failed to take that day. He was overruled by General Haig who told him to exploit southern gains by launching an attack between Longueval and the Bazentin Ridge onto the German second line positions.

The British Fourth Army would now operate south of the main road between Bapaume and Albert, while the Reserve Army (later renamed the Fifth Army) commanded by General Sir Hubert Gough would engage the Germans to the north of the road (See Map Somme (North) which shows this clearly).

Haig's proposal was as follows:

- The British Fourth Army should launch an attack between Mametz Wood on the left and Bernafay Wood on the right. This would mean that four divisions would attack and be bounded by woods on either side;
- The four divisions which would be used to carry out this attack were from left to right the 21st, 7th, 3rd and 9th Divisions;
- The 21st would attack Bazentin-le-Petit Wood and Bazentin-le-Petit;
- The 7th Division would attack Bazentin-le-Grand Wood and Bazentin–le-Grand, before going on to assist the 21st Division to capture Bazentin-le-Petit;
- The 3rd Division would capture the centre ground between the 7th Division to its left and 9th (Scottish) Division to its right;
- The 9th Division would attack Longueval and the adjacent Delville Wood;
- Their goal was to secure the territory between Bazentin-le-Grand and Longueval, thus gaining a firm position on the German second line which ran between these locations;
- Lastly they would attack High Wood. Rawlinson optimistically thought that a cavalry attack would successfully overcome German defenders in High Wood.

Between 2 July and the date of the proposed offensive, three key positions had to be taken before operations could proceed. This was because as the attack moved forwards there were German positions that would be on either side of the attacking forces and would be able to fire at them from the sides.

On one side these positions were at Contalmaison and Mametz Wood (to the west), and on the other side at Trônes Wood (to the east) and this can be understood by looking at Main Map Somme (South 1).

- Contalmaison and Mametz Wood were captured with great difficulty and loss of life by the 23rd Division and the 38th (Welsh) Division, respectively;
- Trônes Wood also had to be captured for the reason explained and this was achieved by the 18th Division on 14 July.

After Bernafay Wood was captured on 3 July, repeated attempts were made to capture Trônes Wood which lay quite close to it (see Figure 7.1). This photograph was taken from the village of Longueval about a mile away from Bernafay Wood. It shows Bernafay Wood to the right and Trônes Wood to the left.

No fewer than eight attacks were launched from the margin of Bernafay Wood towards Trônes Wood between 8 and 14 July. The first seven attacks failed because insufficient artillery and inadequate numbers of men were used to deal with a very heavily defended position. Trônes Wood was finally taken by the 18th Division on 14 July.

Figure 7.1 Bernafay Wood to the right and Trônes Wood to the left taken from the village of Longueval; Trônes Wood was captured by men of the 18th Division on 14 July 1916.

The 18th Division attacked and captured Trônes Wood at the same time as the 21st, 7th, 3rd and 9th Divisions attacked towards their objectives. The men in these four divisions advanced at right angles to the men in the 18th Division. Had the 18th Division been unsuccessful, this would have meant that Germans within Trônes Wood could have directed machine gun fire against the soldiers advancing towards Longueval. This final attack on Trônes Wood succeeded because adequate resources were allocated and used to make it a success. The most important reason for success was that enough artillery pieces had been made available to provide a density of fire four times greater than on 1 July.

Rawlinson made a strong case for a night assault in the days leading up to the attack. This was because No Man's Land was more than 1,000 yards wide on the right flank and the cover of darkness would allow men of the 9th and 3rd Divisions to leave their front line positions and advance some distance into No Man's Land to await zero hour at 0325. They would not have so far to go to reach the German front line. Haig at first thought Rawlinson's proposal was impractical, and that complex troop movements in the dark would prove too difficult, but he finally agreed to it.

There was, in fact, another and much more important reason why the assault on 14 July was successful. There was much more artillery available to support the attack. Men crept into No Man's Land while a hurricane bombardment went over their heads into the German positions. It destroyed the German barbed wire and trenches. At the start of the attack (zero hour) a creeping barrage using high explosive for the first time allowed the men to advance rapidly into enemy positions. Regardless of whether it was dark or not, if the soldiers had encountered uncut German barbed wire in No Man's Land, the commotion in getting through this would certainly have alerted German defenders to the danger. Fortunately, the artillery barrage commencing on 11 July, which preceded the attack and was maintained up until the start of the attack, had been very effective.

The 3rd and 9th Divisions took up their advanced positions in No Man's Land under cover of this barrage, which also helped to conceal their presence. There was a further five minute intense bombardment which began at 0320. The German front line and barbed wire were completely pulverised. The intense barrage was the key to success. Without the destruction of the German barbed wire and trenches, a night attack would have stood no greater chance of success than one launched in daylight.

Objectives were soon achieved. Bazentin-le-Petit Wood, Bazentin-le-Petit, Bazentin-le-Grand and Bazentin-le-Grand Wood were captured on the left. At the same time the 9th (Scottish) Division quickly captured most of Longueval (except for a small part at the far end of the village, with some adjacent orchards) and a small part of Delville Wood.

British and Indian cavalry were duly brought up to charge up to High Wood, but by the time they got there it was early evening, and their attack was unsuccessful. The most important reason for failure was that artillery support at this far limit of the attack was not available because it took a great deal of time and effort to position guns and to register them on targets before beginning. The advance had outstripped effective artillery support and left the cavalry exposed to German fire.

Begin your journey at the village of Montauban. Travel along the D64 till you reach a cross-road with the D197. Go straight across and then go past Bernafay Wood on your left until you reach Trônes Wood. Stop at the Memorial to the 18th Division which is situated near the road in front of the wood on the left of the D64 as you go along it and reflect on what happened at Trônes Wood. By the time the attack on Trônes Wood had finished, the British line ran along close to the far side of the Wood, the edge which faces the village of Guillemont, that is a short distance away along the D64, and can be clearly seen less than a mile away. Go along the road to the edge of Trônes Wood which faces Guillemont. A few hundred yards in front of you is the Cross of Sacrifice at Guillemont Road Cemetery.

As you stand at this position, looking towards the Cross of Sacrifice, here are some facts to reflect on:

- Here you will find the grave (I.B.3) of Raymond Asquith, the son of the British Prime Minister Herbert Asquith. A Lieutenant in the Grenadier Guards, he was killed on 15 September 1916, fighting with the Guards Division during the battle of Flers-Courcelette when tanks were used for the first time (Chapter 10);

- Close as it is to Trônes Wood, Guillemont was not captured until 3 September 1916 by the 20th Division with additional help from the 16th (Irish) Division. There had been many failed attempts before this happened. Such failures were again due to too few soldiers attacking over too narrow an area which allowed German artillery fire to inflict heavy casualties;

- One of the early failures at Guillemont involved the 10th King's (Liverpool Scots) on 7 August. The Battalion medical officer (Captain Noel Chavasse) won a Victoria Cross in the field between your current position and Guillemont Road Cemetery. He repeatedly went out into this field, which was in No Man's Land and despite heavy hostile fire brought back wounded to his regimental aid post. He also went out to recover identity discs from the dead, so that family members at home would not hold out any false hopes that their loved ones were still alive. Chavasse won a second VC on 31 July 1917 on the opening day of 3rd Battle of Ypres. Sadly he sustained a penetrating abdominal wound, underwent an emergency abdominal operation at a Casualty Clearing Station (No 32) at Brandhoek, near Ypres, but died of complications on 4 August. He is buried in Brandhoek New Military Cemetery and was the only individual to win two VCs in the Great War.

Figure 7.2 Guillemont Road Cemetery with Guillemont village beyond; Noel Chavasse (10th King's) won the first of his two Victoria Crosses in the field in foreground of this photograph.

Now retrace your steps and go back along the D64 until you come to the junction of the D64 and D197 which is at the side of Bernafay Wood. Go straight across the junction, and stop before you reach Montauban. If you look through the fence to your right, you can see the rectangular expanse of territory that was attacked on 14 July.

To the left (refer to the photograph as you look) you can see a wooded area, which is actually made up of three (Mametz, Bazentin-le-Grand and Bazentin-le-Petit) Woods. Straight ahead of you in the far distance is High Wood. To the right of High Wood is Delville Wood together with the houses of the village of Longueval just visible in front of the trees. To the extreme right of the photograph you can see the corner of Bernafay Wood. Just out of the photograph to your left is the village of Montauban.

The British front line on 14 July was beyond the crest of the field in front of you. This was in Montauban Alley Trench which you have seen in Chapter 2. The front line then curved round the front of the village as you are looking ahead (to the north) then around the margin of Bernafay Wood which is again in front of you at the furthest away edge of the wood and then down towards the far side of Bernafay Wood (which is the side facing Trônes Wood where you have just been).

Figure 7.3 Looking from Montauban towards High Wood on the skyline; to the right of High Wood is Longueval with Delville Wood adjacent to it. The corner of Bernafay Wood can be seen on the right foreground. To the left may be seen the overlapping Bazentin-le-Grand, Mametz and Bazentin-le-Petit Woods which are not clearly distinguishable on this photograph.

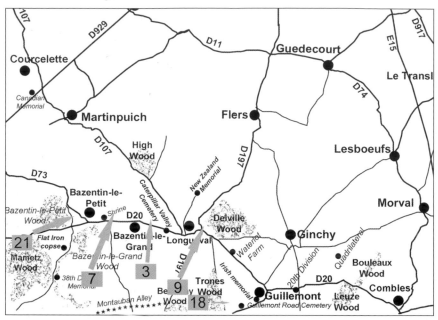

Figure 7.4 Diagram of attacking Divisions on 14 July 1916; No Man's Land was very wide on the front of the 9th (Scottish) and 3rd Divisions and so they moved forward into it under the barrage before the attack began.

In Figure 7.4 the five divisions that launched the attack on 14 July 1916 are shown. To summarise their positions and objectives:

- The 18th Division attacked towards Trônes Wood to your right;
- The 9th (Scottish) Division attacked from positions well out in No Man's Land ahead of your present position towards Longueval. No Man's Land was more than 1,000 yards wide, and the cover of darkness and ferocious artillery bombardment meant that these men could make their way unnoticed into No Man's Land;
- Men from the 3rd Division were positioned over to your left on the left-hand side of the 9th Division and they too attacked from positions well out into No Man's Land. Their objective was to take the centre ground between the 9th Division on their right and the 7th Division on their left;
- The 7th Division attacked Bazentin-le-Grand and Bazentin-le-Grand Wood, before going on to help the 21st Division capture Bazentin-le-Petit;
- The 21st Division was at Mametz Wood over to your far left and it launched its attack towards Bazentin-le-Petit Wood and continued to Bazentin-le-Petit on the Bazentin Ridge.

Now leave your position at the fence and go along the D197 up a slight incline towards Longueval which you can see. As you reach the far end of Bernafay Wood stop for a moment. To your right you are level with the British front line which extended along Montauban Alley (to your left). As you move beyond Bernafay Wood, you are in No Man's Land, which was an exposed area more than 1,000 yards wide at this point. Men from the 9th Division made their way forward under cover of darkness from here and used the bombardment to get as close as they possibly could to German front line near Longueval.

Nearby is Bernafay Wood Cemetery on your left and Longueval Road Cemetery on your right on your as you make your way to Longueval. You can clearly see Delville Wood to the right of the village. The 9th Division captured most of Longueval and the adjacent corner of Delville Wood. When you reach the village, turn left onto the D20 towards Contalmaison. Stop when you reach Caterpillar Valley Cemetery which is about half a mile on the left.

Caterpillar Valley Cemetery is an ideal location to be able to understand events as they unfolded on 14 July. You should go to the wall of the cemetery in the far distance as you enter the cemetery gate (this is the southern wall). Looking straight ahead from this wall, the village of Montauban is visible on the skyline and is easily recognised because of its unusual and unique bulbous church spire. To the left is Bernafay Wood where you have just come from.

Figure 7.5 Montauban from Caterpillar Valley Cemetery with Bernafay Wood to the left; the 9th (Scottish) Division attacked towards Longueval, and its men would have come towards you across the ground to the left of the photograph while men from the 3rd Division would have advanced across the ground to the right of the photograph between the 9th Division to their right and 7th Division to their left.

The attack by men of the 9th Division came directly towards you from their positions in No Man's Land. To their left, which to confuse, is actually to the right as you look from your current position) the 3rd Division came across the fields in front and to your right.

Looking to the right from your position (a westerly direction) along the skyline from Montauban, you can discern the ground captured by the 18th Division on 1 July. The strongly fortified position of the Pommiers Redoubt would have been on the skyline. On a clear day, you can just make out the cross of sacrifice at Danzig Alley Cemetery that is in the 2 o'clock position approximately. Pommiers Redoubt would have been roughly half-way between Montauban and Danzig Alley Cemetery. You cannot see the village of Mametz captured by the 7th Division as it is below the skyline.

If you continue looking round to the right, in the middle distance, there is a heavily wooded area, composed of Bazentin-le-Grand Wood in the foreground and Mametz Wood just visible above the fields to the right. The 7th Division attacked towards Bazentin-le-Grand and its wood, whilst beyond it the 21st Division attacked from the northern margin of Mametz Wood towards Bazentin-le-Petit and its wood. The 7th Division assisted the 21st Division to capture Bazentin-le-Petit.

Now move to the front gate of the cemetery, and look across the road (D20) you came here along straight ahead (this is to the north). High Wood is seen on the skyline on the crest of the ridge in front of you.

Figure 7.6 Looking to the right along the ridge between Montauban and Mametz (beyond and to the right) from Caterpillar Valley Cemetery; men from the 30th Division captured Montauban on 1 July advancing from their front line which was half a mile on the far side of the village running from left to right. Pommiers Redoubt, approximately mid-way along the ridge, was captured by men of the 18th Division. This was one of the few successes of 1 July.

Figure 7.7 This shows Bazentin-le-Grand Wood and Mametz Wood just visible beyond it. Bazentin-le-Grand Wood was captured by men of the 7th Division on 14 July.

Figure 7.8 High Wood, from the gate of Caterpillar Valley Cemetery; the failed cavalry charge took place towards High Wood in the early evening of 14 July through the field. High Wood remained in enemy hands until 15 September.

Look to your left and on the same side of the road as High Wood you can see Bazentin-le-Petit Wood. The village of Bazentin-le-Petit is considerably larger that Bazentin-le-Grand and is up a fairly steep incline. Both these villages and their respective woods were captured on 14 July by late afternoon. This resulted in the attacking British forces now having a firm foothold on the Bazentin Ridge. Still standing at the cemetery gate, look to your right and you will see the nearby village of Longueval and Delville Wood is clearly visible behind it and to its left.

Men of the 9th Division entered the ruins of Longueval within a few minutes of starting the attack on 14 July, and they also approached a strongly fortified German position called Waterlot Farm a few hundred yards to the south of Delville Wood on the road between Longueval and Guillemont which cannot be seen but is in the distance to your right. Waterlot Farm was not taken till 17 July. By the end of the day on 14 July, the 9th Division had captured part of what you can see in front of you (also shown in this photograph). They had taken most of Longueval apart from the top end of the village to the left. They had taken the bottom corner of Delville Wood closest to the village.

After the successes on 14 July, as previously explained, the British turned their attention to the Germans who were still occupying High Wood. Rawlinson, having been previously criticized by Haig for his cautious 'bite and hold' policy, demonstrated signs of undue optimism when he ordered the cavalry to attack High Wood through the fields on your immediate left.

Figure 7.9 This view of Longueval and Delville Wood was taken from Caterpillar Valley Cemetery Gate. Most of the village was captured on 14 July by men of the 9th Division apart from the northern part of the village and adjacent orchards which were close to where the sheep are grazing.

It had been thought that High Wood was practically empty of Germans and could be captured easily. However, this was not the case because there were enemy reserves in the wood. The cavalry attack was to be made by the Secunderabad Brigade, which arrived after making its way over the shell-pocked terrain between Montauban and where you are standing. The attack failed and High Wood remained in German hands until 15 September. From Caterpillar Valley Cemetery gate, take a moment to reflect that you would have seen cavalry charging through the fields in front of you, horses and men falling as they rode to death and glory towards High Wood.

Leave Caterpillar Valley Cemetery and continue along the D20 away from Longueval (this is in a westerly direction). As you go, you will travel along the road that was crossed by the attacking 3rd Division. To the left you will see Bazentin-le-Grand Wood in the middle distance, while to your right is High Wood as you already know. You will reach a turning to the left sign-posted Bazentin-le-Grand. Men from the 7th Division would have crossed the road here on their way up towards Bazentin-le-Petit. There is, a short distance beyond the turn-off to Bazentin-le-Grand, a small copse of trees in a hollow of the road on the right side. Stop here and, looking very carefully because it is easy to miss, you will see a bronze crucifix within the trees. You will notice gaping wounds in the figure's right thigh and armpit. This statue was here in 1916. The 'wounds' appear to be the result of shell splinters. Perhaps they were inflicted by the creeping barrage on 14 July.

Figure 7.10 Damaged crucifix.

As you stand here you will also become aware that this is a very sheltered spot. Had you been here you would have been protected from shellfire coming from behind High Wood. This was a place where men would congregate before going forward or coming back down to rest. It was also a place where casualties could be sheltered with some degree of safety before being carried to the advanced dressing station which you will visit shortly.

Now carry along the main road until you come to a T Junction a few hundred yards ahead of where you are now. Bazentin-le-Petit is signposted to the right. The wood ahead of you on the left is Mametz Wood. Men from the 21st Division left their positions from the wood, before crossing the road and moving up towards Bazentin-le-Petit Wood on the other side of the road, and to the village of Bazentin-le-Petit beyond. If you turn right and go up the hill to the village of Bazentin-le-Petit itself, you will appreciate that it is quite a steep incline. Once you reach the top of the village, you are on the Bazentin Ridge.

Now go back down the hill to the T Junction again and turn right on to the main road. Almost immediately you are on the road there is a turn off to the left and this is signposted for Flat Iron Copse Cemetery. Continue along this small road until you come to this cemetery and stop at the gate. There was an advanced dressing station here that was used for those wounded in the action on 14 July.

One of the wounded who was brought past here later in July 1916 was poet and soldier Captain Robert Graves, now attached to the 2nd Battalion Royal Welch Fusiliers, who had sustained an extremely severe chest wound. A piece of shell splinter went in one side of his chest wall and came out the other, missing everything of importance in between! It was thought that he would die, and his commanding officer, assured that this would be the case, actually sent word home that Graves had "bought it". The next morning, when he was unexpectedly still alive, he was sent back down the line. On reaching London, he was able to read his own obituary in *The Times* and he himself put in a notice saying that contrary to popular belief, Captain Robert Graves was alive and well and ready to receive visitors![1]

You will notice that the track continues onwards beyond the cemetery. This leads to the 38th (Welsh) Division Memorial Dragon opposite Mametz Wood, which you have already visited (see Chapter 3). If you follow this track and go past the memorial you soon reach a fork in the road. If you take the left fork and go up a steep incline, a minor road from Contalmaison soon joins the road from the right. Keep going and you will arrive at Mametz.

---

1   Graves, R., *Goodbye to All That* (London: Jonathan Cape, 1929. Reprinted Harmondsworth: Penguin Books, 1960), p.187.

This pathway to Mametz was known as "Death Valley." It was the route that soldiers took from Mametz to reach the front line up at High Wood. It was also the way casualties were evacuated from Flat Iron Copse Advanced Dressing Station to casualty clearing stations further back.

The Germans of course knew that this was the principal access route to the front at High Wood, and frequently shelled the area. Death could strike here at any time. After reflecting on some of the events which took place in proximity of where you are standing, you can retrace your steps towards the D20 and go back the same way you came and you will reach Longueval.

As you enter Longueval you will see the Pipers Memorial on your left at the crossroads. It is a modern memorial that was opened in July 2002 and on the nearby wall you will discern the regimental badges of pipers killed during the war. Traverse the crossroads, keeping in mind that most of Longueval was captured by 9th Division on 14 July whilst the buildings and orchard at the northern end of the village remained in German hands. Follow signs for the South African Memorial and stop when you reach Delville Wood a short distance on your left. Only the bottom part of the wood near where you are was captured that day.

The attack on 14 July can only be described as a limited success. The offensive ended in failure in front of High Wood, because there was no longer effective artillery support and men and horses were no match for the machine gun bullet!

EVENTS FOLLOWING THE LIMITED SUCCESS OF 14 JULY 1916

You can reflect on what happened from your position at the gate guarding the entrance to the South African Memorial. The starting point for these events is here in Delville Wood. South Africa had sent a brigade to fight on the Western Front. It was attached to the 9th Division. Most New Army divisions first saw action on the Somme in 1916, but the 9th and 15th (Scottish) Divisions fought at Loos the previous year. Due to massive losses, the 9th Division was reinforced with the South African Brigade that was now tasked with securing the remainder of the much-contested wood.

Within the first hour of attack on 15 July and by 0700 they had taken the southern part of the wood and continued moving forwards towards the northern and eastern parts. Progress appeared steady and most of the wood was thought to have been secured by mid-day. Nevertheless, despite having forced the defenders to the northern portion of the wood, the South African Brigade found itself surrounded on three sides because of the shape and orientation of the woodland area in relation to the enemy lines. This meant that the attackers would be exposed to artillery fire from three sides. The Germans subsequently withdrew. This allowed their artillery to bombard the beleaguered South Africans without fear of inflicting casualties on their own defending infantry. Resultant casualties were enormous. Of the 776 South Africans who perished during the five days' savage fighting (relief occurred on 20 July) only 113 have known graves.

The Germans launched a large counter-attack on the afternoon of 15 July 1916. Retention of the captured ground was impossible, and the Germans reoccupied the majority of the lost positions gained at such great cost. They were, in due course, subjected to annihilating shellfire in the same way as the South Africans had been.

The Germans, still in occupation of the northern extremity of Longueval, could fire on the South Africans from the northern part of the wood. On 16 July, the 11th Royal Scots (9th Division) made an unsuccessful attack on the north part of Longueval and adjacent orchards, while the South African Scottish made another effort to secure the remainder of Delville Wood. Over the course of the following ten days, other (3rd, 18th, 7th and 5th) divisions were deployed to take Delville Wood and Longueval and the orchards.

General Rawlinson, in the aftermath these failed attempts to take Delville Wood, called for a broad front attack against key positions that had defied capture thus far. This took place on the night of 22/23 July. The objectives included High Wood, Delville Wood and Guillemont; six divisions were tasked to do this.

Figure 7.11 illustrates the six divisions employed and the starting times for their attacks. Whilst their attacks were supposed to be co-ordinated there were no fewer than four separate starting times. The element of surprise was lost shortly after the attack on Wood Lane (situated between High Wood and Delville Wood) by 5th Division. Fighting around Delville Wood continued until 27 July, when the fresh 2nd Division, supported by the firepower of 368 guns, cleared the wood. The Germans, however, managed to regain part of it in early August. Here they remained until driven out on 3 September.

Delville Wood, which today is almost exactly the same as it was before the war, was purchased by the South African government in 1920 and the trees replanted. Before the war, it was divided by rides where villagers once strolled during tranquil pre-war Sundays. By July 1916, all that remained were uprooted trees and shattered stumps. Enter Delville Wood through the main entrance opposite. Immediately in front of you is the impressive and imposing South African Memorial and behind the memorial are the museum and the Cross of Consecration. Walk around the left-hand side of the memorial and you will enter the wood. The trees are separated by wide avenues (wider than they were before the war) which have the same names of streets as they had on trench maps during the war. You will see the remains of trenches and there is one tree protected by a metal cage. This is a hornbeam tree that is the only tree surviving from the war.

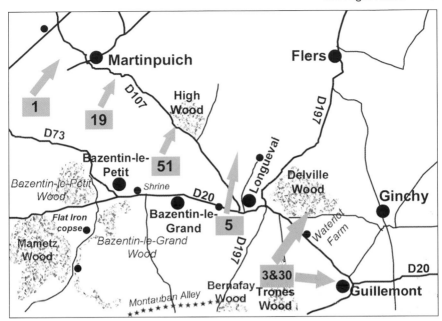

Figure 7.11 This sketch illustrates the poorly coordinated night attacks on 22/23 July There were four different jumping-off times; 5th Division attacked at 2200 on 22 July, 1st and 19th Division at 0030 on the 23 July followed at 0130 by 51st (Highland) Division. The 3rd and 30th Divisions attacked at 0340.

Figure 7.12 Remnants of trenches in Delville Wood.

Nearby you will see another memorial to two soldiers who were awarded the Victoria Cross as a result of their heroic actions on 20 July 1916. These men were Corporal J.J. Davies[2] and Private A. Hill[3], 10th Battalion Royal Welsh Fusiliers. It is difficult to image what conditions must have been like but their award citations might help you to understand:

> On the 20th July 1916, at Delville Wood, Corporal Davies and eight men were surrounded during an enemy counter-attack. Taking cover in a shell hole, they repulsed the attackers with grenades and rapid fire. He then followed up the retreating party of Germans and bayoneted several of them. All the officers had become casualties, Corporal Davies, badly wounded in a shoulder, took charge and led two attacks and kept a tight control of the reserves.

> On the 20th July 1916, at Delville Wood, when the battalion had deployed under very heavy fire for an attack Private Hill dashed forward, when the order to charge was given, and meeting two of the enemy suddenly, bayoneted them both. He was sent later by his platoon sergeant to get in touch with the company, and finding himself cut off and almost surrounded by some twenty of the enemy, attacked them with bombs, killing and wounded many and scattering the remainder. He then joined a sergeant and helped him to find the way back to the lines. When he got back, hearing that his Company Officer and a scout were lying out wounded, he went out and assisted in bringing in the wounded officer, two other men bringing in the scout. Finally, he himself captured and brought in as prisoners two of the enemy.

As you walk around the wood you will see a small obelisk which is at the site of the South African headquarters during the battle.

Across the road from the South African Memorial is Delville Wood cemetery which contains 5,523 British and Dominion graves. Approximately 3,593 are of 'Soldiers of the Great War, known unto God'. Brought here from the surrounding battlefields after the war it is a prime example of a concentration cemetery. The last burials were actually in 1984 – the bodies of three unknown men were found during construction of the South African Museum (Plot XIII, Row J).

2　http://www.delvillewood.com/davieshill2.htm
3　Ibid.

HIGH WOOD

Now return to Longueval and make your way to High Wood. Return to the D20 out of Longueval on the road to Bazentin-le-Petit. Just before Caterpillar Valley Cemetery you will see the D107 leading to Martinpuich on your right; High Wood is along the road to your right. Stop here. It is almost impossible to imagine just what it would have been like here. Harry Lunan (1/5th Gordon Highlanders) has left a poignant description of this area during the ill-fated night attack on 22/23 July:

> I played my company over the bloody top right into the German trenches. It was stupid as hell ... Men falling all around me; falling dead...it was bloody horrible..... I just played whatever came in to my head, but I was worried about tripping on the uneven ground, which interrupted my playing. The enemy fire was murderous; the men were falling all around me. I was lucky to survive. Hearing the pipes gave the troops courage ... The Germans were scared of the bloody pipes.[4]

---

4 Article from *Sunday Express* November 14, 1993 and *The Jock Column* March 1994. http://gordonhighlanders.carolynmorrisey.com/page8.htm

Chapter 8

Thiepval, 1 July 1916

This chapter focuses on the 32nd and 36th (Ulster) Divisions, both of which were New Army Divisions. The way in which the battalions of the 32nd and 36th Divisions lined up on 1 July 1916 is shown in Figure 8.1. The battalions making up the two divisions are shown in Tables 8.1 and 8.2.

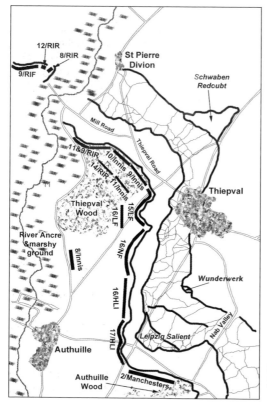

Figure 8.1
32nd and 36th Divisions
1 July 1916.

Table 8.1 32nd Division infantry orders of battle 1 July 1916.

14th Brigade	96th Brigade	97th Brigade
19th Lancashire Fusiliers (3rd Salford Pals)	16th Northumberland Fusiliers (Newcastle Commercials)	11th Borderers (The Lonsdales)
1st Dorsets	2nd Royal Inniskilling Fusiliers	2nd King's Own Yorkshire Light Infantry
2nd Manchesters	15th Lancashire Fusiliers (1st Salford Pals)	16th Highland Light Infantry (Glasgow Boys Brigade)
15th Highland Light Infantry (Glasgow Tramways)	16th Lancashire Fusiliers (2nd Salford Pals)	17th Highland Light Infantry (Glasgow Commercials)

Pioneers 17th Northumberland Fusiliers (Newcastle Railway Pals)

Table 8.2 36th (Ulster) Division infantry orders of battle 1 July 1916.

107th Brigade	108th Brigade	109th Brigade
8th Royal Irish Rifles (East Belfast)	11th Royal Irish Rifles (South Antrim)	9th Royal Inniskilling Fusiliers (County Tyrone)
9th Royal Irish Rifles (West Belfast)	12th Royal Irish Rifles (Central Antrim)	10th Royal Inniskilling Fusiliers (County Derry)
10th Royal Irish Rifles (South Belfast)	13th Royal Irish Rifles (County Down)	11th Royal Inniskilling Fusiliers (Donegal and Fermanagh)
15th Royal Irish Rifles (North Belfast)	9th Royal Irish Fusiliers (County Armagh, Monaghan and Cavan)	14th Royal Irish Rifles (Belfast Young Citizens)

Pioneers 16th Royal Irish Rifles (2nd County Down)

The 32nd Division was given the task of capturing the village of Thiepval and then to advance and take a strongly fortified position called Mouquet Farm in the German second line. The 36th Division, advancing on the left of the 32nd Division was to attack and take the German front line before proceeding to capture the Schwaben Redoubt, another strongly fortified position close behind the front line (Figure 8.1). It was also given the responsibility of attacking along both banks of the River Ancre and along the adjacent steep slopes of the Ancre valley (see Main Map Somme (North)).

Begin your journey at the Thiepval Memorial to the Missing where you can park your car or bicycle if you are being more energetic! Make your way from the car park and through the visitors' centre to the memorial itself, which bears the names of 73,357 British and South African soldiers, as well as sailors from the Royal Naval Division, who died here and who have no known grave. Canadian soldiers who died on the Somme and have no known grave are commemorated at the Vimy Memorial, whilst Australians are commemorated at Villers Bretonneux. New Zealand soldiers who died are commemorated near to where they fell, and on the Somme this is at Caterpillar Valley Cemetery, which will be discussed further in Chapter 10.

When you walk around the Thiepval Memorial, there is a tranquil irony about the place. The Poet Laureate, John Masefield visited what he referred to as "The Old Front Line" in 1917 after the German withdrawal to the Hindenburg Line. From here he wrote:

> Corpses, rats, old tins, old weapons, rifles, bombs, legs, boots, skulls, cartridges, bits of wood & iron & stone, parts of rotting bodies & festering heads lie scattered about. A more filthy, evil hole you cannot imagine.[1]

Now stand with your back to the memorial and face the large grassy area in front of the memorial. Walk forward until you reach a retaining wall with a seat in front of it. Look straight ahead. You will see a farm on the crest of a hillside approximately a mile and a half away. This is Mouquet Farm, which if you remember was one of the objectives for the 32nd Division on 1 July. It was a fortified strongpoint on the German second line.

Figure 8.4 was taken from close to Mouquet Farm and gives an idea of how far men from the 32nd Division would have had to advance to take their objective had they been successful in capturing Thiepval.

Now make your way from the Thiepval Memorial to an obelisk that commemorates the 18th Division. To reach it, go to the exit of the car park from where you will see the obelisk at the edge of a field close to the roadside of the D151. It is here because Thiepval was finally captured on 26 September 1916 by men of the 18th Division (See Chapter 9). Stop when you reach the obelisk and stand with your back to Thiepval on your right. Look straight ahead towards the tall tower partially hidden by trees on the right side of the road. Known as the Ulster Tower, it commemorates men of the 36th (Ulster) Division.

The first objective of the 32nd Division was to capture Thiepval, which you can see to the right from where you are standing. This was one of the most difficult tasks of the day because Thiepval is built on a ridge some 450 feet in height. The British positions were around the base of this high ground in the

---

1   Dyer, G. *The Missing of the Somme* (London: Hamish Hamilton, 1994), p.126.

Figure 8.2 Thiepval Memorial to the Missing.

Figure 8.3 Mouquet Farm seen from the Thiepval Memorial; Mouquet Farm is on a hillside with a commanding view over the ground between the German front line which was approximately at the level of the perimeter fence and the German second line which ran through Mouquet Farm.

Figure 8.4 Taken from Mouquet Farm; the German front line ran round the near side of the Thiepval Memorial; it was the key defensive position in the German second line. Men of the 32nd Division were given the task of capturing it on 1 July 1916. The village of Thiepval can be seen to the right.

Figure 8.5 Looking from 18th Division Memorial towards Thiepval Wood; the British front line was within the margin of Thiepval Wood. Advanced parties of Ulstermen crept out into No Man's Land before 0730 on 1 July in order to shorten the distance they had to go to the German line which ran through where Ulster Tower is today.

low-lying area round about. (You will get a better idea of the task they faced at the next observation point). Wherever the British attacked around Thiepval, they had an uphill climb towards German positions.

The 36th Division advanced from the margin of Thiepval Wood. This is the dense wood on the other side of the road from the Ulster Tower as you stand in your present position. The dividing road (D73) was known as 'Mill Road' in 1916 because of the close proximity of a mill situated astride the Ancre River at the bottom of a steep hill. The site of the previous mill can be reached if you proceed down Mill Road.

Connaught Cemetery is situated in front of Thiepval Wood. This is your next observation point. If you look beyond the cemetery within the same line, you can just see the spire of the church steeple at Hamel, a village on the opposite bank of the River Ancre, just behind the British front line.

The German front line on 1 July ran parallel to the British line and came very close to the position now occupied by the Ulster Tower. Mill Road was in No Man's Land. The German line then ran up towards Thiepval, and if you now turn to your right 90 degrees and face towards the village, the line would have passed between the village and the Thiepval Memorial to the Missing, which would have been in No Man's Land. The British line skirted round the margin of Thiepval Wood before passing through the fields below your present position. You will get a better idea of its position when you visit the next observation point.

The 36th (Ulster) Division was assigned the task of capturing a strong point behind the German front line known as Schwaben Redoubt. It was to the right of the Ulster Tower as you look from your present position. Lying beneath it was an underground warren of accommodation blocks for soldiers, storage and medical facilities.

The men of the 36th Division were also given the job of taking a small village called St Pierre Divion, which is down in the deep valley at the bottom of Mill Road. You cannot see St Pierre Divion from your present position because it is tucked in this side of the valley. In the valley is a small river called the Ancre, which is a tributary of the River Somme. In addition, the 36th Division was tasked to capture the ground along the far bank (the north side) of the River Ancre.

Facing the British at Thiepval was the 26th Reserve Division. The German defenders had prepared strong defenses over a long period of time and their intention here was to defend in great depth. Thiepval had been turned into a fortress. To the south of Thiepval, on the far side of the Memorial to the Missing from your present position, some battalions of the 32nd Division had major defensive obstacles to overcome which you will visit.

Now make your way to Connaught Cemetery and, on reaching it, proceed to the corner of the cemetery wall closest to Thiepval. Turn and face the 18th

Division obelisk. Figure 8.6 was taken from here back towards Thiepval. You can see the corner of Thiepval Wood, which marked the divisional boundary between the 36th and 32nd Divisions and the 18th Divisional Memorial from where you have just come. You can also see the Thiepval Memorial, which was built on the grounds of Thiepval Château, and which was in No Man's Land as already indicated. Thiepval is to the left and was behind the German front line. The British front line ran from the corner of Thiepval Wood and curved round the lower part of the field in the photograph. You will appreciate that there is a significant incline in the field leading up to the 18th Division Memorial. The men of the 32nd Division who went up this field on 1 July were the 15th and 16th Lancashire Fusiliers (1st and 2nd Salford Pals). Their casualties soon littered this field.

These men were, in fact, observed by Lieutenant-Colonel Crozier as they struggled up the hill towards Thiepval. Crozier was commanding officer of the 9th Royal Irish Rifles of the 36th (Ulster) Division. He was standing at the margin of Thiepval Wood, close to where you are standing, waiting to usher his men into the attack. In his autobiography, *A Brass Hat in No Man's Land* he subsequently recollected:

> My eyes are riveted on a sight I shall never see again. It is the 32nd Division at its best. I see rows upon rows of British soldiers lying dead, dying or wounded, in No Man's Land. Here and there I see an officer urging on his followers. Occasionally I can see the hands thrown up and then a body flops to the ground.[2]

One may well pause to consider Crozier's perception of a division "at its best" was when soldiers were being slaughtered by machine gun fire. Had you been in this position on 1 July, the field below the 18th Division Memorial would have been littered with the bodies of dead and wounded British soldiers.

Figure 8.7 shows the village of Thiepval taken from Connaught Cemetery. You can appreciate its elevated position when you see the steep gradient of Mill Road rising up to the village. The 32nd Division battalions from the 16th Northumberland Fusiliers (Newcastle Commercials) and 2nd Royal Inniskilling Fusiliers which followed in support of the Salford Pals met with exactly the same fate. Indeed, German infantry were able to stand on their parapets to take aim without fear of being hit by return fire.

On the far side of where the Thiepval Memorial stands, the German line formed a salient on the downward slope of a steady gradient at the tip of which was the Leipzig Redoubt. The capture of Leipzig Redoubt was the

---

2   Crozier, F.P., *A Brass Hat in No Man's Land* (London: Jonathan Cape, 1930), p.102.

Figure 8.6 View from Connaught Cemetery looking back towards the Thiepval Memorial; the British front line ran round the corner of Thiepval Wood and round the lower slope of the field ahead; the men of the 32nd Division had to climb the slope to reach the enemy front line at the top of the hill.

Figure 8.7 Thiepval village taken from Connaught Cemetery; this was a very heavily fortified village with concrete reinforced cellars and interconnecting tunnels. It was bristling with machine guns that directed deadly flanking fire against the 36th Division after the 32nd Division attack had failed.

task given to part of the 32nd Division and this is where your next viewpoint will be. Return to Thiepval and turn right onto the D151. Follow signposts for Authuille. Proceed downhill; be aware that you are descending a steep gradient. If you are on a bicycle, you won't have to pedal to reach Authuille! The point to be made here is that the heavily fortified village of Thiepval was on the top of a hill and attacking battalions of the British 32nd Division were in most disadvantageous positions around the bottom of the hill. Wherever they attacked was uphill with all the inherent difficulties this posed.

Just after you enter Authuille, there is a road on your left, not numbered, with a signpost directing you to Lonsdale Cemetery. Follow this signpost, and make your way to the cemetery about a mile away. As you go, there is a steep gradient going up this time! Stop when you reach the cemetery gate and turn around to face the Thiepval Memorial.

The German line came round the right side of the Thiepval Memorial as you look towards it and swept round the hillside above your position at the cemetery gate. It formed a jutting bulge opposite the British line known as the Leipzig Salient. Within it was a network of trenches and strong points. Its tip was the Leipzig Redoubt that had numerous machine gun positions and was very heavily defended indeed.

Figure 8.8 This photograph was taken from the entrance to Lonsdale Cemetery which is on the approximate position of the British front line on 1 July. The tip of the Leipzig Redoubt was straight ahead at approximately the level of the rough grass in the foreground. This was the only part of the German front line to be taken by the 32nd Division that day. The Wunderwerk was in the 2 o'clock position half-way towards the trees (beyond the Leipzig Redoubt).

There were two additional strongpoints that gave the defenders a major tactical advantage. To the north was the Wunderwerk (Figure 8.1) which was half-way between your current position at Lonsdale Cemetery gate and the Thiepval Memorial in the 2 o'clock position (as you face the Thiepval Memorial). The second was the Nordwerk (Figure 5.8) which was approximately the same distance away as the Wunderwerk and in the 4 o'clock position. The photograph was taken from the gate of Lonsdale Cemetery and the tip of the Leipzig Redoubt would have been approximately at the level of the slightly rougher area of grass in the foreground just beyond the field of unripe grain as shown in Figure 8.8.

Men of the 16th Highland Light Infantry (Glasgow Boy's Brigade) and 17th Highland Light Infantry (Glasgow Commercials) came through Authuille Wood (directly behind your position facing the memorial) on their way to the front line on the night of 30 June/1 July. Their headquarters were in the wood. The two Glasgow battalions formed the spearhead for the attack on Leipzig Redoubt. The 16th attacked to the left of the tip of the redoubt, while the 17th fought directly opposite the tip of the redoubt (Figure 8.1). Shortly after the whistles blew and the men went over the top, they were struck by a hail of machine gun bullets from the Wunderwerk as they tried to struggle forward. To their horror and dismay, the artillery bombardment had not destroyed the barbed wire, which was still intact. The 16th HLI could not progress any further and survivors took shelter in shell holes. By ten minutes after zero hour, the 16th HLI had lost half its strength.[3]

Companies of 17th HLI – advancing on the immediate right – at least managed to reach and hold part of the trench system at the tip of the Leipzig Redoubt. One of their men, James Youll Turnbull won the Victoria Cross here; the subsequent citation outlines the deed:

No. 15888 Sergeant JAMES YOUNG TURNBULL[4], late Highland Light Infantry.

For most conspicuous bravery and devotion to duty, when, having with his party captured a post apparently of great importance to the enemy, he was subjected to severe counter-attacks, which were continuous throughout the whole day. Although his party was wiped out and replaced several times during the day, Sergeant Turnbull never wavered in his determination to hold the post, the loss of

---

3   Chalmers, T., *History of the 16th Battalion The Highland Light Infantry* (Glasgow: John McCallum & Co., 1930), p.36.
4   http://en.wikipedia.org/wiki/James_Youll_Turnbull

which would have been very serious. Almost single-handed he maintained his position and displayed the highest degree of valour and skill in the performance of his duties. Later in the day this gallant soldier was killed whilst bombing a counter-attack from the parados of our trench.

Turnbull's grave is in Lonsdale Cemetery (Plot IV; Row G: Grave 9). The total casualties amongst 17th HLI amounted to 22 officers and 447 other ranks killed, wounded and missing. The 32nd Division sustained 3,949 casualties in total on 1 July 1916.

Figure 8.9 was taken from some distance away from a farmyard above the heights above the north bank of the Ancre and shows various locations. You can see the Ulster Tower, Thiepval Wood and Mill Road. You can also see the Thiepval Memorial to the Missing and if you look to the right of the memorial you can see an area clear of trees. This is where the Leipzig Salient swept down the hillside and the tip of this redoubt dominated the ground held by the British 32nd Division positions near the top of Authuille Wood, which is on the extreme right of the photograph.

A young soldier of the 17th HLI, Private Bentley Meadows, who would be commissioned later in the war and who subsequently was killed, kept a diary. His account of moving into the line on the evening of 30 June is especially

Figure 8.9 This photograph was taken from a farmyard half-way up the hill from the village of Hamel towards Auchonvillers. It shows Mill Road, Thiepval Wood and Thiepval Memorial to the Missing. The Leipzig Salient was in the open area to the right of the Thiepval Memorial. The top end of Authuille Wood may be seen in the extreme right of the photograph.

poignant, particularly as so many of the men were about to be killed and wounded the following morning:

> The evening of ' Z ' day, the 30th of June, we marched off by platoons. The thunder of the heavy guns as we passed through their belt was almost unbearable, and nearer the lines long lines of eighteen-pounders were giving ' battery fire' down long rows of twenty batteries, some-times all speaking at once. We entered "Oban Avenue "at the right end of the village of Authuille. It was the "up" trench for the advance and "Campbell Avenue" the "down." Both trenches had been deepened, in some places, to twelve feet, and were fairly safe from shrapnel. The line in which we were to spend the night had been blown almost completely out of existence and it was difficult to find sufficient cover for the men. I and the bomber who was next to me in the line found a corner and there slept for the night. We were once disturbed by the enemy destroying a trench mortar store situated close to where we slept. Daybreak came and still there was no word of ' zero.' We made some breakfast, and about half-past five word was passed along that zero was 0730, and to move into battle positions. We moved to the right until we were in contact with the next Company. At 0625 the final bombardment commenced. Every gun was firing ' gunfire ' and the rush of metal overhead was extraordinary. The reply was feeble. At 0725 we left the trench and walked over to within 60 yards of the barrage. At 0730 the barrage lifted and we rushed the front line defenses, destroying the garrison, in and out of dug-outs. I have few definite memories from the time we first saw the Germans to the time the machine gun swept us down outside the Leipzig Redoubt.[5]

Meadows described the Leipzig defenses and the remorseless nature of the fighting:

> The nature of the Leipzig defenses, a maze of trenches and under-ground saps, made advancing into the area where this projected out towards the British front line extremely hard. One was continually attacked in the rear.
>
> What seemed dug-outs were bombed, and when passed numbers of the enemy rush from them, they being really underground

5   Arthur, W.J., I.S. Munro, *The Seventeenth Highland Light Infantry, Record of War Service 1914-1918* (Glasgow: David J. Clark, 1920), pp.42-47.

communications with their rear defenses. The whole fighting was merciless and no quarter was given or taken. One of the battalions opposing the British was a students' battalion from Bavaria. The enemy used explosive and dum-dum bullets, and they sniped off any of our wounded lying exposed in the open.

It was not permitted to stop to take back prisoners or to stop to dress a wounded chum but it was permitted to stick the bayonet of a wounded man's rifle in the ground and thus to mark the spot where he lay. The Germans observed this and watched for any movement in the heap beside the standing rifle. Men coolly fired at each other at point blank range and sniping became the chief cause of casualties.[6]

Before leaving Lonsdale Cemetery, consider that the furthest ground gained by the 32nd Division was here. It was just a few yards into the tip of the Leipzig Redoubt and a long way from Mouquet Farm two miles away!

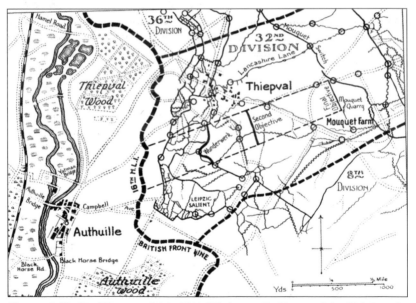

Figure 8.10 32nd Division I July 1916 (Chalmers, T., *History of the 16th Battalion The Highland Light Infantry.* Glasgow: John McCallum & Co., 1930).

---

6   Munro, *The Seventeenth Highland Light Infantry*, pp.42-47.

Return to Authuille along the road you used to reach Lonsdale Cemetery. Go to the church and stop. You will find a memorial to the three Glasgow HLI battalions at the church doorway. Return to Thiepval and proceed down the D73 (Mill Road) in the direction of the Ulster Tower. Once you reach Thiepval Wood to your left, you are level with the front line of the 36th (Ulster) Division, which was in the margin of Thiepval Wood and extended down to and across the River Ancre where men of the division also attacked along the far embankment of the Ancre valley. The German front line was parallel to Mill Road and further to your right and passed through the position now occupied by the Ulster Tower.

The area behind Ulster Tower was the strongly fortified Schwaben Redoubt. Its relation to the capture of Thiepval on 26 September 1916 will be explained in detail in Chapter 9. As you proceed along Mill Road, you will encounter a signpost directing you up a track to the right to Mill Road Cemetery. Stop at the entrance to the track and look along Mill Road in the direction of Connaught Cemetery. Thiepval Wood behind Connaught Cemetery looks very peaceful now, but the Somme has a deep tranquil irony. Edmund Blunden in his celebrated *Undertones of War*, one of the most descriptive of Great War memoirs, described entering Thiepval Wood from the valley of the Ancre on the other side of the wood. He was looking for Gordon House, which was a company headquarters, to deliver a message. The following description was written some months after 1 July.

> There is a track across the lagooned Ancre. A trolley line crosses too, but disjointedly: disjointedness now dominates the picture. When we have passed the last muddy pool and derailed truck we come to a maze of trenches … and Thiepval Wood is two hundred yards on, scowling, but at the moment dumb: disjointed, burnt, uncharitable. Let us find, for we must, Gordon House, a company headquarters, and we scuttle in the poisoned presence of what was once fresh and green around unknown windings of trenches.[7]

Blunden got lost, because he went too far and inadvertently emerged from the margin of the wood adjacent to Mill Road. Here he was immediately spotted by German observers and was targeted by the German guns:

> Shell after shell hurtles past our heads into the inundations of the Ancre, below this shoulder of brown earth, lifting as high as the hill wild streaming sputtering founts of foam and mud.

7   Blunden, E., *Undertones of War* (London: Richard Cobden-Sanderson, 1928. Reprinted London: Penguin Classics, 2000), p.84.

At last he found Gordon House:

> A stained face stares out amongst the chalk and tree fibres. "I shouldn't stand there if I were you: come in". "No, I'm alright: don't want to be in the way." "Come in, blast you; just had two men killed where you are".[8]

Proceed up the track to Mill Road Cemetery. Many of the gravestones have been laid flat, because there is so much subsidence here due to the remaining underground network of tunnels.

Return to Mill Road and turn right. You will pass Connaught Cemetery on your left and Ulster Tower on your right. Stop in the lay by outside the Ulster Tower.

Figure 8.11 Mill Road Cemetery; the horizontal headstones are unusual; if placed upright they would topple over due to the underground network of tunnels and chambers which make the ground unstable and liable to subsidence.

8   Ibid., p.85.

Figure 8.12(a) and **(b)** Ulster Tower; 8.12 (b) was taken from the approximate position of the Beaucourt Redoubt. Mill Road Cemetery, Ulster Tower, Mill Road, Thiepval Wood and Thiepval Memorial are marked, as is the position of the Schwaben Redoubt.

The Ulster Tower commemorates the men of the 36th Division whose objectives on 1 July were Schwaben Redoubt and St Pierre Divion, which is down at the bottom of Mill Road in the valley of the Ancre. The Ulstermen also held the line on the far (northern) embankment of the Ancre, and were given the task of attacking along the latter to secure Beaucourt Station. (See Main Map Somme (North)). The Ulster Division, therefore, was involved in fighting on both north and south banks of the Ancre. See Figure 6.1 for the 36th Division infantry order of battle. Go into the Ulster Tower and pay a visit to the café which also has a selection of books. Leave there and turn right by the guest tables and proceed to the perimeter fence. Look straight (due north) ahead.

You are standing on the German front line. Beyond the fence the ground dips away in front of you to the valley of the Ancre. There was a German strongpoint on the hillside more than a mile away at the 2 o'clock position called the Beaucourt Redoubt. It held a commanding view of this area (See Figure 8.13). The Schwaben Redoubt was some 150 yards beyond the tower, to your right. The British line was to your left just within the margin of Thiepval Wood, so you will get an idea of how far the Ulstermen were expected to advance.

The attack on the north side of the Ancre was a disaster. While the wire had been cut by the artillery bombardment, men advancing in the river valley met very stiff opposition and Beaucourt Redoubt escaped the attention of the British artillery. It poured fire into Ulstermen as they appeared over the

Figure 8.13 At Ulster Tower looking towards Beaucourt Redoubt; the Beaumont-Hamel position is shown, as is the Beaucourt Redoubt site.

skyline and halted further progress. This had very serious implications for the attack on Schwaben Redoubt because after the attack on the north bank of the Ancre petered out within three hours of zero hour, machine gunners in Beaucourt Redoubt brought enfilade fire to bear on the Ulstermen assaulting Schwaben Redoubt.

You will now visit the approximate location of the Beaucourt Redoubt. Leave the Ulster Tower and rejoin Mill Road. Turn right and go down the steep hill into the Ancre Valley. St Pierre Divion is along a secondary road to your right before you cross the river. There is an unmanned railway crossing to negotiate as you continue straight ahead. Turn right and proceed to Beaucourt when you reach the road junction with the D50. Take the D163 towards Beaumont-Hamel, and stop when you have climbed onto the high ground between the two villages (See Main Map Somme (North)).You should stop before you reach a signpost directing you to Frankfurt Trench Cemetery.

This photograph was taken from the approximate position of the Beaucourt Redoubt. You will now understand just what commanding views the German defenders had over the fighting below as you look towards the clearly visible Thiepval Memorial. You can also see the Ulster Tower and have a clear view of the margin of Thiepval Wood. Look at the field adjacent to the Ulster Tower (See Figure 8.14) and you will see the old German front line and support trench. It depends entirely on what time of year you visit, since the former trench tracings are only visible after the fields have been ploughed and before

Figure 8.14 View from Beaucourt Redoubt over towards Thiepval Wood; the chalk marks through the ploughed field are traces of the German defences.

the crops begin to grow. The Schwaben Redoubt was to the left behind the German front line trenches. Men from the 36th Division would have been clearly visible and within the range of machine guns from this position.

The attack from Thiepval Wood made good progress at first. The front line German trenches were badly damaged by shellfire and the wire was well cut by the bombardment. The Ulstermen penetrated the Schwaben defences and secured a portion of the Redoubt before advancing beyond. They would have been moving from right to left across the fields beyond where the tower now stands. It appeared to observers that they were on the verge of a significant local success.

They had, however, penetrated too deep into the enemy line and on too narrow a front. The collapse of their attack on the northern side of the Ancre coupled with the complete failure of the 32nd Division to their immediate right (south) meant that German fire could be brought to bear from both flanks of the Ulstermen advancing from Thiepval Wood.

British reserves attempted to deploy in No Man's Land from Thiepval Wood to support earlier gains at Schwaben Redoubt, but hostile artillery brought down a curtain of fire along the length of Mill Road and the British front line. This prevented reinforcements getting forward.

By this time, German reinforcements were arriving and counter-attacks increased in frequency as the afternoon wore on. Many Ulstermen who had gone beyond Schwaben Redoubt, were killed and wounded. The shattered survivors fell back to the Redoubt. By now there was complete chaos and attempts to deploy the 49th Division (in reserve) failed with heavy losses. By the afternoon of 1 July, the Ulstermen were in a hopeless position. On 3 July, survivors were still making their way back from the Schwaben Redoubt to the jumping-off line in Thiepval Wood.

Lieutenant-Colonel F.P. Crozier described leading his men out from Thiepval Wood into No Man's Land on 1 July:

> I cross the fire trench ... I wait on the edge of the wood. Machine guns open fire on us from Thiepval village; their range is wrong: too high I say to Hine. I survey the situation still; more machine gun fire: they have lowered their sights: *pit, pit,* the bullets hit the dry earth all round.[9]

The 9th Royal Irish Rifles passed out of the front line into No Man's Land to lie down on Mill Road to re-group. Sprayed with machine-gun fire and

---

9   Crozier, *A Brass Hat in No Man's Land*, p.104.

bombarded by shells, many were killed and wounded at the margin of Mill Road. The survivors pressed on across No Man's Land. Crozier later observed:

> The dead no longer count. War has no use for dead men. With luck, they will be buried later; the wounded try to crawl back to our lines. Some are hit in so doing, but the majority lie out all day, sunbaked, parched, uncared for, often delirious and at any rate in great pain. My immediate duty is to look after the situation and not bother about the wounded men.[10]

Returning to his headquarters, he found that many of those killed and wounded during the preceding days had been collected there. Suddenly there was a commotion outside, because large numbers of men in field-grey were coming towards them. Perhaps this was a counter-attack. Somebody opened fire with a machine gun, until it was recognised that these men were German prisoners. A few Ulstermen also returned stating that they had enough and were not going to continue. A young officer tried to stop them, but they pushed by. Crozier observed: "He draws his revolver and threatens them. They take no notice. He fires. Down drops a British soldier at his feet".[11]

Crozier's battalion had some 70 men left out of 700 after the battle was over. One young officer, who fled prior to the attack, was discovered in a nearby village. He was not court martialed because Crozier considered that anyone who could have given evidence at his trial was deceased: "So he goes home to Ireland, no longer a soldier, but as an officer resigned, where he enters business and makes a fortune! Such is the reward for spineless behaviour on the battlefield".[12]

This unnamed officer was more fortunate than Private James Crozier, who had enlisted at the age of 16 in 1914. Lieutenant-Colonel Crozier (no relation) made a pre-embarkation promise to the young Crozier's mother that he would look after his underage namesake.

In early 1916, clearly disorientated, confused and sickened by war, the young Crozier abandoned his post and was duly tried for desertion. He was shot at dawn on 27 February 1916 on the recommendation of Lieutenant-Colonel Crozier. The firing squad failed to find its target and the officer in charge was obliged to step forward and put a bullet through young Crozier's head.

---

10 Ibid., p.106.
11 Ibid., p.110.
12 Ibid., p.112.

> Inside the little garden the victim is carried to the stake. He is far too drunk to walk. As he is produced I see he is practically lifeless and quite unconscious. He has already been bound with ropes. There are hooks on the post. We always do things thoroughly in the Rifles. He is hooked on like dead meat in a butcher's shop.[13]

Because of this broken promise to the young boy's mother, Lieutenant-Colonel Crozier attempted to have his name added to a list of field casualties. He failed and Mrs. Crozier was duly notified that her only son had been shot for desertion. As a result she was denied the normal allowances payable on the death of a next-of-kin.

Total casualties sustained by the 36th Division on 1 July were 5,104 killed, wounded and missing. The only apparent gain made by the now shattered 32nd and 36th Divisions was a small section of the Leipzig Redoubt.

---

13 Ibid, p.84.

Chapter 9

Mouquet Farm, Thiepval, Schwaben Redoubt and the Ancre Heights

MOUQUET FARM

In Chapter 8 the failed attack on Thiepval on 1 July 1916 was considered and the reasons for its failure were explained. Thiepval was eventually captured on 26 September and this chapter will explain how that came about and how subsequent attacks led to the capture of the high ground near the formidable village fortress. These actions were to become known as the Battle of the Ancre Heights. To begin with, what took place at Mouquet Farm will be considered because events there played an important role in determining what subsequently happened. Mouquet Farm was a heavily fortified German position midway between Thiepval and Pozières. It was an integral part of the German second line defense system which ran from Grandcourt in the Ancre Valley through the Windmill near Pozières, (see Main Map Somme (North)) before running along the Bazentin Ridge, through Longueval (Chapter 7), and then onto Guillemont. The best place to begin is in Pozières, from where you should take the D73 towards Thiepval. After travelling approximately half a mile, look back in the direction of the village for the excellent panoramic view. The radio mast on the left is an important landmark.

Beneath the mast, the obelisk of the Tank Memorial is just visible on the far side of the main road between Albert and Bapaume. The notorious Windmill site, the highest point on the Pozières Ridge, is directly opposite the memorial on the near side of the road. The German second defensive line ran through the Windmill, where Australian and French flags may be seen if you use binoculars. Observation from your current position gives an idea of the distance the 2nd Australian Division had to cover in order to capture the Windmill. The 4th Australian Division relieved the exhausted 2nd Division on 6 August. The former would play a major role in attacks on Mouquet Farm over the following days and weeks.

Continue along the D73 in the direction of Thiepval. Stop when there is a clear view of a small clump of mature trees ahead adjacent to the road, with some farm buildings to the right of the trees on the crest of a hillside. This is

Figure 9.1 Looking towards Pozières and the Windmill position adjacent to the radio mast; Pozières is out of the photograph on the right. Men from the 4th Australian Division attacked across the fields to the position from which the photograph was taken as they fought their way towards Mouquet Farm.

Figure 9.2 Looking towards Mouquet Farm; it is situated on the crest of a hill, which gave it a commanding position. The approximate position of Zollern Redoubt is marked. It was half a mile from Mouquet Farm.

Mouquet Farm and within the clump of trees there is a small memorial which also provides information about what happened here.

As already stated, Mouquet Farm was an integral part of the German second line system. There was a warren of underground tunnels beneath it that connected to adjacent positions. This second line was supported near here by two additional strong points, Zollern and Stuff Redoubts, at a distance of approximately half a mile and a mile, respectively, from Mouquet Farm.

In terms of strategy, it was considered that if Mouquet Farm could be captured, then Thiepval would be vulnerable to a combined frontal, and rear attack from Mouquet Farm. Of course, when Mouquet Farm had been an objective of a frontal attack only on 1 July, there had been complete failure. The capture of Pozières on 22/23 July, and of the Windmill on the high point of the Pozières Ridge on 4 August, made it possible to attack Mouquet Farm from the direction of Pozières. General Sir Hubert Gough (GOC Reserve Army) was well aware of this and he urged an immediate attack. The 4th Australian Division was given the task of capturing Mouquet Farm. On 8 August 1916, the 4th Division began to push towards Mouquet Farm from the direction of Pozières and the Windmill. At the same time, British Divisions on their left pushed towards the same objective. As they advanced they pushed out a salient, which is quite simply a part of the line that juts into the enemy line like a tongue. The salient driven towards Mouquet Farm had a narrow base; there was only a short distance between one side of it and the other. This made it extremely vulnerable to attack from German positions situated on three sides of the expanding salient. Undeterred, Gough persisted with his plan as British and Australian forces slowly converged on Mouquet Farm between the first week in August and the beginning of September.

Exhausted divisions had to be relieved frequently and the British 12th, 25th and 48th Divisions all fought here as well as Australian 1st, 2nd and 4th Divisions. By the beginning of September, the Australians too were exhausted and were withdrawn from the attack. The Canadian Corps comprising the 1st, 2nd and 3rd Canadian Divisions replaced the Australians on 5 September. They too failed to take Mouquet Farm. So trying to get into the correct position to be able to attack Thiepval from the rear was proving very difficult.

Continue further along the D73 until a lay by in the road is reached where you will find the commemorative plaque to Australian soldiers who fought and died here.

It is inscribed with the following words:

Mouquet Farm, situated on Pozières Ridge was a central bastion in the German defence position during the battles of the Somme from July to October 1916. The shattered farmhouse was then located to the left of the farm road on the crest before you. Its deep cellars and

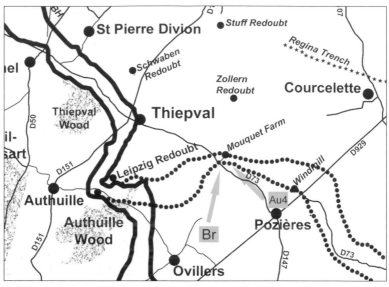

Figure 9.3
Sketch map showing the attack on Mouquet Farm; the further British and Australian soldiers advanced the more they pushed out a deadly salient in front of them.

Figure 9.4 Commemorative Plaque to Australian soldiers at Mouquet Farm.

tunnels were connected to a complex network of German trenches in the fields.

On 5 August, the Australians were first to attack this stronghold, having just incurred a devastating loss of 17,000 men in the capture of Pozières, only one kilometre away. The Australians proceeded to claw their way up the slopes to Mouquet Farm each day in a nightmarish landscape deluged by artillery fire. Both sides fought to the death over small sections of trench. After a month of this combat, the exhausted Australians with 5,300 casualties were relieved on 5 September just outside the farm ruins by the Canadians. Twenty-five days later the farm fell to the British.

The war would pass over this ridge again in 1918. Many of the men who fought and were lost in 1916 remain beneath this land forever, unknown, but never forgotten by their homeland, Australia.

Go on a few yards further to the farm track leading up to Mouquet Farm and stop. Look straight along the road towards Thiepval. The road you are on enters the village in the 12 o'clock position. The Thiepval Memorial is in the 10 o'clock position, approximately one mile away. The Zollern and

Figure 9.5 Looking towards Thiepval from Mouquet Farm; the Thiepval Memorial is at the 10 o'clock position. The 32nd Division would have crossed the intervening fields on its way to capture Mouquet Farm if things had gone according to plan on 1 July. The visitor can well appreciate that the route from Mouquet Farm approaches Thiepval from the rear.

Stuff Redoubts are in the 2 o'clock position, so follow that line of direction through the fields. Stuff Redoubt, the further away of the two redoubts is roughly the same distance from your point of observation as the Thiepval Memorial. Zollern Redoubt is half-way between Stuff Redoubt and Mouquet Farm. The approximate position of Zollern Redoubt is indicated on Figure 9.2. The importance of these redoubts will be considered later in this chapter.

Figure 9.6 is a photograph of Mouquet Farm as it is in the present day. If you turn round from your observation point at the bottom of the track and look up the drive towards the farm buildings, you can reflect on the numbers of soldiers who were killed, wounded or missing trying to capture this place. The numbers of casualties sustained by various assault divisions are shown in Table 9.1.

Attempts to take Mouquet farm were ill-conceived and cost a great many lives with absolutely nothing to show for it. Mouquet farm was finally taken on 26 September by the 11th Division, when on the instructions of General Sir Douglas Haig, the Reserve Army finally launched a four-division attack on a broad front with the aim of capturing both Thiepval and Mouquet Farm (See below).

Continue from Mouquet Farm towards Thiepval. Stop as you enter Thiepval at the junction with the D151. You will see the 18th Division Memorial visible

Figure 9.6 Mouquet Farm today. The farm was on the other side of the farm track in 1916. Its position was strategically located on the crest of a hill. It had tunnels connecting it to the German second line defensive system.

Table 9.1 Losses sustained by Australian, Canadian and British at Mouquet Farm.

Division	Number of casualties
1st Australian Division	2,650
2nd Australian Division	1,300
4th Australian Division	4,650
Canadian Corps	2,800
12th Division	1,450
25th Division	1,700
48th Division	3,650
Total	18,200

in the ten o'clock position in the field adjacent to the road and close to the Thiepval Memorial car park. Go there, stand with your back to it and gaze towards Thiepval Wood.

The following is a brief outline of the military situation before the four divisions attacked on 26 September: Thiepval Wood is to your left and the Ulster Tower to the right. The British front line was on the edge of Thiepval Wood, before curving around the bottom of the field in front of your position at 18th

Figure 9.7 18th Division Memorial looking towards Thiepval Wood and Ulster Tower; the British front line was within the margin of Thiepval Wood. The German line ran through where the Ulster Tower is today. Mill Road was in No Man's Land. The front lines remained in the same position from 1 July to 26 September.

Division Memorial. The German front line was parallel to the British line and would have passed through Ulster Tower, before approaching Thiepval. Swinging in front of the village it curved behind where the Thiepval Memorial stands today. If this all sounds familiar (see Chapter 8), it is because the front lines remained in exactly the same positions between 1 July and 26 September. The photograph shown in Figure 9.7 is one you have seen before and emphasises this fact.

The Schwaben Redoubt was a large rectangular network of interconnected trenches behind the position occupied by the Ulster Tower. Look from your present observation point beyond the trees to the right of Ulster Tower. This gives the approximate position of this strongpoint, part of which was briefly occupied by the 36th Division on 1 July (See Chapter 8).

On 3 September, the 49th Division was tasked with making a frontal attack on Schwaben Redoubt following a preceding short bombardment. The assaulting infantry left the cover of their front line in Thiepval Wood. Had you been here you would have observed men rushing across Mill Road in a forlorn attempt to reach Schwaben Redoubt. The attack did not succeed and Lieutenant-General C.W. Jacob (GOC II Corps) subsequently blamed the failure of the assault on the lack of "martial qualities" of the men. Gough too accused the men of having poor discipline and motivation.[1]

THIEPVAL, 26 SEPTEMBER 1916

Since the plan to capture Mouquet Farm and envelop Thiepval from the rear had failed, it was decided to make a broad frontal (6,000 yards) attack on 26 September. The assaulting divisions of the Reserve Army are shown in Figure 9.8.

On the right, the 1st and 2nd Canadian Divisions attacked from Courcelette – captured on 15 September (See Chapter 10). Their task was to take Regina Trench which was a short distance beyond Courcelette. The 11th Division would capture Mouquet Farm, Zollern Redoubt and Stuff Redoubt. Thiepval itself would be attacked by the 18th Division advancing from the same front line as the 1st and 2nd Salford Pals on 1 July. Proceed to Thiepval and stand by the church. By 26 September, nothing remained of the houses but there were concrete reinforced cellars and a warren of tunnels underneath and in the surrounding area. As you stand on this spot you can imagine men making painfully slow progress as they clambered over the rubble. Heavy machine gun fire came from the chateau ruins until a tank intervened. German snipers were everywhere. The village was finally secured on 27 September.

---

1   Prior R & Wilson T., *The Somme* (New Haven: Yale University Press, 2005), p.249.

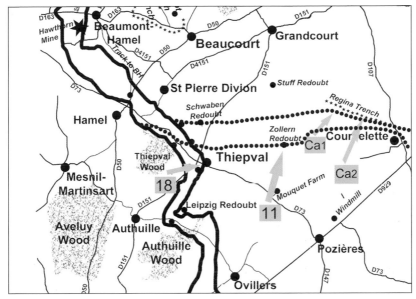

Figure 9.8 Sketch Map showing the attacking formations 26 September 1916.

Second Lieutenant T.E. Adlam (7th Bedfordshire Regiment) won a Victoria Cross near where you are standing. His citation reads:

> When an attack at Thiepval came under heavy machine gun and rifle fire, he ran from shell hole to shell hole under fire, collecting grenades and gathering men for a rush on an enemy held village. Despite receiving a leg wound he led the rush, captured the village and killed its occupiers.[2]

Thiepval had fallen. You will now have an opportunity to find out what happened to the 18th Division, 11th Division and 1st and 2nd Canadian Divisions after 26 September. By the end of "The Battle of the Ancre Heights" (1 October-11 November) the British possessed most of the high ground that dominated the Ancre Valley. Of particular importance was the capture of the Schwaben Redoubt (See Figure 9.9).

The 11th Division captured the rubble that had been Mouquet Farm and by 27 September had advanced slowly north to take Zollern Redoubt and then

---

2   Arthur, M., *Symbol of Courage* (London: Pan Macmillan, 2005), p.258.

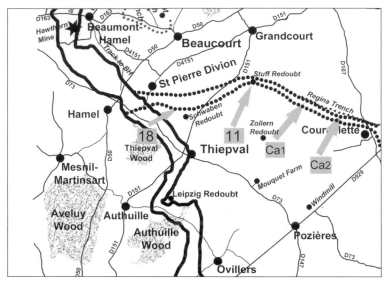

Figure 9.9 Sketch Map showing the progress made during the Battle of the Ancre Heights during which the British captured Schwaben Redoubt, Mouquet Farm, Zollern and Stuff redoubts. Regina Trench defied capture till 11 November 1916.

had a foothold on the Stuff Redoubt after much bitter close quarter fighting. Stuff Redoubt was finally taken on 9 October, although the Germans still held the northern part of the position (See Main Map Somme (North)).

To understand the 18th Division's epic capture of Schwaben Redoubt, leave Thiepval church and proceed along the D151 towards Grandcourt. You will pass a track to your left which takes you over the Schwaben Redoubt into St Pierre Divion. First, proceed along the D151 for a mile until you are level with a cemetery which is on your right. This is Grandcourt Road Cemetery. The final line reached by the British Reserve Army by the close of the Battle of the Ancre Heights crossed the road nearly level with this cemetery. To reach it, continue for half a mile until you arrive at a secondary road on the right. Follow it to Grandcourt Road Cemetery. Continue past the cemetery for roughly the same distance you travelled to get from the D151 to Grandcourt Road Cemetery. You are now in the vicinity of Stuff Redoubt.

Now retrace your steps to the D151 and turn left. Proceed in the direction of Thiepval. Stop when you reach the narrow road to the right. This will lead you behind the Ulster Tower. If on foot or bicycle, you can proceed along the track and down into St Pierre Divion in the valley of the Ancre. Be aware that the descending track is unsuitable for vehicles. It does, however, provide splendid views of Thiepval and the Ancre Valley.

Figure 9.10 View to Thiepval from Schwaben Redoubt. Thiepval Church may be seen, as can Mill Road, which was in No Man's Land. The German front line passed between the Thiepval Memorial and where the church stands today.

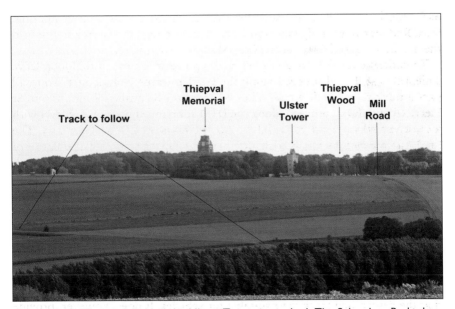

Figure 9.11 The track behind the Ulster Tower is marked. The Schwaben Redoubt was between this position and the tower. Thiepval Wood and the Thiepval Memorial can also be discerned. The track descends into St Pierre Divion in the Ancre Valley.

Stop when you are level with the Ulster Tower (Figure 9.11). The track you are on is marked with an arrow corresponding to your current position. The Schwaben Redoubt would have been in the field between your position and the tower.

The 18th Division's next task was to capture the Schwaben Redoubt. Bitter fighting would last from 28 September to 6 October, after which it gained possession of most of the redoubt apart from the section nearest to where the high ground falls away to the Ancre Valley ahead of you. Artillery was of little use here amongst the warren of deep dugouts where defending Germans were well protected from shellfire. The only way to clear them out was for the infantry to move forward step by bloody step. Fighting was confused and degenerated frequently to hand to hand engagements in mortal combat. On 14 October, the 39th Division, which had replaced the 18th Division, attacked the Schwaben Redoubt, and finally evicted the Germans from their last toe-hold on the Schwaben Redoubt.

To all intent and purposes, the Battle of the Ancre Heights was over. Continue along the track till the ground falls away. It can be seen (as marked in the photograph) descending steeply between the trees to the village of St Pierre Divion. Before you descend, look towards the village of Hamel below you. It was behind the British front line, so you can clearly appreciate the German "bird's eye view" of everything that went on in the British sector round about. It was thus very important to gain control of this dominating high ground before further offensive operations could be carried out. Proceed down the track to join the D4151 at St Pierre Divion.

FOOTNOTE

The Canadian failure to capture Regina Trench on 26 October was followed by repeated efforts that continued until the last futile attack on 8 October. The barbed wire remained uncut by the barrage and the Germans took the opportunity to reinforce it at zero hour. The attack was made by the 1st and 3rd Divisions. Most of the attackers were shot down in front of the wire. Gough blamed the failure on the Canadians. On Sunday 8 October, General Haig remarked in his diary: "Gough was of the opinion that the Canadians (3rd Division) had not done well. In some parts they had not left their trenches for the attack yesterday. The Canadian 1st Division which had attacked north-west of Le Sars and gained some trenches had been driven out again".[3] Gough made no mention of this in his memoirs:

---

3 Sheffield, G., J. Bourne, *Douglas Haig: War Diaries and letters 1914-1918* (London: Weidenfeld & Nicolson, 2005), p.239.

Figure 9.12 View from Heights above the Ancre to Hamel. Hamel was only a few yards behind the British front line The Germans had commanding views from here and could spot troop movements to and from the front line from positions in the rear.

> On 17 October the Canadians were at last withdrawn for a well-earned rest, leaving, however, their 4th Division to fight under the order of II Corps, and to take a glorious part in the final victory of the Somme in the Battle of Beaumont-Hamel, which took place on 13 November.[4]

The 4th Canadian Division came into the line opposite Regina Trench in mid-October. On 21 October, attacking on a broad front with the 39th, 25th and 18th Divisions, it attacked Regina Trench, suffering crippling casualties for no apparent gain. The 4th Division launched a final successful attack on 11 November 1916. It had taken the Canadians 42 days to capture Regina Trench. Approximately 8,000 men were killed, wounded and missing to achieve this.

Amongst Canadians killed on 8 October was Piper J.C. Richardson of the 16th Battalion (Canadian Scottish). James Cleland Richardson was born in 1895 at Bellshill in Lanarkshire and emmigrated to Canada. He volunteered to return and fight. Richardson was awarded a posthumous VC[5].

---

4   Gough, H., *The Fifth Army* (London: Hodder & Stoughton Ltd., 1931), p.151.

5   http://www.cmp-cpm.forces.gc.ca/dhh-dhp/gal/vcg-gcv/bio/richardson-jc-eng.asp

> For most conspicuous bravery and devotion to duty when, prior to attack, he obtained permission from his Commanding Officer to play his company 'over the top'; as the company approached the objective, it was held up by very strong wire and came under intense fire, which caused heavy casualties and demoralised the formation for the moment. Realising the situation, Piper Richardson strode up and down outside the wire, playing his pipes with the greatest coolness. The effect was instantaneous. Inspired by his splendid example, the company rushed the wire with such fury and determination that the obstacle was overcome and the position captured.

Later, after participating in bombing operations, he was detailed to take back a wounded comrade and prisoners. After proceeding about 200 yards Piper Richardson remembered that he had left his pipes behind. Although strongly urged not to do so, he insisted on returning to recover his pipes. He was never seen again.

At the end of November, the 4th Canadian Division left the Somme to join the other three Infantry Divisions of the Canadian Corps at Vimy Ridge near Arras, where they would achieve fame during the capture of Vimy Ridge in April 1917. The four Canadian divisions fought together for the rest of the war. After their experience on the Somme, they never trusted General Sir Hubert Gough again.

Chapter 10

The Battle of Flers-Courcelette, 15 September 1916 and the Battles of Morval and Le Transloy

Following the limited success of the attack on 14 July 1916, the British line in the southern part of the battlefield did not significantly move forward until 15 September. The Fourth Army launched a costly array of piecemeal attacks against Delville Wood, High Wood and Guillemont after 14 July for little or no gain and a mounting toll of casualties. There was, however, a new secret weapon that would be used for the first time in an attempted breakthrough. This was the tank. Unfortunately, the early tanks had many problems which limited their effectiveness. For example, they were mechanically unreliable and prone to frequent breakdowns. They were also very slow and cumbersome, moving at approximately 2mph (slower than the pace of advancing infantry). Crews became progressively worn down by carbon monoxide fumes which, as a result of the primitive exhaust system, quickly filled the cabin.

Nevertheless, General Haig decided that tanks would play a major role in the coming offensive and considered they would help to make a significant tactical contribution to the forthcoming attack. The consequent surprise the new technology would engender would prove advantageous. Haig's plan was ambitious indeed and can be summarised as follows:

- The Fourth Army would endeavour to capture three German lines;
- They would then move on to capture German gun positions beyond;
- The Reserve Army would cooperate in a supporting role;
- The Fourth Army would have between 36 and 42 tanks; Reserve Army would have 18 to 24 tanks;
- Cavalry would be held in readiness in the event of a breakthrough.

Rawlinson thought that Haig's plan was overambitious. A following compromise was agreed upon:

- The first objective would be the German front line;
- The second objective was the village of Flers;
- The third objective was the ground to the right (east) and left (west) of Flers;
- The fourth objective was the capture of Combles, Guedecourt, Lesboeufs and Morval (Main Map Somme (South 2));
- The attack would be made by 11 Divisions all of which would be allotted tanks (See Figure 10.1).

The British front line extended from Leuze Wood on the right to the Windmill site near Pozières on the left. Figure 10.2 shows the ground gained by the British divisions on 15 September.

At the beginning of September, the British front line extended along the northern aspect of Delville Wood and then took a sharp right-angled bend down the right margin (east) of Delville Wood to Trônes Wood. The villages of Guillemont and Ginchy remained in German hands. German artillery was able to direct its fire on Delville Wood from positions to the rear of Ginchy and Guillemont as well as from the north around Flers. British attacks on Guillemont failed because they were poorly co-ordinated and insufficient resources were employed to deal with a formidable and stubborn defence.

Haig directed Rawlinson to exert his position as commander of the Fourth Army to ensure better co-ordination of action between divisions. Unfortunately, Rawlinson continued to allow his divisional commanders to persist with piecemeal attacks. Rawlinson did not seem to regard the overall co-ordination of Fourth Army activity as his responsibility and he had a tendency to leave matters in the hands of formation (corps and division) commanders. He attributed failure to lack of initiative and poor training of the infantry rather than to his own military shortcomings.

Guillemont and Ginchy would have to be captured before a major offensive could proceed otherwise the British would have been enfiladed by machine gun fire. Prior to being taken to consider what happened on 15 September, you will be given time to understand the capture of Guillemont and Ginchy.

Start from the junction of the D197 and D64 near the village of Montauban. Go along the D64 travelling away from Montauban and past the entrance to Bernafay Wood, which was captured by the 9th (Scottish) Division on 3 July 1916. Continue along the D64 beyond the margin of Bernafay Wood that faces the adjacent Trônes Wood. As you look to your left, men from the 18th Division came across this field to capture Trônes Wood on 14 July. You will pass a small 18th Division Memorial on your left that commemorates this action. Keep going till you reach the right margin of Trônes Wood and stop

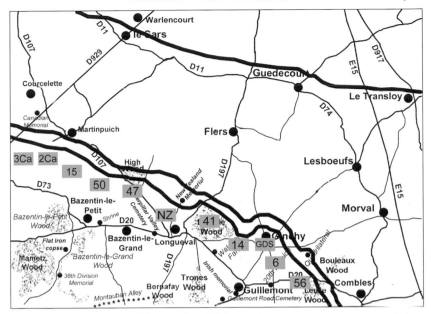

Figure 10.1 Attack on 15 September 1916.

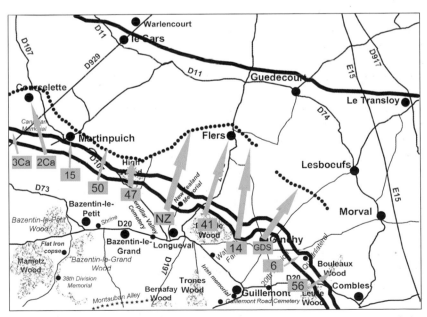

Figure 10.2 British gains on 15 September – the dotted line shows gains made by the various Divisions.

at the bottom of a rough track just at the end of the trees. Looking straight ahead, you will see Guillemont Road Cemetery. Beyond it is Guillemont in the 12 o'clock position. Its capture was deemed essential prior to 15 September. You will also see Ginchy in the far distance at the 10 o'clock position; this too would have to be captured.

You may remember that the field between your position and Guillemont Road Cemetery is where Captain Noel Chavasse won the first of his two Victoria Crosses. This occurred on 9 August when the 10th King's (Liverpool Scots) conducted an unsuccessful attack on Guillemont (See Chapter 7).

Now go on till you are just past Guillemont Road Cemetery and look beyond it (to the north). You will see Delville Wood. The village of Ginchy is to the right of Delville Wood. By the end of July 1916, Delville Wood had been captured and the British front line ran along the right margin of Trônes Wood where you have just come from and then up to the right margin of Delville Wood which you can discern from the cemetery. It then went along the right side to the far end of the wood, before running to the left along the furthest (northern) end of the wood.

Guillemont was captured on 3 September by men of the 20th (Light) and 16th (Irish) Divisions. They did this by digging trenches at right-angles to their front line quite far up beyond the end of Trônes Wood. Thus they managed to get closer to German positions. They also managed to do another crucial thing. Because Guillemont had been bombarded by British artillery for so long,

Figure 10.3 The village of Guillemont; Guillemont Road Cemetery's Cross of Sacrifice is in the foreground.

Figure 10.4 Photograph taken from Guillemont Road Cemetery with Delville Wood in the distance; Ginchy is to the right of Delville Wood. Flers, midway between Delville Wood and Ginchy, is approximately two miles distant.

hostile machine gunners had moved to the sides of the village to avoid being killed or wounded by shellfire. By digging out beyond the village, the British outflanked them, and this greatly assisted in overcoming the defences and the capture of what was left of Guillemont. The subsequent assault was over a wide area. This meant there were fewer German guns available to target the soldiers attacking Guillemont. Using similar tactics, the 16th Division stormed Ginchy on 7 September. The scene was at last set for the next major offensive.

Looking from your position at Guillemont Road Cemetery to beyond (east of) Guillemont, you will see Leuze Wood. This was where the British line was on 15 September. Proceed there now. Continue along the D64 to Guillemont and pass a memorial to the 16th Division outside the church. Turn right onto the D20. After approximately a quarter of a mile, you will pass a memorial to the 20th Division. Both these divisions contributed to the capture of Guillemont. Keep straight on the D20 till the road goes between woods on both sides of the road. Leuze Wood (captured on 6 September) was on the right and German occupied Bouleaux Wood on the left.

If you stop now you are in the position of the 56th (London) Division, which was on the right flank of the attack on 15 September. The small town of Combles is a short distance beyond the wooded area. The objective of the 56th Division was to capture Bouleaux Wood and make progress north of Combles. At the same time, adjacent French divisions would attack and make

Figure 10.5 Guillemont with Leuze Wood beyond; the right flank of the British attack came through Leuze Wood.

progress south of Combles, thereby forcing the defenders to withdraw. The 56th Division would also form a protective flank to allow the 6th and Guards Divisions to advance and capture Morval and Lesboeufs, respectively.

The 56th Division had been assigned three tanks, two of which broke down before reaching the jumping-off position. It had previously been decided prior to the preliminary barrage that "avenues" approximately 100 yards wide would remain open during the bombardment to allow the tanks to pass through these gaps unmolested by shellfire. Unfortunately, this meant the enemy remained relatively untouched, thus giving the machine-gunners time to place their weapons and open fire with devastating results.

The infantry of the 56th Division sustained heavy casualties from machine gun fire. The single tank that did make it to the starting line assisted in a small advance from the vicinity of Leuze Wood. British infantry advancing up the shell-free "avenues" were cut to pieces by machine gun fire. This unfortunate circumstance allowed the Combles defenders to pour fire onto the right flank of the British attack.

Retrace your steps till you reach the crossroads where the 20th Divisional Memorial is located and take the secondary road (D20e) on the right leading to Ginchy.

Proceed towards Ginchy on the D20e. You will remember that the British line ran from Leuze Wood to Ginchy. It ran across the fields on the right as you

Figure 10.6 Ginchy: 6th Division attacked the Quadrilateral across the fields to the right of the road.

make your way to the village. Stop half-way and look to the field on your right. This is where 6th Division attacked before advancing towards Morval. The Quadrilateral Redoubt was a very strong defensive position roughly midway between Leuze Wood and Ginchy. The British artillery had hardly damaged this formidable defensive work. Of the three tanks attached to 6th Division, only one went into action on 15 September. The tank was coming across the field to your right and it poured machine gun fire into the Quadrilateral before bullets striking its boilerplate hull caused slivers of white hot metal to break off and fly around inside its cramped confines.

The Germans also had a supply of armour piercing bullets, which had been procured to penetrate the metal shields that British snipers used to protect themselves. These bullets were now utilised to penetrate the tank's armour. The tank commander ordered a withdrawal. There was no creeping barrage directed against the Quadrilateral as the men moved forwards because it had been assumed that the preliminary barrage and supporting tanks would have destroyed the stronghold. This was a grave error and extremely heavy casualties resulted for no gain whatsoever.

Now continue your journey to Ginchy. On reaching this village your journey will keep straight on the D20e. First, make a brief foray along the minor road to the left which is signposted to Longueval (no designated road number). Delville Wood is to your right. Stop half-way between Ginchy and the margin of Delville Wood and look through the fence on the right. You can just see the church spire of Flers in the distance (north) between the electric pylons. Flers was one of the main objectives of 15 September.

Looking to the right you will observe the area where the Guards Division attacked from the far (northern environs) side of Ginchy towards Lesboeufs moving ahead and to the right (north east) away from the village, whilst straight ahead in the gap between Ginchy and Delville Wood, the 14th Division attacked towards the right side of the distant village of Flers.

Now return to Ginchy and turn left, following the D20e to Flers. The Guards advanced from Ginchy towards Lesboeufs to the northeast. They made some progress, but lost momentum before they reached Lesboeufs. As you look around, you will realise that the terrain ahead (to the north) of Ginchy is much flatter and is quite featureless compared with the wooded areas behind (to the south).

The Guards Division had ten tanks allocated to it but these were of little help. Five broke down before they had reached the jumping-off position and the remainder wandered about in a seemingly aimlessly way. They did not seem to have any recognisable aims although they were supposed to move ahead of the infantry and reach the first objective five minutes ahead of the infantry, before proceeding to attack the second objective.

Figure 10.7 Looking towards Flers in the distance; this photograph was taken from the midpoint between Delville Wood and Ginchy (see Figure 10.4). Men from the 14th Division attacked from here towards the right (east) of Flers.

Once again German defenders were able to exploit the tank "avenues" and were able to bring about uninterrupted fire that caused many casualties amongst the advancing infantry. One badly wounded Guardsman was future Prime Minister Harold MacMillan. He sustained bullet wounds to his left thigh and pelvis. Carried back to Ginchy by stretcher-bearers, he managed to scramble back through the village rubble where he was picked up and taken to an advanced dressing station for medical attention. His wounds became badly infected and he required several operations over the following three years and suffered persisting discomfort for the rest of his life.

The Guards made some progress towards Lesboeufs and gained 2,000 yards over a 1,500 yards wide front. However, the villages of Combles, Morval and Lesboeufs, which were supposed to have been secured by the 56th, 6th and Guards Divisions were still some distance away. Such was the failure of tanks on this part of the battlefield that few Germans would have been aware of their existence.

From your position on the D20e, turn round and look towards Delville Wood and the water tower to its front. The 14th Division attacked between where you are standing and the near edge of Delville Wood.

If you turn 90 degrees to your right, and look along the top (north) margin of Delville Wood then you will see High Wood on the skyline; the New Zealand Memorial is set against the trees.

Figure 10.8 Delville Wood as seen from Ginchy; the water tower is at the southeast corner of the wood. The 14th Division attacked towards the point where the photograph was taken on their way towards Flers.

Figure 10.9 Looking from Ginchy towards High Wood with the New Zealand Memorial visible; the line of trees in the middle distance marks the line of the D197 that runs between Flers and Longueval. The slope of the hillside on the near side of the memorial protected New Zealand soldiers from machine guns in High Wood as they advanced from left to right on both sides of the D197. On the far side of the memorial advancing New Zealanders also sustained losses from machine-guns in the wood.

The 41st Division attacked from the northern end of Delville Wood directly towards Flers. The New Zealand Division launched its assault from between Delville Wood and High Wood. The 14th, 41st and New Zealand Divisions made the greatest advances of the day. They were allocated 17 tanks of which 12 went into action. You can imagine the scene as you gaze towards High Wood. Nearest to you, men of the 14th Division would have passed from left to right across the field to your front. They were hit by machine gun fire from German positions behind you and suffered heavy casualties. Captain Harold Mortimore set out in tank D-1 at 0515 from the side of Delville Wood. He commanded the first tank to lead out men from the 14th Division. Some of the tanks did manage to advance beyond the right (east) of Flers, where they came under artillery fire as they traversed the flat and open ground.

The preliminary bombardment, which opened on 12 September, had been very effective where the 41st Division advanced; very few defenders survived. Despite the prevalence of the aforementioned tank avenues, the majority of defenders were killed or wounded. Thus the British infantry were rendered less vulnerable and advanced without incurring heavy losses.

Figure 10.10 The village of Flers taken midway on the road between Ginchy and Flers; this was the furthest point reached in the attack on 15 September. Units from the 41st Division were advancing on both sides of the road towards the village aided by tanks, which were successful on this part of the battlefield.

Proceed to Flers along the D20e. The tanks allocated to 41st Division were more effective than others, and for a time at least were able to operate in advance of the infantry. Perhaps this was due to the fact that most German defenders had been killed or wounded by the British artillery, or perhaps the terrain was easier to negotiate. Flers was overrun and the tanks made a significant contribution to the success. When men of the 41st Division entered Flers, the German barbed wire was uncut, so they waited for their tanks (which had by then fallen behind) to catch up and flatten the wire.

This allowed the infantry to advance through the main street in Flers. When you get to the village, there is a T Junction with the D197. Turn right and continue along the main street. On 15 September, a tank lumbered up this very street in the direction you are going. This was Tank D-17, commanded by Lieutenant Stuart Hastie, who came from Edinburgh. This resulted in the famous press headline "A tank is walking up the High Street of Flers with the British infantry cheering behind" The nickname of the tank was *Dinnaken*, which roughly translates to 'I don't know'.

Stop when you reach the 41st Division Memorial. Look at the house, if you cannot recollect the name of Hastie's tank, next to the memorial. A painting of the celebrated vehicle is above the door of the building.

Figure 10.11 The 41st Division Memorial at Flers; it was the most successful formation on 15 September.

Now retrace your steps down the main street. Keep straight on as you pass the junction of the D20e and D197. Proceed along the latter to Longueval. This route will take you over the ground attacked by the New Zealand Division. Note the excellent view of Delville Wood ahead. High Wood is hidden by a contour to your right. As you travel towards Longueval, men from the New Zealand Division would have been coming towards you from the margin of Delville Wood on the left and along the hillside on the right. They were attacking towards the ground to the left (west) of Flers, where they formed a defensive flank just beyond the village. For the New Zealanders, 15 September was their baptism of fire on the Western Front. Supported by four tanks, they pushed up the corridor between Delville Wood and High Wood. The accompanying tanks (coming from the direction where you are standing) were in the thick of the action despite the fact that none of them had reached the starting line in time!

Their artillery barrage was effective, and as they pressed forward, the men advancing towards you along the hillside on your right would have been protected from machine gun fire from their left flank. Troops attacking above the skyline beyond the summit were engaged by heavy fire from High Wood.

Figure 10.12 was taken from the village of Montauban two miles away to the south and shows High Wood. Caterpillar Valley Cemetery is marked. The

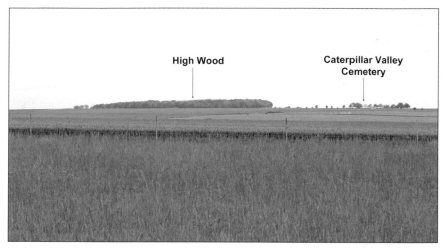

Figure 10.12 This photograph, taken from Montauban, shows High Wood; Caterpillar Valley Cemetery is marked to the right of High Wood; the New Zealand Memorial is beyond the cemetery and to the right, and is out of sight.

New Zealand Division advanced from the right side of High Wood, moving away from the camera position in the direction of Flers, whilst sustaining heavy casualties from machine gun fire from High Wood.

Continue towards Longueval. Just as you reach the village, and before you reach the outskirts, look for a signpost which directs you to the New Zealand Memorial. Take this road and you will arrive at the memorial. Standing with your back to the memorial, turn round facing back down the road you have just come up. You can see Delville Wood and the northern part of Longueval. The New Zealand Division began its advance through the northern part of the village.

Figure 10.9 was taken from Ginchy. It shows the New Zealand Memorial silhouetted against the fringe of High Wood beyond. Remember the New Zealanders were advancing between High Wood and Delville Wood. Any soldiers advancing between your position at the memorial and High Wood were exposed to machine gun fire from the latter. The slope of the hillside between the memorial and Delville Wood falls away rapidly. Troops advancing here were not visible from High Wood. A glance at Figure 10.9 allows you to appreciate this. Now leave the New Zealand Memorial and retrace your steps to re-join the D197. Turn right and you will reach the centre of Longueval. Turn right onto the D20 (signposted to Contalmaison) and continue to Caterpillar Valley Cemetery. Stop and go in. Take note of the New Zealand Memorial to the Missing on the left. This wall bears the names of New Zealanders who fought on the Somme and have no known grave.

Figure 10.13 Looking towards Delville Wood and Longueval from the New Zealand Memorial; Bernafay Wood is visible and Montauban is on the skyline.

Figure 10.14 New Zealand Memorial to the Missing at Caterpillar Valley Cemetery.

You will not find their names on the Thiepval Memorial, as they are always commemorated near where they fell and where they lie to this day. In 2004, the remains of an unidentified New Zealand soldier, "Known only unto God", were removed from here. They now rest in the Tomb of the Unknown Warrior at the National War Museum in Wellington. Return to the cemetery entrance and look to your right towards Longueval. The New Zealand Division began its attack from the north end of the village.

Leave Caterpillar Valley Cemetery and turn back towards Longueval. Turn left onto the D107 that takes you to High Wood. On the right of the road you will observe the 47th (London) Division Memorial set against a backdrop of trees. Ahead of you to the left is the London Cemetery and Extension. Stop at the entrance of the cemetery.

Three divisions were positioned on a line extending from High Wood to the Albert – Bapaume Road which is approximately half a mile from your position at the cemetery. The 47th (London) Division, 50th Division and 15th (Scottish) Division were deployed from right to left. The 47th Division attacked High Wood; the 50th Division attacked the ground between the left of High Wood and Martinpuich, and the 15th (Scottish) Division attacked the village.

Tanks proved incapable of providing effective support in High Wood. They were quite unable to make their way through the broken tree stumps that

Figure 10.15 Looking towards Longueval from Caterpillar Valley Cemetery; the right side of the New Zealand Division attacked from the village towards Flers, which is nearly two miles ahead and to the left of the position where you are standing.

Figure 10.16 High Wood with Thistle Dump Cemetery in the foreground; the London Cemetery entrance is visible near the left margin of High Wood. The 47th (London) Division attacked High Wood. The New Zealand Division attacked on the right; 50th Division on the left.

remained following repeated bombardments. The 47th Division made slow progress and sustained many casualties but finally cleared the Germans from High Wood. Hostile machine gun fire also inflicted severe casualties on the divisions attacking on either side of High Wood. The 50th Division made very little headway, New Zealand battalions assaulting to the immediate right of High Wood also came under sustained heavy machine gun fire. Proceed to the far wall of the London Cemetery and Extension and look straight ahead for a superb view of the southern battlefield for the period 1 July to 15 September.

Proceed towards Martinpuich. Men from the 50th Division would have been passing from left to right across the road in front of you as they advanced between the 47th and 15th Divisions.

Pass through Martinpuich (captured by the 15th Division on 15 September) and carry on to the busy Albert and Bapaume Road (D929). Albert is five miles to your left. Cross the road keeping a careful eye out for oncoming traffic! You have now passed from the Fourth Army sector to that of Reserve Army. The 2nd and 3rd Canadian Divisions fought here on what was the left flank of the 15 September offensive. Having crossed the road, you will immediately see a signpost denoting a Canadian Memorial which is adjacent to the main road. Go there and you will see Courcelette.

Go to the perimeter of the memorial area and look towards the radio mast at Pozières. The Canadian front line was at the Windmill site adjacent to where

Figure 10.17 Canadian Memorial at Courcelette with the village beyond.

the radio mast now stands. Units of the 2nd Canadian Division attacked in this direction towards Courcelette. The Canadian front line extended from near Mouquet Farm (Chapter 9), where the 3rd Canadian Division attacked and then swept round the Windmill site where the line adjacent to the road was held by the 2nd Division. Before the attack began on 15 September, Canadians of the 2nd Division infiltrated forward towards your position here at Courcelette, shortening the distance they had to go to launch their attack on the village, at which point they were assisted by tanks. The Canadians used different tactics with their allocation of tanks. Rather than use them in advance of the infantry they employed their six to follow behind the infantry in a "mopping up" role. As a result, they did not employ 'avenues' with the result that the supporting artillery proved much more effective than that of the Fourth Army.

Between the Canadian front line and Courcelette was a fortified sugar beet factory which was situated approximately half-way between your current position and the Windmill. Its defenders, cut off by the advancing infantry, were soon overwhelmed with the help of a tank christened *Crème de Menthe*.

The attackers retained their objective in the face of fierce local counter-attacks and Courcelette remained in Canadian hands. Leave your position at the Canadian Memorial and return to the D929. Turn right and proceed 600 yards to the Windmill. Look to your left as you go. The Canadians would have been attacking towards you. Beyond them were assaulting units of the 15th

Division moving towards Martinpuich, the church spire of which can just be discerned.

Stop at the Windmill site with the Australian and French flags flying above it. Look back towards Courcelette in the direction you just came from. This panorama provides an idea of how far the 2nd Canadian Division advanced on 15 September.

ANALYSIS OF THE ATTACK ON 15 SEPTEMBER

You have now travelled over the entire length of the attack on 15 September. The two Canadian Divisions of the Reserve Army succeeded in capturing Courcelette, but failed to take Mouquet Farm, which was their other objective that day. As you have seen from your journey round the battlefield, the British Fourth Army had mixed success. The British Fourth Army sustained approximately 30,000 casualties on 15 September. It was a major tactical error to employ shell-free "avenues". This almost certainly contributed to the high numbers of casualties. The tanks contributed less than had been anticipated. Many broke down before the starting line was reached, while others broke down during the battle. Only between Delville Wood and Flers were tanks of any real use to the Fourth Army, while in the Reserve Army sector the Canadians employed them profitably in a mopping up role.

Figure 10.18 Looking towards Courcelette from the Windmill; the 2nd Canadian Division attacked Courcelette from here.

With one or two exceptions, British artillery did not achieve a high enough density of fire on 15 September. It would seem that Generals Haig and Rawlinson learned very little from the success on 14 July when there had been a much higher density of fire. It would be 1917 before British barrages became more effective and late 1918 before artillery superiority made set piece actions unstoppable. The Battle of the Somme was the genesis of effective artillery tactics.

On the evening of 15 September 1916, General Rawlinson issued an immediate order for a further full scale attack the following day. This was not possible because of heavy losses and exhaustion. A few piecemeal attacks were carried out instead. The 6th Division finally captured the Quadrilateral and the New Zealand Division gained some ground north of Flers. These isolated actions were reminiscent of the small and costly attacks which had occurred following the assault on 14 July.

General Haig decided that a further major offensive would take place on 25 September. Known as the Battle of Morval, a formidable artillery bombardment began on the day before. This provided a much greater density of fire compared with that on 15 September. On this occasion tanks were held back to deal with fortified villages immediately after the infantry cleared the forward enemy positions. There was no need to leave the pre-arranged avenues free of artillery fire. As result, the barrage was brought to bear along the entire length of the German front line. By late afternoon on 25 September 1916, the villages of Lesboeufs and Morval were in British hands and Guedecourt and Combles were taken the following day.

Haig ordered the Fourth Army to advance even further and capture Le Transloy through which the next enemy defensive line passed. No fewer than seven failed attacks were made against the Le Transloy defences, the last on 5 November 1916. By then, very heavy rain had turned the battlefield into a quagmire of tenacious mud. The unfortunate situation was further exacerbated by the German practice of keeping their machine gunners well to the side or to the rear of their front line thus avoiding losses to British artillery. Stalled by the mud and novel German tactics, Rawlinson's Fourth Army was exhausted. Deprived of reinforcements, it would contribute nothing more to the Battle of the Somme.

The Battle of the Ancre, 13 November 1916 and 63rd (Royal Naval) Division

> The study of mankind is undoubtedly man, and one can only see man in his natural state when untrammelled by the artificial conventions of modern society. Where can this be better studied than in a front line trench, or during an attack in which death is always hovering near, often in its most revolting forms, and consequently men are seen as they are, not as they wish to appear, and not as our super-civilisation makes them appear.[1]

In Chapter 9 it was explained how Thiepval was finally taken on 26 September 1916, and how further progress was made to capture the Schwaben Redoubt and portions of high ground overlooking the Ancre valley beyond. The Germans were still in possession of St Pierre Divion, a small village tucked into the side of the southern slope of the valley.

Following the partial success of the Battle of Morval on 25 September (Chapter 10), the British Fourth Army was unable to make further progress and heavy rain had turned the battlefield into a quagmire. General Sir Douglas Haig badly needed success because he was soon due to attend an inter-allied conference at Chantilly to discuss plans for 1917. If he could present his political masters and French ally with something positive, it would strengthen his bargaining position. He turned to his protégé, General Sir Hubert Gough (GOC Reserve Army) to provide him with that success.

The Reserve Army, (renamed Fifth Army on 30 October) was tasked with making progress up and to the north of the Ancre valley. As a necessary preliminary, the Battle of the Ancre Heights (Chapter 9) was fought in part to gain control of Schwaben Redoubt which occupied a dominant position over the Ancre. This achieved, it was now possible to launch what would be the

---

1 Sparrow G. & J.N. MacBean Ross, *On Four Fronts with the Royal Naval Division* (London: Hodder and Stoughton, 1918), passim. p. 117.

last major engagement (Battle of the Ancre 13-18 November) of the Battle of the Somme.

THE PLAN OF ATTACK

The plan was to advance along both sides of the Ancre, to secure the villages of St Pierre Divion and Beacourt situated to the south and north of the river, respectively. There would also be an attack between the Ancre and Serre at the northern limit of the battlefield. This called for the capture of Serre, Beaumont-Hamel and the high ground north east of the latter where two German trenches designated Munich and Frankfurt were situated.

On 1 July, the objectives for the British Fourth Army north of the River Ancre had been the same, but as the following chapters will illustrate, no progress was made on 1 July, nor in the intervening weeks between 1 July and 13 November. Start your journey at Thiepval. Go along the D73 (Mill Road) and down the hill to a bridge over the Ancre. Stop and face upstream.

To your right, the 39th Division attacked along the steep valley on the south side of the Ancre. Its task was to capture St Pierre Divion and clear the steep southern slopes of the valley. There were many deep dugouts in the village but the preliminary bombardment, which began on 6 November, was very

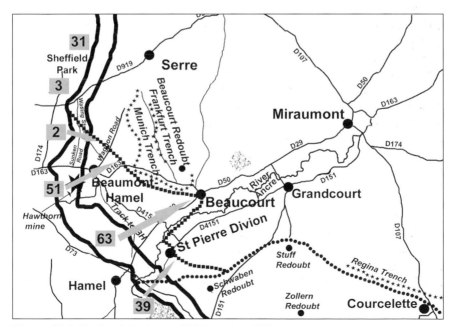

Figure 11.1 Battle of the Ancre 13 November 1916.

Figure 11.2 Battle of the Ancre: To the right (south) 39th Division attacked St Pierre Divion, while to the left (north) the 63rd Division attacked Beaucourt. The Ancre was the divisional boundary.

effective and this was a major contributory factor to the successful assault. Approximately 1,380 prisoners were taken. On the immediate right, the 19th Division formed a defensive flank against counter-attacks.

The 63rd (Royal Naval) Division attacked along the slopes to your left. Dense fog made it difficult for troops to advance although it provided some cover. The assault began at 0545 after a preliminary barrage which did not increase in the minutes leading up to the attack. This was done so as not to alert the enemy of the imminent danger.

Retrace your steps and turn into the D4151 to visit St Pierre Divion. You will notice there are very steep banks to the right. There were entrances here that led to the tunnels and chambers beneath the Schwaben Redoubt which is over to your right behind the Ulster Tower. Men of the 39th Division attacked along what is now the D4151. At the far end of the village there is a steep track. This leads onto the heights above St Pierre Divion and the site of Schwaben Redoubt. The track is very steep. Avoid it unless you are fit for the task. Proceed for about 300 yards. As you ascend, look back towards Hamel on the north bank of Ancre. The river, tucked beneath the steep hillside, is not visible from here. You can, however, see a road (D50) that runs between Hamel and Beaucourt which was captured by the 63rd (Royal Naval Division) on 13 November.

Figure 11.3 The Ancre heights: Hamel, which was just behind the British front line on 13 November, is visible. The road with the steep embankment behind is the D50 which runs between Hamel and Beaucourt. The Ancre cannot be seen as it is hidden by the steep hillside the cyclist (co-author) is ascending. Men of the 39th Division passed from right to left across this hillside on 13 November.

On 13 November, units of the 39th Division attacked along the steep hillside you are ascending as well as in the valley below. They were moving from right to left as you climb. They cleared the Germans from the steep slope and from St Pierre Divion at the bottom of the hill the cyclist is ascending.

Go another couple of hundred yards and look back. Figure 11.4 was taken from the Schwaben Redoubt area looking north towards Hamel. St Pierre Divion is among the trees in the foreground on the near side of the Ancre. The rear area village of Hamel is on the opposite bank. The trees to the right in the middle distance mark the location of Newfoundland Memorial (See Chapter 12). The village on the horizon with church spire just visible is Auchonvillers.

Retrace your steps down the hillside. On 13 November attacking units of the 39th Division moved down this same track to the road below. Here they encountered fleeing elements of the St Pierre Divion garrison.

Return to the Ancre Bridge. It marked the boundary between the 63rd Division to the north of the Ancre and the 39th Division to the south. It is worth remembering that on 1 July, the 36th Division attacked on the north side of the Ancre as well as from Thiepval Wood to the south. This was too much to ask and whilst it made relatively good progress to the south, it made no progress north of the Ancre.

Figure 11.4 View beyond the Ancre valley to the north from Schwaben Redoubt; the trees in the foreground are in the Ancre valley. The village of Hamel is seen on the hillside beyond. The trees on the skyline to the right mark the position of Newfoundland Memorial Park (Chapter 12). The church spire of Auchonvillers is just discernible on the distant skyline.

63RD (ROYAL NAVAL) DIVISION

The Royal Naval Division was formed in 1914 at the direction of First Lord of the Admiralty, Winston Churchill. There were too many sailors for the number of available ships and surplus naval reservists were made into a land-based fighting unit. It saw action early in the war when Belgian forces were besieged in Antwerp following the German invasion in August 1914.

The Royal Naval Division fought at Gallipoli in 1915 and by the end of that campaign there were relatively few of the original sailors remaining. Reconstituted with reinforcements and an army brigade, it came under the jurisdiction of the War Office in 1916. The 63rd Division was responsible for a front of 1,200 yards on 13 November. Its task was to advance over this wide front and capture the village of Beaucourt in the Ancre valley. It was also to advance along the adjacent hillside, eventually reaching the final goal of Munich and Frankfurt Trenches, where it would link up with the 2nd Division that was tasked with capturing the same objectives after traversing Redan Ridge (Chapter 15).

Geoffrey Sparrow and James Ness MacBean Ross were medical officers and subsequent co-authors of *On Four Fronts with the Royal Naval Division*, an illuminating and light-hearted narrative and quite unlike many of the inter-war divisional histories and related personal accounts.[2] Sparrow became an important comic artist and illustrator after the war and the book is liberally illustrated with his sketches.

Proceed towards the D50, carefully crossing the railway line as you go. Turn right onto the D50 and stop at Ancre British Cemetery. Following the German withdrawal to the Hindenburg Line in the spring of 1917 (see Chapter 17), the battlefield was cleared and a number of cemeteries, of which Ancre British Cemetery (then called Ancre River No 1 British Cemetery, V Corps Cemetery No.26) was one. There were originally 517 burials, almost all of the 63rd Division from 13 November and of the 36th Division from 1 July. After the armistice the cemetery was greatly enlarged when more graves from battlefield clearances and several small burial grounds were brought here. There are 2,540 casualties buried or commemorated here of whom 1,335 are unknown.

You will appreciate that it lies in a hollow. Men from the 63rd Division who were attacking here had to pass through this hollow during the attack. They passed from left to right (as you face the Cross of Sacrifice) from the front line to German positions on the hillside to the right side of the cemetery.

Immediately beyond the cemetery, an entrance opens into a minor road that runs parallel to the main road for a hundred yards towards Beaucourt before it turns sharply to the left and climbs over the hillside to Beaumont-Hamel becoming a rough track completely unsuitable for cars.

If you are in a car, then continue along the D50 till you reach the D4151 to your left. You will now be on Station Road which leads to Beaumont-Hamel, although you need not go the entire way. The important thing to note is that you are in a valley with quite steep slopes to both left and right. Men from the 63rd Division who advanced along the hillside north of the Ancre had to cross from left to right as you are looking towards Beaumont-Hamel.

If you are taking the adventurous route (the small track), turn into it immediately beyond the cemetery gate. It is a steep and rough climb. Stop for a moment and glance back the way you have come. Men of the 63rd Division crossed the fields from right to left as you look down into the Ancre valley.

Imagine the scene on 13 November. Sparrow and MacBean recalled:

Men had gone over the top close behind the creeping barrage. On a frantic signal from the alarmed German infantry, the enemy artillery

2 Sparrow G. & J.N. MacBean Ross, *On Four Fronts with the Royal Naval Division* (London: Hodder and Stoughton, 1918), passim.

Figure 11.5a Ancre British Cemetery, which is located in a natural hollow; the British front line was to the left of the cemetery and the German front line to the right. It is situated in what was once No Man's Land. The steep valley had to be negotiated by the 63rd Division.

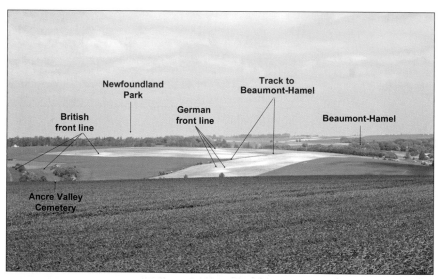

Figure 11.5b Taken from the site of the Schwaben Redoubt, the top of the Cross of Sacrifice of Ancre British Cemetery is marked, as is the track leading to Beaumont-Hamel (see text). The field chalk marks reveal the sites of British and German trenches.

opened up on the advancing troops of the Royal Naval Division, and men began to fall, killed or wounded. The scene in No Man's Land is indescribable. The ground is a mass of shell craters and almost impassable. The cries of the maimed and dying mingle strangely with the shriek of our own shells overhead and the explosions of hostile shells around us. That period of waiting is now over. The medical officer has his time fully occupied injecting morphia into the badly wounded, whilst his orderlies affix tallies marked with the dosage. Shell dressings and first field dressings are applied and the wounded are collected into groups in any spot which affords some shelter from the shells which are bursting around. The ambulance bearers now arrive and carry the cases back to their advanced dressing station. The battalion medical personnel have to push on so as to keep in touch with the battalion, but on the way, numerous cases are hastily treated and got into cover. Large batches of prisoners are now beginning to come across No Man's Land. These are at once commandeered to carry wounded back.[3]

Figure 11.6 Looking back towards Ancre valley from the steep slope of track leading to Beaumont-Hamel; the heavily wooded area immediately behind the cyclists marks the Ancre valley. The Thiepval Memorial and wood are also discernible. Authuille Wood is visible on the far right of the photograph.

3   Sparrow G. & J.N. MacBean Ross, *On Four Fronts with the Royal Naval Division* (London: Hodder and Stoughton, 1918), p.133.

Make your way towards Beaumont-Hamel. Note Station Road leading from the village to the river valley below. There were numerous dugouts in the chalk cliffs on the far side of the road. At this point, the 63rd Division's left would have been in touch with 51st Division's right.

Emerging at Station Road (one of the objectives of the 51st (Highland) Division on 13 November), the track eventually brings you out at Beaumont-Hamel just past the village cemetery. On reaching Beaumont-Hamel, turn almost back on yourself to connect with the D4151 (Station Road) and proceed toward the Ancre valley, the upper area of which was traversed by the 63rd Division.

A visit to Ancre British Cemetery – traversing the track between the cemetery and Beaumont-Hamel – and an exploration of nearby Station Road will give some idea of the ground covered by the 63rd Division. Beaucourt was the final objective.

On reaching the junction with the D50, you will observe a building (a snack bar and disco at the time of this writing). Turn left towards Beaucourt. At the

Figure 11.7 Looking down to Station Road and the Beaumont-Hamel cliffs within which there were German dugouts; the village of Beaumont-Hamel is also discernible; the positions of Munich and Frankfurt Trenches were on the high ground beyond and to the right of the latter. They were to the far (northern) side of the D163 between Beaumont-Hamel and Beaucourt. Beaucourt Redoubt was near the summit of the D163 just off the photograph to the right. (Photograph courtesy of Mr J.D. Holmes FRCS).

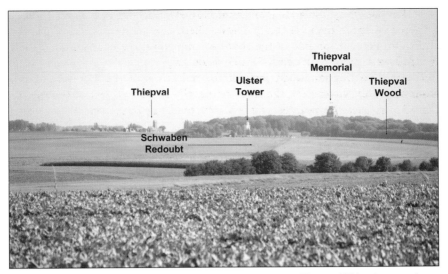

Figure 11.8 The view from Beaucourt Redoubt towards Thiepval Wood; men of the 63rd Division should have reached the position on 13 November after making their way along the valley from right to left. The River Ancre cannot be seen as it is deep within the valley. You can get an impression of the steepness of the slope as it descends to the treetops below. It was too difficult a task and they failed to link up with 2nd Division advancing from Redan Ridge.

village outskirts you will see a memorial commemorating the actions of the 63rd Division in this area.

Its attack started well but German resistance stiffened as the infantry approached Beaucourt. Lieutenant-Colonel Freyburg, temporarily commanding the Hood Battalion, pushed on into the outskirts of the village. He won a Victoria Cross for his actions, as his following citation reads:

> After leading an attack through the enemy's front line trenches at Beaucourt, Somme, his battalion became disorganised, so he rallied the men, leading them in a successful assault on the second objective, during which he was twice wounded. Throughout the following day and night, the battalion held the ground gained unsupported. When reinforced the following day, he led an attack in which a village [Beaucourt] was taken and five hundred German prisoners captured. Despite two further wounds, he refused to leave the line until he had issued his final instructions.[4]

---

4   Arthur, M. *Symbol of Courage* (London: Pan MacMillan, 2005), p. 260.

Freyberg went on to division and corps command in the Second World War. He became New Zealand Governor-General after the war.

Battlefield conditions were appalling and the all-pervasive mud made it almost impossible to move. Thus it was that the maximum advance made during the Battle of the Ancre was at Beaucourt.

The 63rd Division's final and, as it turned out, unreachable goal, was, traversing the high ground parallel to the valley to Munich and Frankfurt trenches near to what is now the D163. This may be regarded as the 'high road' between Beaumont-Hamel and Beaucourt (Main Map Somme (North)). To understand the task from a terrain perspective, proceed to Beaucourt and turn left on to the D163.

Stop when you reach a signpost that directs you to Frankfurt Trench Cemetery. The 63rd Division was supposed to link up with the 2nd Division near this spot. The latter should have been coming round Beaumont-Hamel from the other side (Chapter 15). As things turned out, neither division reached the final objective.

Chapter 12

Y-Ravine and Beaumont-Hamel,
1 July and 13 November 1916

The remaining chapters of this book are divided into two parts: the first part deals with events on 1 July 1916; the second chronicles what occurred on 13 November and ensuing days. It is convenient to explain things in this way because no gains were made on the northern part of the battlefield on 1 July. Indeed, the front lines remained in almost exactly the same position the following November. The VIII Corps (Lieutenant-General Sir Aylmer Hunter-Weston) was responsible for the attack north of the River Ancre on 1 July.

If following guide chapters sequentially, proceed from Beaucourt along the D50 to Hamel. Take the road (D73) to the right to pass through Hamel. Climb the steep hill to Auchonvillers. On reaching the summit you will see a car park. To the right and opposite this car park is the entrance to Newfoundland Memorial Park. This land was purchased by the Canadian Government in 1921 and officially opened by Field Marshal Earl Haig on 7 June 1925.

On entering the park you will see a shallow trench running parallel and very close to the road. This was called St John's Trench. You will come to understand the significance of this later but not at the present moment! Proceed to the 29th Division Memorial. The elite 29th Division was a Regular Army formation, which had fought at Gallipoli in 1915. The infantry orders of battle of its component battalions is reproduced in Table 12.1.

One of its component units was the 1st Battalion, Royal Newfoundland Regiment. Newfoundland was at that time an independent dominion and did not become part of Canada until 1949. Fishing was the dominant industry and the majority of its men hailed from small fishing communities.

A caribou, the emblem of the Newfoundland Regiment, stands in a prominent position ahead of you. The bronze figure, with its gaze fixed towards the once formidable German defences, is an evocative symbol of Newfoundland's Great War sacrifice. Climb the monument steps to the viewing area. Standing beneath the great caribou you will see the site of the British reserve trench, front line trench and No Man's Land – still pock-marked with shell craters.

Table 12.1 29th Division infantry orders of battle 1 July 1916.

86th Brigade	87th Brigade	88th Brigade
1st Battalion, Lancashire Fusiliers	1st Battalion, King's Own Scottish Borderers	1st Battalion, The Essex Regiment
1st Battalion, Royal Dublin Fusiliers	1st Battalion, Royal Inniskilling Fusiliers	1st Battalion, Royal Newfoundland Regiment
2nd Battalion, Royal Fusiliers	1st Battalion, Border Regiment	2nd Battalion, The Royal Hampshire Regiment
16th Battalion (Public Schools Battalion), The Middlesex Regiment	2nd Battalion, South Wales Borderers	4th Battalion, The Worcestershire Regiment

Pioneers 2nd Monmouths

The German front line is at the far end of the park. It skirted round a very important natural tactical feature known as Y-Ravine, which runs at the bottom from left to right (west-east) from the caribou. Y-Ravine greatly added to the strength of the German defences. Within its steep banks were deep dugouts. It also provided a relatively safe communication route to Beaumont-Hamel. This allowed the defenders to rapidly deploy reinforcements where and when necessary (See Figure 12.3).

Figure 12.1 Newfoundland Memorial.

Figure 12.2 Panorama from the viewing platform of Newfoundland Memorial Park. The British front line, No Man's Land and the German line are marked. The Memorial to the 51st Division is just beyond the latter position. It faces towards Beaumont-Hamel, which is a short distance beyond.

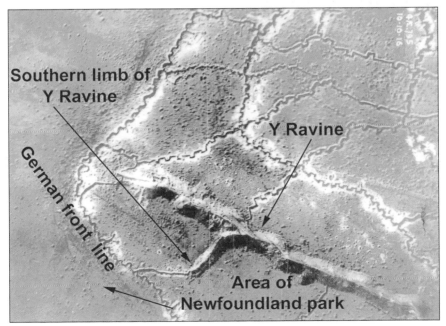

Figure 12.3 Aerial photograph of Y-Ravine circa 1916.

PLAN OF THE ATTACK, 1 JULY 1916

The attack objective was Beaumont-Hamel. The 29th Division (87th Brigade) occupied the British front line approximately 100 yards in front of you. It attacked down the slope towards Y-Ravine in the distance. The battalion lineup is shown in Figure 12.4. The 86th Brigade attacked further to the left over ground dominated by the Hawthorn Redoubt. The difficulties it encountered will be explained in Chapters 13 and 14.

A large mine was detonated beneath Hawthorn Redoubt at 0720, 10 minutes before zero hour. The VIII Corps barrage moved onto targets beyond the German front line leaving attacking troops at the mercy of hostile machine gun fire.

To your front right were men of the 1st Royal Inniskilling Fusiliers; directly to your front were the men of the 2nd South Wales Borders, with the 1st Battalion Border Regiment just behind them.

The assaulting battalions, on leaving their trenches, came under devastating direct and indirect machine-gun fire. Some of these were located in the high ground to the rear of Beaumont-Hamel and Beaucourt Redoubt was in

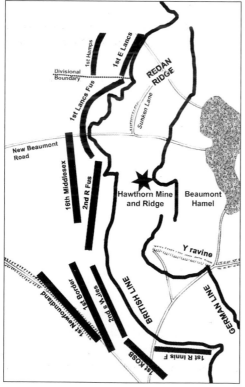

Figure 12.4
Situation of 29th Division on 1 July 1916. Y-Ravine was a natural feature that presented a major obstacle in this part of the battlefield.

the two o'clock position as you look from the caribou. There was a machine gun position in the Schwaben Redoubt (Chapter 8). Machine guns from the Hawthorn Redoubt, to your left, would have enfiladed the men as they rushed forward (See Figure 13.5).

Worse still were the machine guns aimed at gaps made by the British in their own barbed wire. This was done to allow troops to pass unimpeded through the obstacles. Men were cut down in great numbers. German accounts state that following the detonation of Hawthorn Mine, defending machine-gunners and riflemen took up position in readiness to meet the anticipated attack.

Waiting in reserve were the 1st Newfoundland Battalion and 1st Essex Battalion. The former had been stationed behind the lines at Louvencourt until the evening of 30 June. Approximately 800 men marched to reach the area of the St John's Trench by 2am on 1 July.

The 1st Border Battalion followed up the attack at 0805 but was halted by heavy fire. Confusion and uncertainty reigned during the heat of battle. Observed flares, which were later identified as German, were erroneously thought to have been the signal that the assaulting divisions had taken their first objective. Thus Major-General de Lisle (GOC 29th Division) gave the order at 0837 for the Newfoundland and Essex battalions to follow up the attack.

The Newfoundland Battalion began its advance at 0915 from its starting position in St John's Road. The men had to cross 250 yards of open ground

Figure 12.5 Photograph from site of Schwaben Redoubt. The trees mark the site of Newfoundland Memorial Park.

before even reaching the British front line. Making their way through their own barbed wire, the Newfoundlanders suffered heavy casualties before entering No Man's Land. One observer said:

> Steadily they advanced to the first line of wire under a heavy machine gun fire, first from the right and then from the whole front. Men began to drop, but not in large numbers, as the enemy had their guns trained on the gaps. The first gaps were reached and men fell in each of them. Those who could not go on did their best to clear the gaps of wounded, killed and equipment.[1]

Survivors continued down the slope in what was becoming an increasingly impossible task. By 0945, the Newfoundland Battalion had been practically destroyed. The wounded able to crawl back to their own line tried to do so for the remainder of the day; attempts were made to retrieve as many of the wounded as possible under cover of darkness. Every single officer who went forward was either killed or wounded. Fourteen officers and 219 men were killed or died of wounds; 12 officers and 374 other ranks were wounded; 91 other ranks were reported missing. When the roll call was taken only 68 men answered. Many had been hit before they reached their own front line and others were found lying between the gaps in the barbed wire. The surviving Newfoundlanders remained in the front line until relieved on 6 July.

The 1st Essex jumped-off, despite the intense machine-gunfire, at 1050; it was an impossible task and within twenty minutes it was called off. Those not killed or wounded returned to the jumping-off trench. A further attack by the 4th Worcesters (88th Brigade) against Y-Ravine was scheduled for later that morning, but such was the disarray in the trenches that they could not reach the front line when ordered to do so at 1130. The attack, not surprisingly, was cancelled.

It soon became clear that the Y-Ravine attack was a complete failure. Major-General de Lisle, observing from the Mesnil Ridge, called a halt to further attacks at 1300. Then at 1425, in anticipation of a German counter-attack, he ordered the front line to be secured. Total losses sustained by the 29th Division were 5,240 killed, wounded and missing.

1   Nicholson, G.L.W., *The Fighting Newfoundlander* (Montreal: McGill-Queen's University Press, 2006), p.270.

PLAN OF ATTACK, 13 NOVEMBER 1916

The 51st (Highland) Division attacked Beaumont-Hamel as part of an offensive by the British Fifth Army that became known as the Battle of the Ancre. In Chapter 11 you visited the Ancre valley where the 63rd Division attacked along the north bank to Beaucourt. The 51st Division moved into the line opposite Beaumont-Hamel in mid-October (See Table 12.2. for infantry orders of battle).

Standing at the Newfoundland Memorial, the battalion lineup (right to left) on 13 November were the 7th Gordon Highlanders and the 6th Black Watch (153 Brigade) attacking towards Y-Ravine. To their left, the 5th Seaforths and the 8th Argyll and Sutherland Highlanders (152nd Brigade), assaulted Beaumont-Hamel from Hawthorn Crater and the Sunken Road respectively (see Chapters 13 and 14).

Their objective was to take Beaumont-Hamel and ascend to the high ground to the left (north east) of the village. You might be able to discern the spire of the village church beyond the far side of Y-Ravine. The next stage of the assault was to advance and capture Munich and Frankfurt trenches (See Figure 12.6).

On the left of the 51st Division, the 2nd Division attacked across Redan Ridge whilst the 63rd Division attacked towards Beaucourt on the right. The plan was for the latter divisions to converge on Frankfurt Trench and press through and beyond the 51st Division. Our primary focus, however, will be on the events connected with Y-Ravine.

The starting point for this attack was Hunter's Trench, which was closer to the German line than on 1 July. From the Caribou Memorial you can see it running to the front from left to right about half-way across No Man's Land. However it is best seen by following the marked pathway to the German front line and Y-Ravine Cemetery. Note the front line previously occupied by the 29th Division on 1 July as you pass.

Table 12.2 51st Division infantry orders of battle 13 November 1916.

152nd Brigade	153rd Brigade	154th Brigade
5th Seaforth Highlanders	5th Gordon Highlanders	7th Argyll and Sutherland Highlanders
6th Seaforth Highlanders	7th Gordon Highlanders	4th Seaforth Highlanders
8th Argyll and Sutherland Highlanders	6th Black Watch	4th Gordon Highlanders
6th Gordon Highlanders	7th Black Watch	9th Royal Scots

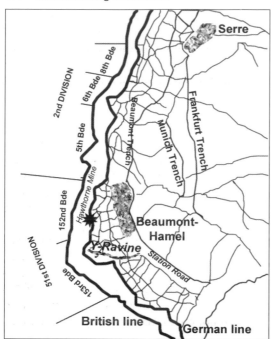

Figure 12.6
V Corps 13 November 1916.

Figure 12.7 Section of British front line on 1 July 1916. Note the crenellated trench pattern. This was done to contain the effect of exploding shells.

Walk until you reach the series of interconnected shell holes that are a couple of hundred yards in front of the original British front line. This was called Hunter's Trench and was the point from where the attack began on 13 November. This decreased the distance to Y-Ravine and lessened the time spent crossing No Man's Land being exposed to German machine gun and artillery fire.

Men from the 7th Gordon Highlanders and 6th Black Watch moved into Hunter's Trench on the night of 12/13 November at 0320, and were ready for the attack to jump off at zero hour the following morning. The attackers pressed forward at 0545 under cover of a dense fog that concealed the advance.

Continue along the pathway until you come to the shorter extremity of Y-Ravine, which is just behind the German front line trench on your immediate left. Gaze down into the depression. There were numerous German dugouts along this portion of the ravine. The 7th Gordon Highlanders and the right flank of the 6th Black Watch were held up by fire from this vicinity.

German resistance was fierce, with 300 to 400 defenders holding out and emerging to face the attacking British from the many deep dugouts; reserves were required to counter the threat. Bombing parties of two companies of 4th Gordon Highlanders (154th Brigade) were dispatched to enter Y-Ravine from both ends from where they eliminated pockets of resistance by painstakingly

Figure 12.8 Hunter's Trench was the starting position for the attack on 13 November. It was considerably closer to the German front line than British front line of 1 July.

Figure 12.9 The German front line trench still shows its depth and strength of defence almost 100 years later.

Figure 12.10 The short extension of Y-Ravine: dugout entrances were in the steep banks. The lengthy extension is amongst the trees. It provided a safe avenue to and from Beaumont-Hamel.

Figure 12.11 Y-Ravine: View from short extension.

clearing one dugout after another until resistance was overcome. Bombing parties of the 6th Gordon Highlanders were also sent to bomb German infantry inflicting casualties on the 6th Black Watch. There was fierce hand-to-hand fighting until the defenders were overwhelmed. Following this, the attackers pressed on to Station Road near Beaumont-Hamel.

The 51st Division had been allocated two tanks and by 1030 they moved on to assist with village clearance. Ground conditions were so poor that the cumbersome vehicles stuttered to a halt. One became stuck between the German first and second lines, the other reached the village.

51st Highland Division Memorial

Continue on until you reach the 51st (Highland) Division Memorial. Its base is carved from Rubislaw granite. The Highland figure is gazing towards Beaumont-Hamel. It was modeled after the likeness of Sergeant-Major Bob Rowan of the Glasgow Highlanders. It was sculpted by George Henry Paulin, and is described 'Bronze Statuette – Memorial to the 51st Highland Division at Beaumont-Hamel 1924'. Beneath is the Gaelic inscription: *La a'Blair s'math n Cairdean* or *Friends are good on the day of battle*. The monument was unveiled by Marshal Ferdinand Foch on 28 September 1924; the final words of his speech were "Sons of Scotland sleep in peace".

Figure 12.12
51st (Highland) Division Memorial.

Another memorial to the 51st Division is close by. The small wooden cross commemorates the Division's costly action at High Wood on 22/23 July 1916 (Chapter 7). Originally erected in the much-contested wood, its emotive inscription reads as follows:

This Cross is erected in memory of the Officers, NCOs and men of the 51st Highland Division who fell at High Wood July 1916.

Figure 12.13
51st Division:
Memorial cross
to the fallen on
22/23 July 1916.

There are three cemeteries within the boundary of Newfoundland Memorial Park. They are of particular interest because the overwhelming number of burials reflect two days' (1 July and 13 November) bloody fighting.

Hunter's Cemetery

This cemetery, once a large shell hole, contains the graves of 46 soldiers from the 51st Division of which forty-one are known. They died capturing Beaumont-Hamel. It has been suggested that the name originated from the Reverend Hunter who was attached to the Black Watch. All except two burials are from the Gordon Highlanders or Black Watch.

Hawthorn Ridge No 2 Cemetery

This cemetery was started by V Corps in early 1917. Originally designated 'V Corps Cemetery No. 12', it contains over 200 graves of which 149 are identified. The majority perished on 1 July. Seven men, however, were brought in and interred there after the armistice.

Figure 12.14 Newfoundland Memorial Park: the 51st Division Memorial is close to the position of the German front line. Hunter's Cemetery and Hawthorn Ridge Cemetery 1 are in the foreground.

Y-Ravine Cemetery

Y-Ravine Cemetery was established by V Corps in early 1917. Originally designated 'Y-Ravine Cemetery No.1', there are approximately 400 casualties interred here of which 275 are identified. Some 61 memorials to those believed to be buried here extend along the inner walls of the cemetery; 38 are from the Newfoundland Regiment.

Figure 12.15 Y-Ravine Cemetery.

Chapter 13

Hawthorn Redoubt,
1 July and 13 November 1916

Chapter 12 examined what happened to the 29th and 51st Divisions at Y-Ravine on 1 July and 13 November 1916. This chapter deals with the problems faced by these two divisions during attacks against a strongpoint called Hawthorn Redoubt. Situated in the northern part of their respective attacks towards Beaumont-Hamel the redoubt was a formidable all-around defensive position north of Y-Ravine and overlooking the famous 'Sunken Road'.

Leave Newfoundland Park from the car park and turn left onto the main (D73) road towards Auchonvilliers. Proceed a short distance to a right turn-off and follow the road to Hawthorn Ridge Cemetery No 1. Alternatively, if seeking a more adventurous route, proceed from Newfoundland Park to Auchonvillers.

Figure 13.1 Auchonvillers from the Newfoundland Park car park.

When you reach a signpost marking Auchonvillers, you will observe a flattened open area to the right near which is the entrance to a track once known as 'Old Beaumont Road', a former main route to the front line that can be cycled or walked upon with ease.

Proceed along the Old Beaumont Road to see old dugout tracings within the embankment of the sunken part of this road. It takes little imagination to perceive that they would have offered protection against German shellfire.

The track curves as it winds its way to join the New Beaumont Road. Approximately 100 yards before it joins the New Beaumont Road there is a right turn-off. Follow this to the top of the ridge and to the site of Hawthorn Redoubt. From there you will see Hawthorn Ridge Cemetery No 1. Go through the gate and to the opposite wall and gaze down toward the New Beaumont Road and its immediate environs. To your sharp right you will see a clump of tall tress which marks the position of Hawthorn Mine Crater. Indeed, trees now grow out of the base of what is a twin crater, the first and second detonated on 1 July and 13 November, respectively.

Taken from the cemetery wall, Figure 13.5 shows the line of the Sunken Road and Argyll and Sutherland Highlanders Memorial marking the former's approximate position. It is important to note that it is possible to see into the lower end of the Sunken Road from the Hawthorn Crater. The Germans stationed in Hawthorn Redoubt were able to do the same.

Figure 13.2 The entrance to the Old Beaumont Road; men began their journey to the front line along this road.

Figure 13.3 The Old Beaumont Road.

Figure 13.4 Hawthorn Mine Crater.

Figure 13.5 View of the Sunken Road from the site of Hawthorn Redoubt. It is possible to see into the bottom end of the Sunken Road from this position. Men from the 1st Lancashire Fusiliers attacked from here only to be struck down by machine gun fire. Redan Ridge is the high ground behind.

You also get an excellent view of Beaumont-Hamel Military Cemetery and the adjacent field, through which men of the 1st Lancashire Fusiliers advanced on 1 July. They jumped-off from the right-hand side of the embankment.

Looking in the opposite direction (south) towards Y-Ravine you will realise that a machine gunner ensconced in Hawthorn Redoubt could pour fire into troops attacking Y-Ravine. There were no trees in the vicinity on 1 July, but you can still discern the grassy slope leading down towards the ravine.

1 JULY

Given its elevated position, Hawthorn Redoubt had commanding views of the surrounding terrain over which the 29th Division would launch its attack. It had to be eliminated before any contemplated advance in this sector. It fell to the men of the 252nd Tunneling Company to construct a mine underneath the Redoubt. A shaft was dug to a depth of 75 feet and a tunnel approximately 1,000 feet in length was dug from behind the British front line near White City to the redoubt. The excavated soil and rock had to be carefully removed and deposited as far away as practical or very carefully camouflaged so as not to arouse enemy suspicion. The chamber was filled with 40,600 pounds of ammonal

Figure 13.6 Looking south towards Y-Ravine from Hawthorn Ridge Redoubt.

Although the original plan had been to detonate the Hawthorn Mine just prior to zero hour at 0730, Lieutenant-General Hunter-Weston (GOC VIII Corps) had other ideas. He wanted to discharge the mine four hours before the main attack in order to allow for the early seizure of the crater rims. General Rawlinson, who wanted all mines to be simultaneously exploded just prior to the infantry assault at 0730, denied Hunter-Weston's request. However, for reasons that remain unclear, the Hawthorn Mine was detonated ten minutes prior to zero. The resultant effect of this was the Germans defenders were alerted.

Everything within the mine's epicentre was completely destroyed. Tons of soil and rock descended killing and burying indiscriminately leaving a crater rim 18 feet high and 100 feet wide. The standard tactical response called for the attacking force to seize the nearer crater rim. As a rule, the enemy did exactly the same and occupied the other side of the crater to prevent complete occupation by hostile forces. Geoffrey Malins, an official war photographer, was in position to film the Hawthorn mine explosion on1 July (See Figure 13.7):

> Then it happened. The ground where I stood gave a mighty convulsion.
> It rocked and swayed. I gripped hold of my tripod to steady myself.
> Then, for all the world like a gigantic sponge, the earth rose in the air
> to the height of hundreds of feet. Higher and higher it rose, and with

Figure 13.7 I July 1916: photograph taken from Malins' position.

a horrible, grinding roar the earth fell back upon itself, leaving in its place a mountain of smoke. From the moment the mine went up my feelings changed. The crisis was over, and from that second I was cold, cool, and calculating.[1]

The Hawthorn Mine left a crater 300 feet wide and 40 feet deep. Companies of 2nd Royal Fusiliers, followed by 16th Middlesex, advancing to occupy the nearer rim of the crater, were targeted by German machine gunners from the far side of the gaping hole. These men were filmed by Malins from the site shown in Figure 13.8. The footage can be seen today in the iconic *Battle of the Somme* feature film first shown to the British public in August 1916.

The enemy rushed machine guns into position on the 18-foot high eastern lip just minutes after the mine explosion. The 2nd Royal Fusiliers were, at first, able to seize the opposite crater rim, but by the end of the day were forced back with heavy losses. Hawthorn Cemetery No 1, situated in the most tranquil of settings, is far removed the ensuing carnage of 1 July.

Generally the mines on the Somme in 1916 were of less value than they should have been. Hunter-Weston's compromise time of 0720 for the

---

I   Malins, G.H., *How I Filmed the War* (London: Herbert Jenkins Limited, 1920), p.162.

Figure 13.8 View from near Malins' position looking towards the field across which the 2nd Royal Fusiliers and the 16th Middlesex crossed on their way to Hawthorn Crater.

Figure 13.9 Hawthorn Cemetery No 1.

detonation of the Hawthorn Mine certainly warned the enemy of an imminent attack. His directive over the entire front of the 31st, 4th and 29th Divisions to move artillery fire away from the German front line to targets in the rear was a major contributory factor to the failure of the 29th Division attack on 1 July as was the failure of the Hawthorn Mine to result in the neutralisation of the Hawthorn Redoubt. As a result, German machine gunners were able to wipe out advancing troops all around them. The Hawthorn Mine on the 29th Division front was the only one north of the River Ancre on 1 July.

THE 51ST (HIGHLAND) DIVISION, 13 NOVEMBER 1916

On 13 November, the Hawthorn Mine was detonated for a second time. The start of the 51st Division's attack was signaled by the detonation of the mine at 0545 when 30,000 lb of ammonal exploded. The 5th Seaforths followed this up by overrunning the smoking crater before moving on to Beaumont-Hamel. This time there was no delay and the debris was still falling when they attacked the crater. The mine had been employed correctly as an integral shock weapon. An effective artillery barrage and immediate deployment of follow-up infantry helped to ensure the mine achieved its goal. From your position in Hawthorn Cemetery No 1, the men of the 5th Seaforths rushed towards the smoldering crater. The dark and foggy conditions made maintenance of direction difficult.

Jumping-off from the left flank in the Sunken Road, the 8th Argyll and Sutherland Highlanders advanced towards Beaumont-Hamel. The 5th Seaforths encountered uncut wire as they made their way toward their next objective. A reserve company of the 6th Gordon Highlanders was ordered forward to assist the now depleted ranks of the 5th Seaforths.

The German second line was breached. Two bombing squads from the 6th Gordons went forward and cleared the third German line. This allowed progress to be made towards the Green Line, which was just beyond Station Road (See Chapter 12). The fighting became so severe that it was impossible to reach the yellow line objective at Frankfurt Trench.

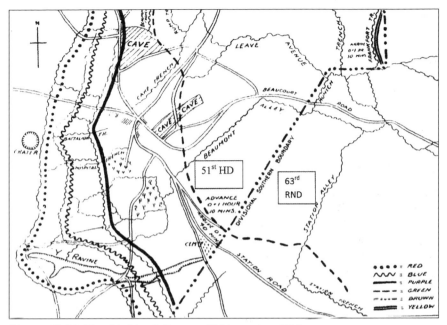

Figure 13.10 51st (Highland) Division 13 November 1916.

Chapter 14

The Sunken Road and Beaumont-Hamel, 1 July and 13 November 1916

THE ATTACK ON 1 JULY 1916

As previously explained, the British Fourth Army attack north of the River Ancre on 1 July 1916 was the responsibility of the 29th, the 4th and the 31st Divisions (which were collectively part of VIII Corps). The overall Commander was Lieutenant-General Sir Aylmer Hunter-Weston.

This chapter first deals with the attack which was made by the 86th Brigade of the 29th Division (its left flank) on 1 July. It takes you to the famous Sunken Road near Beaumont-Hamel. The 29th Division (GOC Major-General Beauvoir de Lisle) was a battle-hardened Regular army formation tasked with seizing Beaumont-Hamel.

Beaumont-Hamel was heavily fortified, containing many cellars in the remnants of the houses, deep dugouts and reinforced ruins surrounded by complex networks of barbed wire. There were also caves in the hill behind the village which offered additional protection. The Germans had the advantage of two years to strengthen the village defences until transformed into an almost impregnable fortress. The 29th Division infantry order of battle for 1 July 1916 is shown in Table 14.1, while the situation on 1 July is shown in Figure 14.1.

The 86th Brigade attacked on either side of what is now the D163. You can reach the jumping-off point either by making your way from Hawthorn Redoubt (See Chapter 13) or by leaving Auchonvillers and proceeding along the D163 towards Beaumont-Hamel. Prior to reaching the latter village, follow the left track to the Sunken Road. You will recognise it by its proximity to the Argyll & Sutherland Highlanders Memorial that marks its entrance.

Walk a few yards into the Sunken Road. This was actually in No Man's Land on 1 July. Stand adjacent to the memorial and face up the slight incline of the road. The British and German front lines ran parallel (right and left, respectively) to the Sunken Road just two hundred yards apart.

Table 14.1 29th Division infantry orders of battle 1 July 1916.

86th Brigade	87th Brigade	88th Brigade
1st Battalion, Lancashire Fusiliers	1st Battalion, King's Own Scottish Borderers	1st Battalion, The Essex Regiment
1st Battalion, Royal Dublin Fusiliers	1st Battalion, Royal Inniskilling Fusiliers	1st Battalion, Royal Newfoundland Regiment
2nd Battalion, Royal Fusiliers	1st Battalion, Border Regiment	2nd Battalion, The Royal Hampshire Regiment
16th Battalion (Public Schools Battalion), The Middlesex Regiment	2nd Battalion, South Wales Borderers	4th Battalion, The Worcestershire Regiment

Pioneers 2nd Monmouths

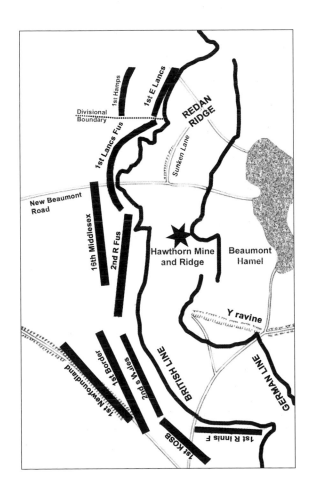

Figure 14.1
29th Division 1 July 1916.

Figure 14.2 Sunken Road: Argyll & Sutherland Highlanders Memorial.

Figure 14.3 General view up the Sunken Road adjacent to Argyll & Sutherland Highlanders Memorial. On 1 July No Man's Land ran parallel to the respective front lines. The British front line was to the left, approximately 75 yards away.

THE SUNKEN ROAD, 1 JULY 1916

The Sunken Road was the jumping-off point for the 1st Lancashire Fusiliers on 1 July. They had fought at Gallipoli in 1915 where six of its members were awarded the Victoria Cross in a single day. Their CO was Lieutenant-Colonel Meredith Magniac, a Regular Army officer commissioned into the Lancashire Fusiliers in 1899. A keen sportsman, he once played test match cricket for England. Equally keen on discipline, he accompanied the battalion to Gallipoli where he earned the respect of subordinates. Subsequent staff appointments were unequal to his personal disposition or taste, so he returned to his beloved battalion prior to the offensive. Taking up his post in the Sunken Road on 1 July, Magniac awaited zero hour with his men.

PLAN OF ATTACK

The village of Beaumont-Hamel was defended by the experienced 119th Württemburg Infantry Regiment (26th Reserve Division)) which had been there for almost two years. The attack plan was relatively straightforward – the entire village was to be secured. As part of the attack, a great offensive mine (See Chapter 13) had been dug beneath Hawthorn Redoubt. This was on the nearby Hawthorn Ridge which formed a promontory of elevated ground guarding the way to Beaumont-Hamel; it also held commanding views over most of the 29th Division sector. The Germans could see into the bottom of the Sunken Road from this position.

Face the main road from the Sunken Road entrance to observe Hawthorn Ridge from the 10 o'clock position. Behind you and upwards to the left as you face Hawthorn Ridge is Redan Ridge. Beaumont-Hamel is nestled between the two and thus protected. The plan was that following the detonation of Hawthorn Mine, the British would rush forwards to seize the crater rims. Note the clump of trees on the ridge top. This marks the mine crater site. Previously viewed from the German's position, you are now seeing what the men of the Lancashire Fusiliers would have seen that day.

WHAT HAPPENED HERE?

The Sunken Road, as previously explained, was in No Man's Land. Turn around and look up the slight incline with the main road directly behind you. The British front line was beyond the embankment to the left; the German line to the right. The German front line extended along the Redan Ridge, then dipped down the hillside to the left and across New Beaumont Road before ascending Hawthorn Ridge on the other side.

Figure 14.4 Hawthorn Mine Crater from the bottom of the Sunken Road.

Figure 14.5 Looking towards Beaumont-Hamel from Sunken Road edge; the ground on the left rises to Redan Ridge, Hawthorn Ridge is to the right. Beaumont-Hamel church steeple is discernible behind the trees between the respective slopes.

Neither the British nor Germans had possession of the Sunken Road, although from time to time both mounted night-time raids to take temporary control of it. The road was relatively exposed and its exact position known to both British and German artillery. On the night of 30 June, men of the 252nd Tunnelling Company dug a Russian Sap (a narrow underground trench with its turf roof remaining in place to conceal passage) from the front line to the Sunken Road. By 0300 on the morning of 1 July, men from B and D companies of the 1st Lancashire Fusiliers made their way through to the road, accompanied by supporting machine-gun and Stokes mortar teams. B Company was closest to you at the bottom end of the Sunken Road. The Sap exit, having been spotted by German observers, was shelled from 0700 with heavy losses amongst the waiting infantry.

The Sunken Road and the Battle of the Somme Film

Geoffrey Malins, the self-described "Official Kinematographer", wrote an emotive account of the Lancashire Fusiliers' last moments in the Sunken Road. He had met many of these men over the preceding days and on 30 June remarked:

> I turned and groped the way back to my shelter and, as I did so, our fire increased in intensity. This was the prelude to the greatest attack ever made in the history of the world, and ere the sun set on the morrow many of these heroes – the Lancashire Fusiliers, Royal Fusiliers, Middlesex, etc. – would be lying dead on the field of battle, their lives sacrificed that civilisation might live.[1]

Malins was asked by Magniac if he would film the men before the attack started. He agreed and with the help of a guide made his way through the British trenches in the early hours of 1 July, carrying his photographic equipment. Crawling on hands and knees into the Russian Sap, Malins descended into a murky passageway approximately 50 yards long, 5 feet high and less than a yard wide:

> Four men passed me, with horrible wounds; another was being carried on the shoulders of his comrades, one arm being blown clean off, leaving flesh and remnants of cloth hanging down in a horrible manner. The shells fell in front, overhead and behind us ... I went down, and crawled along over the dead bodies of some of our lads killed only a

---

1   Malins, G.H., *How I Filmed the War* (London: Herbert Jenkins Limited, 1920), p.152.

few minutes before. It couldn't be helped. Purgatory, in all its hideous shapes and forms, could not possibly be worse than this journey. It seemed years getting through that hellish fire.[2]

Look back from the main road towards the slight incline and look closely at the bank on your left. Through the vegetation you will see likely spots where the sap might have emerged (See Figure 14.6).

Rushing across the Sunken Road to avoid hostile fire from Hawthorn Redoubt, the Lancashire Fusiliers took cover under the opposite bank. The overgrown vegetation prevents one from seeing Hawthorn Crater.

Malins described how the men appeared when he emerged from the sap. The men were on the right-hand side embankment as you glance up the Sunken Road in the opposite direction from the main road. Malins was above the Lancashire Fusiliers, aiming his camera down towards the Auchonvillers – Beaumont-Hamel Road:

> I had to take every precaution in getting my machine in position, keeping it close to the bank, as a false step would have exposed the position to the Bosche, who would have immediately turned on H.E. shrapnel, and might have enfiladed the whole road from either flank. I filmed the waiting Fusiliers. Some of them looked happy and gay, others sat with stern, set faces, realising the great task in front of them ... Cheer up, boys," I shouted to the men as I parted from them, "best of luck; hope to see you in the village." "Hope so, sir," came a general chorus in reply.[3]

Malins' famous photograph of soldiers sitting with bayonets fixed corresponds exactly to where the members of the group of present day travellers are sitting (see Figure 14.7). The film clip is well-known and can found and can be easily viewed on-line by entering 'Somme Sunken Road' and 'Somme Lancashire Fusiliers'.

Carefully make your way up the embankment and look over the embankment towards Beaumont-Hamel. It was customary for men to have a tot of rum prior to an attack. George Ashurst, a surviving Lancashire Fusilier, later observed:

> We had all received a stiff tot of rum and some of the officers and NCOs had certainly had a very stiff tot, which was very plain to some of us who did not have access to the stone jar, or carry flasks.[4]

---

2   Ibid., pp.155-156.
3   Ibid., p.158.
4   Ashurst, G., *My Bit; A Lancashire Fusilier at War, 1914-18* (Marlborough: Crowood Press, 1987), pp.87-109.

Figure 14.6 View along the Sunken Road: Russian sap is on the left bank.

Figure 14.7 Visitors at the Sunken Road.

THE ASSAULT

The Hawthorn mine erupted at exactly 0720. The ground shook as the Lancashire Fusiliers, sheltering against the embankment, observed a flaming mass of debris hurl headlong into the clear blue sky. At exactly 0730 the whistles blew and the men of B and D companies jumped-off in the direction you are now facing. You can if you wish, clamber out of the Sunken Road in the same way. Beaumont-Hamel is less than 400 yards away. The attackers, having moved out of the Sunken Road, rushed across the field shown in Figure 14.8.

The men were now in the open and hopelessly exposed to German machine gun fire. To the right they would have been aware of the smouldering mine crater on Hawthorn Ridge. They might also have been aware of terrible machine gun fire coming from the smoking rim of the crater which was cutting them down relentlessly. The mine – detonated at 0720 – alerted the enemy of the imminent attack. The 2nd Royal Fusiliers and 16th Middlesex, having failed to secure the crater (Chapter 13) allowed surviving enemy machine-gunners to pour relentless enfilade fire into the advancing Lancashire Fusiliers. Most were cut down straight away or within seconds of leaving the Sunken Road (See Figure 14.8 for the area as it is today). Meanwhile, A and C Companies, attempting to enter the Sunken Road after zero hour, were also engaged by machine gun fire. Suffering numerous casualties, they never reached B and D. Corporal Ashurst recalled:

> Looking around, my God, what a sight. The whole road was strewn with dead and dying men. Some talking deliriously, others calling for help and asking for water. Some fit men like myself were bandaging wounded comrades or holding a water bottle to some poor fellow's lips.[5]

Lieutenant-Colonel Magniac reorganised his command whilst attempting to obtain reinforcements. Approximately 75 effectives were all that remained at 0815. The redoubtable CO, under cover of a renewed Stokes mortar barrage, ordered another, albeit unsuccessful, advance. Ashurst, joining in this second assault, was forced to seek shelter in No Man's Land:

> Hundreds of dead lay about and wounded men were trying to crawl back to safety; their heart rending cries could be heard above the rifle fire and bursting shells. As I lay there watching their painful efforts to get back to our line, I noticed these poor fellows suddenly try to rise to their feet and then fall in a heap and lie very still. Surely Fritz wasn't killing these unfortunate men. Shells whistled over my head

---

5   Ibid., pp.87-109.

Figure 14.8 Men of the 1st Lancashire Fusiliers passed over this field on their way to Beaumont-Hamel.

and dropped amongst the poor fellows, blowing dead men into the air and putting others out of their agony. As I gazed on this terrible scene I asked God to help me.[6]

Magniac was ordered to make a third attack during the early afternoon, but it was futile. Reserves proceeding up the Sunken Road suffered massive casualties before reaching the jumping-off point. Orders for this attack were subsequently cancelled. The position was evacuated following this debacle. One officer (with Ashurst as NCO) and 20 other ranks were left to hold the position overnight:

We collected our dead comrades, took off their identity discs, and placed the bodies together tidily. When darkness came at last stretcher bearers came swiftly across the open from our lines, collected the wounded and carried them back to our trenches ... All of the wounded were evacuated from the road during the night and dawn broke just one officer, myself and twenty men, along with the dead were in the road.[7]

6 Ibid., pp.87-109.
7 Ibid., pp.87-109.

Seven officers had been killed and 14 wounded; other rank losses amounted to 156 killed, 298 wounded and 11 missing. The Lancashire Fusiliers remained in the line until 3 July, after which they withdrawn for rest and refit.

CAPTURE OF BEAUMONT-HAMEL, 13 NOVEMBER 1916

The 51st (Highland) Division came to Beaumont-Hamel in mid-October 1916. Commanded by Major-General Montague Harper, it had been involved in failed attacks at High Wood the previous July and August. It was unfortunate that the 51st Division's badge bore the letters 'HD', as – in the aftermath of these previous failures – the Territorial Force formation acquired the unfortunate nickname 'Harper's Duds'. This perception was about to change. Our immediate concern is with the actions of the Division's component 152nd Brigade. A glance at Table 14.2 will give you the order of battle of the battalions making up the 152nd Brigade.

The 8th Argyll and Sutherland Highlanders attacked from the position around the Sunken Road, whilst the 5th Seaforths stormed Hawthorn Mine Crater. The first task was to capture Beaumont-Hamel and, passing through the village, occupy the high ground – including Munich and Frankfurt trenches to the northeast (See Chapter 12). As you stand facing Beaumont-Hamel, these formidable trenches were on the left-hand side beyond the village (See Chapter 15).

On the left, the 2nd Division would attack Redan Ridge, whilst the 63rd Division attacked Beaucourt and the high ground north of the Ancre Valley. Their first objectives gained, the divisions would launch a converging attack on Munich and Frankfurt trenches before pressing-on to the next objective (See Chapter 11).

Assigned objectives (See figure 14.10) were as follows:

* Green Line: Station Road and the village of Beaumont-Hamel;
* Yellow Line: Frankfurt Trench and intermediate (Pink, Blue, Purple) lines;

Table 14.2 51st (Highland) Division orders of battle 13 November 1916.

152nd Brigade	153rd Brigade	154th Brigade
5th Seaforth Highlanders	5th Gordon Highlanders	7th Argyll and Sutherland Highlanders
6th Seaforth Highlanders	7th Gordon Highlanders	4th Seaforth Highlanders
8th Argyll and Sutherland Highlanders	6th Black Watch	4th Gordon Highlanders
6th Gordon Highlanders	7th Black Watch	9th Royal Scots

Figure 14.9
51st (Highland Division)
13 November 1916.

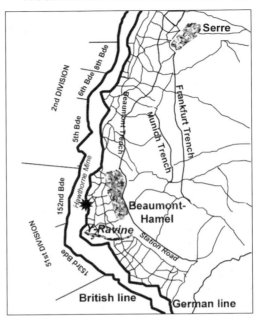

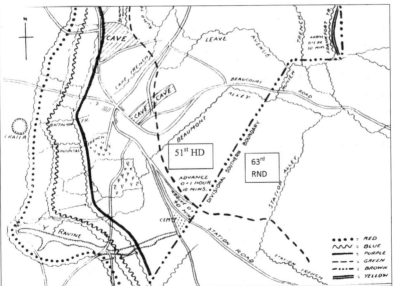

Figure 14.10 51st Division: map denoting (green, pink, blue, purple, yellow) objectives on 13 November 1916. Having captured Beaumont-Hamel, the division failed to make further significant progress. Munich and Frankfurt trenches remained in enemy hands. (Bewsher, F.W., *The History of the Fifty First (Highland) Division*. Edinburgh: William Blackwood and Sons, 1921, opposite p.114).

The attack was delayed by bad weather until 13 November. The preliminary barrage commenced on 20 October. Night patrols subsequently confirmed the barbed wire had been effectively cut. Battalions of 152 Brigade, their kilts sodden, encountered deep mud during the march forward, rear units only arriving at the jumping-off position less than two hours before zero hour giving them little time to get everyone in position. Men were instructed to avoid coughing for fear of alerting the enemy. Water bottles were to remain full to prevent the racket of half-empty bottles on the march. Taking up positions in the frontline, the assault battalions awaited the approach of zero hour:

> The most unimaginative loon, particularly if it is not his maiden fight, knows that there are many men assembled with him who in an hour or two will see the dawn break for the last time. The stoutest-hearted cannot help reflecting on what his own fate is to be, and on the odds for or against his being hit; if hit, will the wound be a "cushy" one, or will he, in the next few hours, be transformed from an able-bodied soldier into a permanent cripple or dead man?[8]

At 0545, the infantry advanced following the detonation of a second Hawthorn Mine. On the left flank of the 51st Division attack, the 8th Argyll and Sutherland Highlanders followed behind a creeping barrage at a pace of 25 yards per minute. This pace was difficult to maintain given the state of the ground. By 0750 the brigades were on the German third line, despite the fact that pockets of the enemy still held out. Bombing squads from the 6th Gordon Highlanders were sent to assist the 6th Black Watch at Y-Ravine and the 5th Seaforths who had encountered uncut barbed wire and suffered heavy losses (Chapter 13).

Proceed to Beaumont-Hamel by the main road as far as Station Road. This was the Green Line objective. The Argyll and Sutherland Highlanders advanced by this same route. They were also on the hillside to your left. The 5th Seaforths would have traversed the higher ground on the immediate right while making their way past Hawthorn Mine Crater and to the village beyond; the Green Line objective was just beyond Station Road.

Figure 14.11 shows Station Road and the village of Beaumont-Hamel. Taken from the rough track between Ancre Valley Cemetery and Beaumont-Hamel (see Chapter 11), you can also see the high ground where Munich and Frankfurt trenches were located. The 51st Division's final goal was, denoted by the latter position, the Yellow Line objective.

---

8 Bewsher, F.W., *The History of the Fifty First (Highland) Division* (Edinburgh: William Blackwood and Sons, 1921), p.111.

Figure 14.11 Station road and Beaumont-Hamel can be seen, with the positions of Munich and Frankfurt trenches indicated.

Make your way to the 51st Division Memorial Flagstaff near the foot of the narrow road leading up to Redan Ridge (See Chapter 15). Losses were heavy and it proved to be impossible to seize the Yellow Line objective. Meanwhile, the 2nd Division, having secured the enemy front line on Redan Ridge, failed to secure Munich Trench due to the all-pervasive mud and uncut barbed wire. Thus there would be no link up with the neighbouring 63rd Division now ensconced in Beaucourt.

A fresh attack was launched towards the Yellow Line on the morning of 14 November. The 7th Argyll and Sutherland Highlanders captured Munich Trench but consequent heavy losses forced them to withdraw. That night, the Royal Engineers dug 'New Munich Trench' some 150 yards west of its German-occupied namesake. Garrisoned before dawn, it provided a much-needed foothold north-east of Beaumont-Hamel.

Overall territorial gains were less than hoped for. Little advantage, despite retention of captured ground and an impressive haul of some 2,000 prisoners, was gained. The 51st Division sustained approximately 2,500 killed, wounded and missing, but its reputation as a shock division was made. Lieutenant-General E.A. Fanshawe (GOC V Corps) subsequently observed with fulsome praise:

The 51st Division leaves this Corps tomorrow to take a place in another part of the line, and although this postpones a well-earned rest, it is also a sure sign of the very efficient state of the Division that it should be called upon to do this by the army after its recent splendid fight. It is evident from the newspapers that all the world looks upon the capture of Beaumont-Hamel as one of the greatest feats in the war, and to those who know the ground and the defences it must be a marvellously fine performance.[9]

---

9   Bewsher, *The History of the Fifty First (Highland) Division*, p.125.

Chapter 15

Redan Ridge, 1 July and November 1916

Chapters 12, 13 and 14 explained what happened to the 29th Division and the 51st (Highland) Division on 1 July and 13 November 1916, respectively. Geographically, the village of Beaumont-Hamel nestles between Hawthorn Ridge to its south and Redan Ridge to its north. This chapter outlines what happened on the Redan Ridge, which was named after a group of front line trenches. The British 4th Division fought on Redan Ridge on 1 July and 2nd Division on 13 November. There are three ways you can get onto or near Redan Ridge from Beaumont Hamel.

First, you can walk (or cycle) to the top of the Sunken Road (see Chapter 14 for details) to the T-Junction near which is a rough track extending from right to left. This was known as 'Watling Street'. As you near the top you'll note it is no longer sunken, but quite open and exposed. In the lower part of the Sunken Road the men would have been offered some protection from German fire.

Stand at the junction of the Sunken Road with Watling Street. Turn right (Beaumont-Hamel is in your 3 o'clock position), to traverse Redan Ridge. There are three ridge cemeteries visible which are in what was No Man's Land, with the German front line just beyond. Whilst walking this pathway, you will pass the entrance to Redan Ridge Cemetery No 2. Alternatively, if you were to turn left onto Watling Street it would take you across the British front line and away from the Redan Ridge until the track joins the D919 road. This is the main road running between the villages of Mailly Maillet and Serre. Of these villages, Serre is in your 10 o'clock position from where you are standing.

The second route to Redan Ridge is by way of Beaumont-Hamel. Locate the 51st Division Memorial Flagstaff and climb the steep and narrow path – just by the memorial – out of the village. This will place you on the exposed and elevated ridge. Note Redan Ridge Cemetery No 2 on the immediate left.

The third route is via Waggon Road. Proceed downhill into Beaumont-Hamel – just past the flagpole – as far as a three-way junction. On your left is a secondary road labeled 'Waggon Road Cemetery' and 'Munich Trench Cemetery'. Turn left, following the signs; this route is the actual Waggon

Figure 15.1 View from the Hawthorn Ridge No 1 Cemetery looking over the Sunken Road, Watling Street and the Redan Ridge. Serre is to the left and Beaumont-Hamel is to the right.

Figure 15.2 Beaumont-Hamel flagstaff where you will see the entrance to the steep and narrow road that leads onto Redan Ridge.

Road of 1916. Follow it to Redan Ridge. Note the steep bank of Waggon Road in close proximity to Beaumont-Hamel which provided shelter from shell fire from the right.

Continue along Waggon Road until the bank becomes less pronounced and finally peters out. Note the exposed ground about. Further on the left is Waggon Road Cemetery and beyond that is Munich Trench Cemetery. British positions on 1 July were on the left. Figure 15.4 was taken from Frankfurt Trench Cemetery, which is on your right (See below).

FIGHTING ON I JULY 1916

One of the 4th Division's objectives was a German strongpoint known as Heidenkopf Redoubt (known as 'Quadrilateral' to the British). It can be found by proceeding along Watling Street as far as the main Mailly Maillet – Serre Road. Turn right and continue past Serre No 2 Cemetery. The formidable Heidenkopf was located in the field close to the main road and just beyond the cemetery.

From Waggon Road the position of the Heidenkopf may be reached by continuing to the end of the former before turning left onto the D919 towards Serre No 2 Cemetery.

Figure 15.3 Standing in Waggon Road and looking towards Beaumont-Hamel, you will see there is a steep bank offering protection from incoming fire from the left.

Figure 15.4 Panorama from the Frankfurt Trench Cemetery looking back across the Redan Ridge.

The second objective on 1 July was to secure the German front line on the forward slope of Redan Ridge. The 4th Division infantry orders of battle are shown in Table 15.1.

As the 4th Division closed in on Beaumont-Hamel from the Redan Ridge side (north), the 29th Division attacked (west and south) directly opposite the village. (See Chapters 12, 13 and 14).

Table 15.1 The 4th Division infantry orders of battle 1 July 1916

10th Brigade	11th Brigade	12th Brigade
1st Royal Warwicks	1st Somerset Light Infantry	1st King's Own
2nd Seaforths	1st East Lancashires	2nd Lancashire Fusiliers
1st Royal Irish Fusiliers	1st Hampshires	2nd Duke of Wellington's
2nd Royal Dublin Fusiliers	1st Rifle Brigade	2nd Essex

Pioneers 21st West Yorks

The Heidenkopf Redoubt/Quadrilateral

The Heidenkopf Redoubt/Quadrilateral was a strongly fortified position projecting from the German front line. This meant that it had an inherent weakness since it could be attacked from the front and from both sides. The Germans were fully aware of the unfortunate tactical predicament in the event of a concerted British attack. Although defended by a small German garrison, measures had been taken to ensure Heidenkopf's destruction by planting a demolition mine beneath the redoubt should it fall into enemy hands. This would be detonated after the garrison had withdrawn to safety.

Despite awareness of Heidenkopf's inherent weakness, the British had little understanding of the German defences along the Redan Ridge. The latter feature was well defended indeed and considered impregnable. The labyrinthine defensive system also included numerous deep dug outs. Such protection allowed them to survive the seven-day bombardment preceding the start of the battle.

The Attack

At 0730 on 1 July, the 1st Royal Warwicks (left flank of 4th Division) attacked the Heidenkkopf. The 1st East Lancashires, followed by the 1st Hampshires, advanced across Redan Ridge on the right flank. The 1st Royal Warwicks captured much of the Heidenkopf. The mine was prematurely detonated and

Figure 15.5 Heidenkopf Redoubt: the site was located in the field on the left. Serre Chapel is seen in the middle distance.

caused the retreating garrison many casualties. To the south, the barbed wire remained intact despite the heavy bombardment.

Companies of the 1st East Lancashires, advancing across No Man's Land, sustained heavy losses from fierce artillery and machine gun fire. German machine-gunners in Serre, in addition to those on Redan Ridge, also brought enfilade fire to bear from the left. (Glance up Waggon Road to view the village).

Ten minutes after zero hour, the support battalions advanced. Some progress was made, as the attackers pushed forward some 300 yards beyond the enemy front line. They sustained heavy casualties including many of their officers. The result was confusion and a serious breakdown of command and control as surviving defenders emerged from deep dugouts to engage the British from the rear. The attack's obvious failure was discerned by 0930 when the order was given to halt. The order came too late for the 2nd Royal Dublin Fusiliers. Following up the preceding waves, the unfortunate battalion suffered heavy casualties. Some were even mistakenly shot down by British troops ensconced in the Heidenkopf.

The attack failed for the same reasons as on other parts of the Somme battlefield:

> British artillery had failed to cut barbed wire obstacles. Defenders were alive and well in deep dugouts and very little of the much needed counter-battery fire had been provided.

FIGHTING ON 13 NOVEMBER 1916

This section covers the same territory described above; the best position – where you are now – is Waggon Road in the vicinity of Waggon Road and Munich Trench Cemeteries. The next major attack on Redan Ridge occurred on 13 November. The 2nd Division's objective was to capture Redan Ridge before pressing on to secure Munich and Frankfurt Trenches. The plan called for a link-up with the 63rd Division which would be closing on these trenches from the other side (south). See Table 15.2 for the 2nd Division infantry order of battle. Face up Waggon Road in the direction of Serre near Waggon Road Cemetery. Munich and Frankfurt Trenches were a few hundred yards on the right.

It rained heavily prior to the 2nd Division's assault. No Man's Land was thus transformed into a sea of deep clinging mud, while continual shelling turned the landscape into an impassable quagmire of water-filled shell holes.

On the morning of 13 November the infantry left their trenches and entered No Man's Land during the period prior to zero. At 0545 there was a massive British bombardment and the Hawthorn Mine was detonated for a second time. Weather conditions remained frightful. A dense fog hindered the

Table 15.2 2nd Division infantry orders of battle 13 November 1916.

5th Brigade	6th Brigade	99th Brigade
17th Royal Fusiliers	1st King's Liverpool	22nd Royal Fusiliers
24th Royal Fusiliers	2nd South Staffordshire	23rd Royal Fusiliers
2nd Oxford & Bucks Light Infantry	13th Essex	1st Royal Berkshires
2nd Highland Light Infantry	17th Middlesex	1st King's Royal Rifle Corps

Pioneers 10th Duke of Cornwall Light Infantry

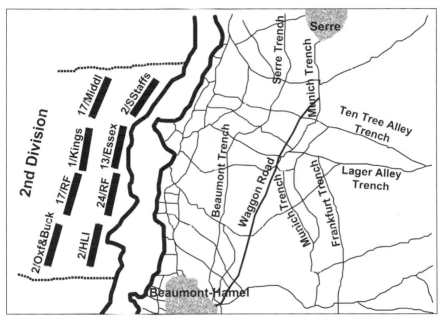

Figure 15.6 Redan Ridge 13 November 1916.

attackers as they negotiated No Man's Land. On the right, the 2nd Highland Light Infantry (HLI) and the 24th Royal Fusiliers made good progress, breaking through the enemy front line and capturing Beaumont Trench and many prisoners. The 2nd Battalion of the Oxfords and Bucks and the 17th Royal Fusiliers then moved forward. The plan called for them to follow up and capture Munich and Frankfurt Trenches.

Unfortunately the fog created orientation difficulties as the battalions tried to cross Redan Ridge; instead of moving forwards towards the German front line, the attackers inadvertently swung round to their left to move in a northerly direction. From your position close to the Waggon Road Cemetery, gaze up Waggon Road towards Serre. The attack was supposed to have crossed the road here from left to right. Advancing in the wrong direction, the assaulting battalions ended up behind Heidenkopf Redoubt before recognising the error. Some elements entered Munich Trench and an even smaller number reached Frankfurt Trench, but, lacking support, they had no option other than to withdraw across Waggon Road to Beaumont Trench.

The position of Munich Trench as you stand in the Waggon Road Cemetery area can be worked out with the help of Figure 15.6; it was just behind you (as indicated by the position of Munich Trench Cemetery). Crossing Waggon Road, it continued (left to right) for approximately 300 yards to your front. The distance between it and Waggon Road increased (in the general direction of Beaumont-Hamel) from Waggon Road Cemetery. Frankfurt Trench was beyond Munich Trench and ran parallel to it.

To understand Munich and Frankfurt Trenches and their relationship to Waggon Road see Figure 15.9.

Figure 15.7 View from Frankfurt Trench Cemetery looking (north) back across the Redan Ridge. Waggon Road and Munich Trench are marked by the position of Munich Trench Cemetery. From that point Munich Trench first came towards you and then ran parallel to and on the near side of Waggon Road.

Figure 15.8 View looking from the British line across Redan Ridge. Waggon Road Cemetery is on the opposite side of the road; Munich Trench and Frankfurt trenches ran almost parallel to Waggon Road.

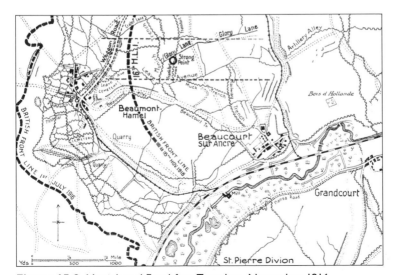

Figure 15.9 Munich and Frankfurt Trenches, November 1916.

Look in the opposite direction (west) of Munich Trench. Beaumont Trench was situated to your immediate front (See Figure 15.6).

On the left flank of the attack, the 2nd South Staffordshire (6th Brigade) advanced through the dense fog. On their left were men of the 3rd Division attacking towards Serre. Further confusion ensued when battalions of the latter division became disorientated. Indeed, instead of moving towards Serre, wayward companies moved to the right and merged with units of the 2nd Division on Redan Ridge!

The 3rd Division failed to capture Serre and survivors retired towards their original front line. Meanwhile, the 17th Middlesex of 2nd Division pushed forward to the first objective. The appalling confusion was almost certainly caused by the dense fog and terrible ground conditions.

The 3rd Division having been repulsed, watchful machine gunners in Serre brought enfilade fire to bear on the 2nd Division. To make matters worse an enemy pocket, still holding out in a section of Heidenkopf Redoubt, began to pour fire on the attackers.

Those men not killed or wounded made their way back to their own lines with the exception of a small party holding out in Beaumont Trench. The 99th Brigade (2nd Division Reserve) was now ordered forward to reinforce the shattered battalions of the 5th and 6th Brigades. Further attacks were launched on Munich Trench at 0630 on 14 November with no result. A counter-attack from Munich Trench forced the British back to Waggon Road. The 2nd Division's attack had been repulsed with heavy loss, the survivors, seeking shelter in Waggon Road, strengthening positions and holding on wherever they could.

On the night of 14 November, the Royal Engineers dug what they called 'New Munich Trench'. This was positioned about 150 yards on your side of the original Munich Trench (still in German hands) site, as you look forwards from Waggon Road Cemetery. Occupied before dawn, it provided a vital foothold on the high ground north-east of Beaumont-Hamel.

As explained earlier, the Heidenkopf was a key German defensive position and although much was in British hands on the morning of 15 November 1916, it was finally completely captured by the 22nd Battalion Royal Fusiliers after its occupying German defenders withdrew to Munich Trench.

British reinforcements were now brought forward to capture Munich Trench. Weather conditions remained poor and the fog thick. The attack, launched behind a creeping barrage, only got within 50 yards of the objective at a cost of approximately 3,000 killed, wounded and missing. The 32nd Division replaced the 2nd Division.

Stop for a moment and reflect on what happened thus far. The situation on 16 November was that Beaumont-Hamel had been captured by the 51st Division with no significant progress beyond the village itself. To the north, the 3rd Division failed to take Serre. The newly-arrived 32nd Division was now opposite Munich Trench. The next attack was planned for 0610 on 18 November. Weather conditions remained terrible, the prevailing fog and mud replaced by snow and subzero temperatures.

32nd Division's component 97th Brigade had four battalions opposite Munich Trench on a front of approximately about 1,000 yards. The 16th Highland Light Infantry (HLI) was situated at Brigade HQ less than half a mile to the west of Waggon Road. This battalion would play a major role in the forthcoming epic struggle to secure Frankfurt Trench.

The 16th HLI set off from White City at 2145 on 17 November. Two broad tapes had been laid on the ground by the 2nd King's Own Yorkshire Light Infantry (KOYLI) between White City and Waggon Road to guide the 16th HLI in the dark. Misfortune dogged the 16th HLI during the march forward when the all-important marker tapes were destroyed and guides provided by the 2nd KOYLI were killed by shellfire. Assisted by map and compass, it took the battalion six hours to reach Waggon Road, stumbling about the shell-scarred landscape before becoming exhausted through sheer effort.

The last of the 16th HLI reached Waggon Road at 0610 in the morning, just as the British artillery barrage began. Without respite and struggling through a blizzard, they crossed Waggon Road and advanced into the wintry distance towards Munich Trench some 200 to 300 yards away. The attackers were met by heavy machine gun fire and shelling and as a result most failed to reach Munich Trench. The British bombardment, having halted before they reached the objective, allowed the defenders to emerge from dugouts relatively unscathed.

At the left side (northern end) of the attack, the distance to Munich Trench was closer than towards the southern end, only being about 200 yards. The 16th HLI, rushing across this narrow divide, succeeded in capturing this portion of Munich Trench. They were soon joined by elements of the 11th Border Regiment. By late morning it was clear that the attack had failed; those who could were now making their way back to the British lines. The survivors of the 16th HLI, still secure in their captured section of Munich Trench, had other ideas! Two companies (D and C)) continued to press forward as far as neighbouring Frankfurt Trench. Their orders were to capture and hold it for an additional 48 hours. The small German garrison of approximately 50 men was duly captured and sent back, only to escape when their escorts were killed by shellfire. C and D companies were followed by surviving elements of other battalions that failed to get through.

By the evening of 18 November, Frankfurt Trench was occupied by roughly 50 fit men. Approximately 50 wounded, many of them mortally, had to be attended to by the increasingly isolated garrison. Placed into one of two nearby dugouts, they were cared for by a designated corporal. There were no medical resources available except for some simple bandages. Those fit enough to fight occupied the other dugout. Thus situated, the tiny party made

Figure 15.10 16th HLI graves in Frankfurt Trench Cemetery.

ready to defend Frankfurt Trench for the stipulated 48 hours. The reality was they were almost cut-off and too far distant for relief or reinforcement.

To defend themselves, they had only four Lewis guns, a limited quantity of small arms ammunition and an extremely limited stock of food and clean water. Temporary succor was provided by obtaining murky water (subsequently purified by boiling) from nearby shell holes and the gathering of food and ammunition from the dead who lay about in large numbers.

By dawn on 19 November they were ready to defend themselves. During the night they carried out repairs to their defences but to their surprise they did not come under German attack. It has been suggested in the history of the 16th HLI that this was because the enemy remained unaware the trench section was occupied.[1]

The Germans remained ignorant of the 16th HLI's presence until 20 November, when a local counter-attack supported by machine-guns and bombs was launched. The now isolated defenders put up a fierce resistance with rifles and Lewis Guns before the Germans fell back. The cost was, unfortunately, too high, many irreplaceable men joining the mounting ranks of killed and wounded. A sergeant belonging to the 11th Borders – one of the few members of other battalions that managed to make their way to Frankfurt

---

1　Chalmers, T., *History of the 16th Battalion The Highland Light Infantry* (Glasgow: John McCallum & Co., 1930), pp 60-61.

Trench – left the trench after dark to bring back reinforcements. Meanwhile, preparations to strengthen the trench were well underway for what would be the third day of a desperate defence.

The sergeant succeeded in getting through on 21 November. A heavy British barrage was then brought to bear on enemy occupied trench sections adjacent to the beleaguered pocket. There was no other immediate help for the surrounded men. Their already limited resources depleted even further, the garrison had to hold out for another night; spotted by British aircraft the following (22 November) day, morale rose following repeated signals that help was on the way.

A second bombardment of adjacent trenches occurred on the fifth day, but no relief force appeared to relieve men grimly determined to hold out for as long as possible. On the sixth day (23 November), the Germans launched a major attack. It was, against all odds, beaten off, the defenders' meagre manpower assets further reduced in the process.

The British rescue plan was entrusted to 300 men of the 16th Lancashire Fusiliers supported by the 2nd Royal Inniskilling Fusiliers. The forlorn hope stalled opposite Munich Trench with the loss of some 250 casualties. A few enterprising elements, having been able to penetrate beyond, subsequently

Figure 15.11 Frankfurt Trench Cemetery: graves of two Lancashire Fusiliers.

retired in the face of fierce fire from the enemy-occupied sections of Frankfurt Trench.

Frustrated thus far, the Germans brought up reinforcements on the following day (24 November). A message promising good treatment if they surrendered was dispatched to the contested trench section. Refusing to give in to the overwhelming force arrayed against them, the depleted companies of 16th HLI somehow managed to repel the subsequent enemy onslaught.

On day eight, a heavy attack retook the lost section of Frankfurt Trench. Only 15 men remained unwounded out of the original garrison of 50; there was no other option but surrender and face captivity. Their epic stand against overwhelming odds was duly recognized by a plethora (1 DSO, 11DCMs and 22 MMs) of bravery awards. The German brigade commander, on viewing the small number of prisoners, remarked: "Is this what has held up the brigade for more than a week?"

Table 15.3 16th HLI at Frankfurt Trench: Summary of Events.

Day Number	Key Events
1	Frankfurt Trench captured by two companies of 16th HLI.
2	Fresh water scarce; has to be collected from shell holes; ammunition stocks replenished from the dead.
3	Sergeant from 11th Border Regiment brings word of the surrounded garrison's plight; German assaults are blunted but relief attempts fail to get through.
4	Hopes raised by aeroplane signals requesting surrounded companies to hold out.
5	Second relief attempt fails; subsequent aeroplane message leaves defenders uncertain whether or not they should remain or fall back.
6	German attacks on front and flanks fail to make headway; eight prisoners taken by beleaguered garrison.
7	German efforts to negotiate surrender rebuffed. Further reinforcements are brought in.
8	Frankfurt Trench defenders overwhelmed in concerted attack; only 15 of 50 remain unwounded after capitulation.

The action at Frankfurt Trench was the last act of the campaign. The embattled 16th HLI, having fought on 1 July at Leipzig Redoubt, held the dubious distinction of fighting on the first and last days of the Battle of the Somme.

CEMETERIES OF INTEREST

Redan Ridge cemeteries are of interest as they are lasting legacies of 1 July and November. Two are in No Man's Land; one is situated near the German front line.

Redan Ridge No 1 Cemetery

The cemetery was developed in 1917 by V Corps as a result of battlefield clearances. It is located on the top of Redan Ridge and lies about midway between the British and German front lines. There are more than 154 graves, with 81 identified; most are from July or November 1916. The majority are from the 4th and 2nd Divisions.

Redan Ridge No 2 Cemetery

This triangular shaped cemetery is also situated in No Man's Land. The largest of the three, it contains the graves of 279 men of the 4th, 29th and 2nd Divisions.

Redan Ridge No 3 Cemetery

Situated in close proximity to the German front line trenches, Redan Ridge No 3 Cemetery contains 67 graves of 2nd Division soldiers of which 33 are unidentified. Twenty of the identified soldiers belonged to three battalions (24th Royal Fusiliers, 2nd Oxfordshire and Buckinghamshire Light Infantry and 2nd HLI).

Waggon Road Cemetery

Situated along the right-hand side of Waggon Road as you walk away from Beaumont-Hamel, Waggon Road Cemetery contains 195 graves of which 36 are unknown. The graves of Lieutenant George Neil Higginson (Row C 30), who led the attempt to rescue the cut-off men of the 16th HLI in Frankfurt Trench, and those of many Inniskilling Fusiliers who accompanied him are located here.

Munich Trench Cemetery

It is situated on left on a narrow patch of grass. It contains the graves of 126 men of whom 28 are unknown. Buried in Row A, Grave 12 is Captain Heinrich William Max Thomas (1st East Lancashire Regiment). Of German descent, he died on 1 July.

Frankfurt Trench Cemetery

Frankfurt Trench Cemetery can be found by following the Beaumont-Hamel – Beaucourt road for approximately 800 yards. Sign-posted on your left, a short walk will bring you there. Containing more than 150 graves, the majority are from the 16th HLI companies cut-off in Frankfurt Trench. Five Lancashire Fusilier burials represent their part in the failed rescue attempt. Two of their graves are shown in Figure 15.11.

Chapter 16

Serre, 1 July and 13 November 1916

This chapter begins by looking at the fortunes of the 31st Division, which was part of VIII Corps under the overall command of Lieutenant-General Alymer Hunter-Weston. The 31st Division (GOC Major-General Wanless-O'Gowan) was composed entirely of men who were volunteers in Kitchener's New Army.

There are, depending on mode of transportation, various ways of getting to the Serre battlefield. Take the D919 (Mailly – Serre Road) towards the latter village if travelling by car until you reach a signpost labelled 'Sheffield Memorial Park'. Follow this to Serre No 3, Queen's, Luke Copse and Railway Hollow Cemeteries. Alternatively, if travelling from Beaumont-Hamel (see Chapter 14), follow the minor road near the 51st Division Commemorative Flagpole over Redan Ridge. This will bring you onto the D919 near Serre.

If on bike or foot, follow the more adventurous route (as directed in Chapter 15) by way of the Sunken Road near Beaumont-Hamel. You will, on reaching the top of the road, arrive at a T-junction with a track (to the right) extending from the direction of Beaumont-Hamel. Turn left to enter what was known as Watling Street. This takes you through some comparatively rough terrain to the D919. Serre Road Cemetery No 2, the largest British burial ground on the Somme, is a short distance away. Be aware the track can be difficult in wet conditions!

Follow the CWGC signposts for approximately 300 yards to Sheffield Memorial Park. The track, although unpaved, is made up of firm stones suitable for vehicles. Its general route crosses what was once No Man's Land. The German line was to your right; the British front line was just within the tree line ahead of you.

There are three cemeteries situated in No Man's Land; the closest is Serre No 3. Queen's and Luke Copse Cemeteries are beyond, the latter in the distance.

The wooded area before you consisted of four separate copses covering a length of approximately 1,500 yards in 1916. Known from left to right as Matthew, Mark, Luke and John they have merged into one over the succeeding years. Proceed to the fence gate at the track's end. The British front line ran just within the treeline.

Figure 16.1 The end of Watling Street at the junction with the D919; the Ulster Tower and Thiepval Memorial to the Missing are visible in the distance.

Figure 16.2 Sheffield Memorial Park: the combined Matthew, Mark, Luke and John copses are in the distance. The British front line was at the edge of the wood. No Man's Land is delineated by the three cemeteries in the middle. The German front line is directly behind you, in front of Serre.

Figure 16.3 View from Serre No 3 Cemetery.

Figure 16.4 The British front line extended along the front of the trees. The Sheffield Pals, Accrington Pals and Leeds Pals occupied positions from right to left. The gate denotes the entrance to Sheffield Park.

Turn around and look towards Queen's Cemetery. This was No Man's Land. Serre is just over the horizon to your front.

ATTACK ON SERRE

The 31st Division was given the task of taking Serre. Battalions attacking from John Copse were given very specific instructions; they were to advance and then to turn 90 degrees to their left to form a defensive flank. This would protect the remainder of the attack as it pressed on to Serre.

The plan also included a diversionary attack by the 56th (London) and 46th (North Midland) Divisions (VII Corps), which were part of the Third Army (GOC General Sir Edmund Allenby). As explained in the introduction, the objective was the fortified village of Gommecourt approximately one mile from your present position. It was hoped this diversion would divert German resources away from the left flank of the Fourth Army. In the event, it did not do so, was very costly and made no useful contribution to the main offensive. The 46th and 56th Divisions sustained 2,455 and 4,314 casualties respectively.

Look to your right towards what was the 4th Division's line. Attacking over the exposed Redan Ridge on 1 July, its only measurable success was the partial capture of Heidenkopf Redoubt (See Chapter15).

SERRE

The Germans occupied Serre in autumn 1914. Approximately 1,000 yards from the British front line, this small rural community's formidable defences commanded a barely discernible slope which had to be traversed if the village was to be captured. The already established fortifications in and around the village were increased following a series of French attacks in June 1915. Construction of dugouts some 30 feet deep and use of existing cellars turned Serre into a seemingly impregnable fortress protected by thick barbed wire obstacles and three lines of trenches.

By July 1916 the German garrison had been in Serre for almost two years. Comprised of 4,200 effectives of the 169th Regiment (8th Baden) and 400 additional men of the 66th Regiment positioned to the north of the village (i.e. to the left as you look towards Serre), the south side of the village was covered by 400 men of the 121st Reserve Regiment. Supported by approximately ten machine gun companies, in terms of numbers and quality of the defences, Serre was going to present one of the toughest of challenges facing the British forces.

Turn around and pass through the gate. Looking to the right along the inside of the fence, you will note the shallow remnant of a British trench dug prior to 1 July. This is where the 11th East Lancashires (Accrington Pals) jumped-off that terrible day.

Figure 16.5 Trench from which the Accrington Pals set out on 1 July 1916.

Table 16.1 31st Division infantry orders of battle 1 July 1916.

92nd Brigade	93rd Brigade	94th Brigade
10th Btn East Yorkshire (Hull Commercials)	15th Btn West Yorkshire (Leeds Pals)	12th Btn York & Lancaster (Sheffield City)
11th Btn East Yorkshire (Hull Tradesmen)	16th Btn West Yorkshire (1st Bradford Pals)	13th Btn York & Lancaster (1st Barnsley Pals)
12th Btn East Yorkshire (Hull Sportsmen)	18th Btn West Yorkshire (2nd Bradford Pals)	14th Btn York & Lancaster (2nd Barnsley Pals)
13th Btn East Yorkshire (Hull T'others)	18th Btn Durham Light Infantry (Durham Pals)	11th Btn East Lancashire (Accrington Pals)

Pioneers 12 KOYLI (Halifax Pals)

The men in the 31st Division were volunteers from the North of England. Answering Lord Kitchener's 1914 call for volunteers, they came from Lancashire, Yorkshire and Durham. Often hailing from the same city or town, they enlisted into the celebrated 'Pals' battalions

THE PALS BATTALIONS AND KITCHENER'S NEW ARMY

Let us return to August 1914 to understand how these 'Pals' battalions came into existence. Lord Kitchener had just been appointed as Minister for War. Instinct told him the conflict would be long and costly. Possessing a professional military man's disdain for Territorial Force personnel, whom he regarded as 'weekend soldiers', he set about increasing the size of the British Army by calling for volunteers to serve three years, or the duration, with the so-called 'New Army'. Men volunteered from towns and cities throughout Great Britain and Ireland for what became known as 'Service' battalions.

New Army battalions were numbered in relation to the local Regular and Territorial battalions, but often went by another albeit unofficial title which indicated where the volunteers came from or the nature of their civilian employment; thus 'Accrington Pals' or 'Hull Commercials'. See Table 16.1 (31st infantry orders of battle) for examples of regimental, regional and employment connections of the Division's New Army battalions.

Pass back through the gate and face Serre. The battalions of the 31st Division faced the village as follows: To your left, looking towards Serre was the left flank of the attack. This was formed by the Sheffield, Barnsley and Accrington Battalions (94th Brigade). However, about half of the 14th York and Lancaster Battalion (2nd Barnsley Pals) were facing the left of the main assault (north) at the far end of John Copse.

The 12th Battalion York and Lancaster Battalion (Sheffield City) was between John and Luke Copse and the 11th East Lancashire Battalion (the Accrington Pals) were on their right as far as Matthew Copse. They would attack Serre head on. The men from Hull were the 10th, 11th, 12th, 13th Battalions East Yorkshires (92nd Brigade). These battalions were held in reserve and played no part on 1 July. Their turn came later on 13 November 1916. To your right, men from the 15th West Yorkshire (Leeds Pals) were preparing to go over the top. Behind were the 16th and 18th West Yorkshires (1st and 2nd Bradford Pals). The 18th Durham Light Infantry remained in immediate reserve to the rear. They would attack Serre from the southwest. The German front line, directly in front, was approximately 400 yards away.

SERRE, 1 JULY 1916

The seven-day bombardment increased in intensity prior to the attack. The earthquake-like tremor and accompanying roar of Hawthorn Mine (Chapter 13) reverberated through the massed ranks of the 31st Division as zero hour approached. Following this, battalions of the 31st Division entered No Man's Land via five Russian saps while VIII Corps gunners adjusted the barrage. Meanwhile, waves of assault infantry clambered out of their trenches to enter No Man's Land only to encounter uncut hostile barbed wire cleverly laid out in open V-shaped channels. The deadly trap was set when enemy machine-gunners sprayed these tempting avenues of approach with devastating effect. Concealed artillery pieces added to the mounting losses.

Look straight ahead; the attackers were about 100-150 yards in front when the German artillery-shelled No Man's Land and the British front line.

Figure 16.6
31st Division 1 July 1916.

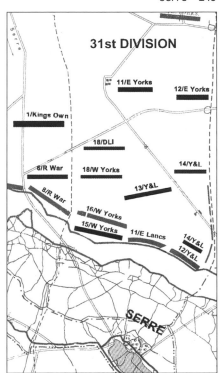

Figure 16.7 View from the Accrington Pals' trench across No Man's Land towards the barely discernible incline leading up to Serre.

The British bombardment had moved onto the German second line trenches and beyond by this time. This allowed the defenders to emerge from dugouts and manhandle machine-guns into position prior to zero hour.

The assaulting battalions rose to their feet at 0730. Murderous machine gun fire and artillery fire made progress almost impossible. The 12th York & Lancaster Battalion (Sheffield City Pals) had been out into No Man's Land the night before and had laid white marker tapes as a guide for the assaulting companies. Unfortunately, they all but disappeared in the bombardment. Confronted by unsuppressed machine-gun fire, the Sheffield Pals and other battalions of the 93rd and 94th Brigades suffered a grim fate and consequent appalling casualties. Many of the wounded sought protective shelter in shell holes or tried to return to the front line. More than 2,000 casualties killed, wounded and missing were sustained during a thirty minutes holocaust of shot and shell.

Captain Arnold Bannatyne Tough, the son of an Accrington family doctor, was a dental surgeon living and working in the town. Responding to Kitchener's appeal, he enlisted in the Accrington Pals. His company, marching forward with full equipment during the night of 30 June/1 July, traversed wet fields and waded through muddy communication trenches to get to their positions from base. Prevailing good spirits waned after an encounter with mass graves and wooden crosses prepared in advance for anticipated losses. Reality set in as even the most unimaginative recognised the fate that awaiting the Battalion. The Accrington Pals arrived at the front line at 0240, just five hours before zero hour.

Tough led the first wave into No Man's Land at 0720 but was wounded almost immediately he left the trench. Zero hour: Tough rose again only to be wounded a second time. Pressing on regardless, he sustained a third and fatal shot through the head. His gravesite (Row D, number 62) can be found in Queen's Cemetery.

Leading the second wave was Captain Harry Livesey who was a director of the family textile manufacturing business in nearby Blackburn. Enlisting with the local Pals he followed Tough's first wave into No Man's Land. At 0730 he stood up, revolver in one hand and walking stick in the other, to follow Tough's company. On the latter's death, Livesey assumed command and rallied the survivors. Pressing on through gaps in the barbed wire, Livesey led his men into the enemy front line trench. Revolver in hand, he gunned down five Germans before taking charge of a trench section. Last seen trying to return

Table 16.2 Brigade Casualties.

Brigade	Casualties
94th	2,000
93rd	1,950

Figure 16.8
Captain A.B. Tough was killed in the
vicinity of these cemeteries.

to the British front line, Livesey vanished and was never seen again. He is commemorated (Pier and Face 6 C) on the Thiepval Memorial to the Missing.

Lieutenant G. Gorse (one of Livesey's subordinates) subsequently wrote home to tell of his company commander's exploits:

> Livesey, who commanded, will I believe be recommended for the V.C.; a very gallant officer, he was hit in the arm getting over the parapet, hit in the chest half-way across, hit in the head on the German wire, and he got into the German trench, cleared a part of it and held it till he was hit in the face by a rifle-grenade, and died.[1]

A few managed to get beyond the German front line. Last seen advancing in the direction of Serre, they disappeared from view and were never seen again. Accrington Pal Will Marshall recollected:

> They [German machine gunners] were just sweeping across; men were falling at either side, all around you. By time I got... there were three of us of my section left, there were only three of us left and by time we'd got to where... we'd only gone about a hundred yards, must have done, to German front line and they'd gone back you know, they weren't there.

1   http://www.pals.org.uk/livesey.htm

And there were just them three of my section left. They were Calvert and another fella; I forget his name at present, and me. Well there weren't another man within 60 yards at either side of us, so you can tell how many had fell up to getting there and we'd only gone about a hundred yards. We'd got to like a big shell hole, where a shell had dropped before, previously, and Calvert and this other boy went round to left and I went round to right of this shell hole, we didn't go down it. Well another shell came and I were blown off my feet flat on to floor. Didn't know where I were for a minute and when I picked myself up, these two were missing. There were only me there. A bit of shrapnel had hit me in th'arm and another piece just across my leg. Well there weren't another soldier within sixty or seventy yards either side of me then.[2]

The Serre attack was a disastrous failure. Still in reserve, 92nd Brigade remained uncommitted to avoid unnecessary losses and as a ready reserve against a possible enemy counter-attack. The 31st Division remained in the line for three more days until relieved on 4 July. Its combined casualties amounted to more than 4,500 killed, wounded and missing. Brigadier General Hubert Conway-Rees (GOC 94 Brigade) subsequently wrote:

As I said before, the attack began at 7.30am, but ten minutes before zero our guns opened an intense fire. I stood on top to watch. It was magnificent. The trenches in front of Serre changed shape and dissolved minute by minute under the terrific hail of steel. Watching, I began to believe in the possibility of a great success, but I reckoned without the Hun artillery. This ten minutes intense bombardment combined with the explosion of twenty tons of dynamite under the Hawthorn Redoubt near Beaumont-Hamel must have convinced any enemy observer that the attack was in progress &, as our infantry advanced, down came a perfect wall of explosive along the front trenches of my Bde & the 93rd. It was the most frightful artillery display that I had seen up to that time and in some ways I think it was the heaviest barrage I have seen put down by the defence on any occasion. At the time this barrage really became intense, the last waves of the attack were crossing the trench I was in. I have never seen a finer display of individual and collective bravery than the advance of that brigade. I never saw a man waver from the exact line prescribed for him. Each line disappeared in the thick cloud of dust & smoke which rapidly blotted out the whole area. I can safely pay a tribute also to the

---

2   http://www.pals.org.uk/marshall.htm

bravery of the enemy, whom I saw standing up in their trenches to fire their rifles in a storm of fire. They actually ran a machine gun out into No Man's Land to help repel the attack.

I saw a few groups of men through gaps in the smoke cloud, but I knew that no troops could hope to get through such a fire. My two staff officers, Piggott and Stirling, were considerably surprised when I stopped the advance of the rest of the machine gun company and certain other small bodies now passing my Headquarters. It was their first experience of a great battle & all that morning they obviously found it difficult to believe that the whole brigade had been destroyed as a fighting unit. Messages now began to pour in. An aeroplane reported that my men were in Serre. The Corps and the division urged me to support the attack with all the force at my disposal. I was quite sure that we had not got anyone into Serre except a few prisoners, but the 93rd Bde on my right reported that their left had got on, whilst the 4th Division beyond them again claimed the first four lines of German trenches & were said to be bombing down our way. It was obviously necessary to attempt to get a footing in the German front trenches to assist these two attacks. The hostile barrage had eased off by now & was no longer formidable so I ordered two companies of the 13th York & Lancs to make the attempt. I did not know that the German barrage was an observed barrage, but thought it was probably mechanical. As soon as this fresh attack was launched down came the barrage again. When people had recovered from the unbalancing effect of this disaster, I was asked whether I recommended making an attack with the 92nd Bde. I said "no", very decidedly. General Ingles came over to see me early in the afternoon and a member of the corps intelligence branch arrived. I gave the whole lot a lecture on the situation as I saw it and at last convinced my own staff that the whole attack was a terrible failure.[3]

BATTLE OF THE ANCRE, 13 NOVEMBER 1916

The Serre sector remained comparatively quiet until 13 November. The 3rd Division took over the section of front you are standing in in preparation for its part in the Battle of the Ancre. British perceptions (Chapter 9) of a weakened and depleted enemy led to the decision to launch another offensive to the north. The preparatory barrage opened on 11 November. With more guns than on 1 July, the bombardment targeted barbed wire obstacles, dugouts and hostile batteries.

---

3   http://www.johndclare.net/wwi3_rees.htm

The 3rd Division jumped off to attack Serre from the trench line where you now stand. Taking up positions on the night of the 12/13 after a long and laborious march, 76th Brigade was on the left and 8th Brigade on the right; 9th Brigade was behind (near La Signy Farm and La Touvent Farm Ridge) in reserve. The Hull Pals (31st Division) were to the north in John Copse. Held in reserve on 1 July, they were part of the approximately 8,000 men awaiting the arrival of zero hour.

At 0500, the attackers moved out into No Man's Land concealed by the thick fog. Visibility being limited to no more than a few feet, they lay down in the mud. The area had not changed much since July, but the Germans, relying on their barbed wire and machine guns, had rebuilt their defences. Worse was to come. Pressing forward, the attackers encountered rotting corpses; disturbing reminders of 1 July. There they lay, decayed and eaten by rats, some entangled in barbed wire. Heavy rain transformed the ground into a quagmire of mud increasingly difficult to negotiate. By 0900 the dissipating fog revealed another costly failure. Once again as on 1 July, men were unable to penetrate the barbed wire; bogged down by mud and wire it was impossible to get through.

Little progress was made on the left where the attackers were struck by a devastating German counter-barrage. To the right, the 10th Royal Welch Fusiliers and the 1st Gordon Highlanders penetrated as far as the enemy fourth line, while on the left, the 13th East Yorkshires (92nd Brigade) progressed as far as the third line before being shelled-out in a tragic friendly-fire incident that reduced the attackers to a mere handful subsequently captured by the enemy.

Orders to halt the attack were dispatched at 1700; the fighting was over. The 9th Brigade, in divisional reserve, remained uncommitted. Situated to the rear of the 8th and 76th brigades, it remained in place as an available reserve. Casualties sustained by the the 3rd and 31st Divisions amounted to 2,816: the 76th Brigade 1,074; the 8th Brigade 927 and the 92nd Brigade 815. Major contributing factors to the reverse were failure to cut the German barbed wire obstacles combined with the muddy conditions.

Serre was never taken. It was not until 21 February 1917 that a patrol of 21st Manchesters discovered the Germans had evacuated the fortress village as a necessary preliminary to the withdrawal to the Hindenburg Line (See Chapter 17).

A JOURNEY AROUND THE BRITISH FRONT LINE

The Sheffield Memorial Park commemorating the Sheffield City Battalion (12th York and Lancaster Battalion) opened in 1936 despite the fact that these trenches were actually occupied by the Accrington Pals on 1 July. Note the various memorials and large shell holes. Many men were killed here before reaching the front line. For example, the 2nd Barnsley Pals lost 30% of its effectives prior to 'hopping the bags'.

Sheffield City Pals Memorial

The Accrington Pals Memorial is constructed of Nori bricks from Accrington. Dedicated in 1991, it commemorates men of the 11th East Lancashire Regiment.

The Chorley Plaque commemorates Y Company 11th East Lancashire Regiment.

The Burnley Pals Memorial commemorates the men of Z Company 11th East Lancashire Regiment.

Unveiled in 1998, the Barnsley Memorial is a black marble structure dedicated to the Barnsley Pals (13th and 14th York and Lancaster).

A wooden cross commemorates Private Albert Bull of Sheffield City Battalion. Discovered in March 1928, his body lies in Serre Road No 2 Cemetery (Grave: XIX E 16).

Railway Hollow Cemetery contains 107 graves of which 44 are unidentified. It also contains the graves of two French soldiers killed in 1915. The ground hereabouts was once home to a narrow gauge railway concealed by the natural contours from inquisitive German eyes.

Serre No 3 Cemetery

Serre No. 3 Cemetery contains 81 graves and four memorials to men believed to be buried within its confines. West Yorkshire Regiment burials predominate.

Queen's Cemetery

This cemetery contains the graves of 311 men (131 unidentified) who died between July and November 1916 and February of 1917. A great many Accrington Pals, including Captain A.B. Tough, are buried here.

Luke's Copse Cemetery

This cemetery has 72 burials (28 unidentified) of which Sheffield City Battalion predominates. A memorial to 2nd Suffolks commemorates losses on 13 November.

Figure 16.9 Large shell crater 50 yards behind the British front line.

Figure 16.10 The Sheffield City Pals Memorial is a substantial brick archway.

Figure 16.11 The Accrington Pals Memorial is a brick wall constructed with Nori bricks and was dedicated to the 11th Battalion East Lancashire Regiment in 1991.

Figure 16.12 The Chorley Plaque commemorates Y Company of the 11th East Lancashire Regiment.

Figure 16.13 Memorial to the Burnley Pals Company of the 11th East Lancashire Regiment.

Figure 16.14 The Barnsley Memorial, dedicated to the Barnsley Pals (13th and 14th York and Lancaster), was unveiled in 1998.

Figure 16.15 The Accrington Pals trench; the wooden cross is a private memorial to Private Albert Bull.

Figure 16.16 Railway Hollow Cemetery: a small gauge railway passed through here in 1916.

Chapter 17

Concluding Remarks

From the Line

Have you seen men come from the Line,
Tottering, doddering, as if bad wine
Had drugged their very souls;
Their garments rent with holes
And caked with mud
And streaked with blood
Of others, or their own;

Haggard, weary-limbed and chilled to the bone,
Trudging aimless, hopeless, on
With listless eyes and faces drawn
Taut with woe?

Have you seen them aimless go
Bowed down with muddy pack
And muddy rifle slung on back,
And soaking overcoat,
Staring on with eyes that note
Nothing but the mire
Quenched of every fire?

Have you seen men when they come
From shell-holes filled with scum
Of mud and blood and flesh,
Where there's nothing fresh
Like grass, or trees, or flowers,
And the numbing year-like hours
Lag on drag on,
And the hopeless dawn

Brings naught but death, and rain
The rain a fiend of pain
That scourges without end,
And Death, a smiling friend?

Have you seen men when they come from hell?
If not, ah, well
Speak not with easy eloquence
That seems like sense
Of "War and its Necessity!"
And do not rant, I pray,
On ' War's Magnificent Nobility '!
If you've seen men come from the Line
You'll know it's Peace that is divine!
If you've not seen the things I've sung
Let silence bind your tongue,
But, make all wars to cease,
And work, and work for Everlasting Peace!

Roderick Watson Kerr MC 1893-1960
*(With grateful thanks to Neil Kerr for permission to
reproduce his Father's poem)*

The Battle of the Somme began on 1 July and ended with a final action on 18 November. It had lasted for four and a half months. It began on a beautiful warm and sunny summer morning and ended in a snowy wasteland of frozen mud. Fought between the villages of Serre in the north and Montauban in the south, a distance of approximately twelve miles, the plan had been for the British Fourth Army to breach the German defences between the two villages. Had this been achieved, the Reserve Army would exploit the breakthrough towards Bapaume. Following this, the cavalry were tasked with keeping German reinforcements at arm's length whilst assisting the Fourth Army's general advance to the north and northeast. The reality was different. The great campaign on which such high hopes were placed petered out in the frozen November landscape around Munich and Frankfurt Trenches. The maximum depth of penetration into German-held territory was less than six miles. Bapaume remained well out of reach three miles behind the enemy front line. Territorial gains from July to November 1916 are shown in Figure 17.1.

The British had employed no fewer than 44 divisions, including 10 predominantly Regular Army Divisions, 25 mainly New Army (Service) Divisions,

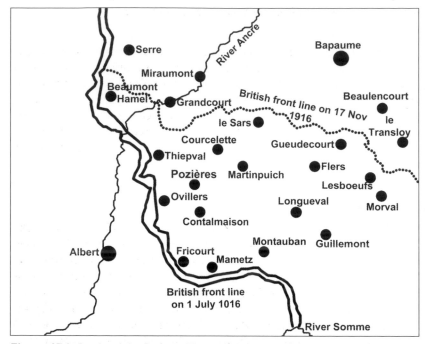

Figure 17.1 Battle of the Somme: Territorial gains July–November 1916.

8 Territorial Divisions and 1 primarily Naval Division. Fifty-eight percent of divisions were New Army. These latter, by and large, were composed of 1914 volunteers. Many joined up in a wave of patriotic fervour. Some enlisted to escape grinding poverty. Others joined to be with their pals. The Dominion contribution to the 'big push' amounted to four Australian and four Canadian Divisions, 1 New Zealand Division and a South African Brigade.

The British Army sustained approximately 432,000 casualties, of which some 150,000 were killed or died of wounds. Death came in many forms: a storm of machine gun bullets; bayonet, bomb or a solitary shot from a sniper's rifle; but because the Great War was first and foremost an artillery war, most fatalities were the result of high explosive or shrapnel shells.

One hundred thousand British soldiers were so seriously wounded that they never served again. Many remained unfit for civilian life. With some notable exceptions (e.g. the 9th and 15th (Scottish) Divisions, both of which suffered heavy casualties at Loos in 1915) the Battle of the Somme was the first time that most of the New Army Divisions were involved in serious fighting. At the close of the campaign, the once inexperienced volunteers had slowly transformed into battle-hardened veterans. The hard-won experience would reap tactical dividends throughout the battles of 1917-18.

FAILURE OF THE ARTILLERY ON THE SOMME

While the outcome of Great War battles depended on good artillery support some historians[1] maintain that Generals Haig, Rawlinson and Gough failed to appreciate this. Overall, the artillery barrage which preceded the attack on 1 July was inadequate despite the expenditure of 1.7 million shells. The deployment of too few guns over too great an area provided a density of fire which, with a small number of exceptions (e.g. in the southern part of the battlefield at Mametz and Montauban), failed to achieve the three objectives of artillery action: (i) the destruction of barbed wire, (ii) destruction of defenders, and (iii) destruction of enemy artillery.

Destruction of barbed wire

German barbed wire remained intact to a large extent. High explosive shells, a vital necessity for barbed wire destruction, were available in limited stocks throughout most of 1916. To have the desired effect, it was necessary for shells to explode instantaneously on contact with the wire or ground surface. In 1916, British high-explosive shells penetrated the ground before exploding, rendering them relatively ineffective. Approximately one third were faulty and failed to explode. They litter the Picardy battlefields to this day. Thus on 1 July, the attackers confronted intact barbed wire which was a major contributing factor to the consequent enormous casualties.

A specially designed fuze (Nr. 106), which instantaneously exploded at the slightest contact, was developed and tested during the latter stages of the battle before entering service in early 1917. From then onwards the BEF had a reliable means of eliminating barbed wire obstacles. Furthermore, because it exploded on the surface, it did not result in crater formation, allowing the infantry to advance more easily. The Battle of the Somme was the catalyst for this important technological development, but experience gained by trial and error cost many thousands of casualties.

Creeping Barrage

A primitive creeping barrage, first used around Montauban and Mametz on 1 July, provided some protection for the advancing infantry. To begin with, it used only shrapnel and it moved too fast, leaving the infantry behind and vulnerable to enemy fire. High explosive was first employed on 14 July and proved much more effective in causing fear and destruction than shrapnel.

---

1   See Prior, R. & T. Wilson, The Somme (New Haven: Yale University Press, 2005). p.49-56, 119-129, 140.

Smoke was added to creeping barrages by Arras in 1917 and helped to conceal advancing infantry. More sophisticated and carefully orchestrated creeping barrages were developed which completely confused and terrified the enemy. Such developments brought the realisation that it was not necessary to destroy German soldiers in deep dugouts, merely to keep their heads down by neutralisation fire till the infantry arrived to deal with them. A prolonged preliminary bombardment was unnecessary, and a hurricane bombardment commencing five minutes before zero hour would achieve this necessary aim while at the same time retaining the important element of surprise.

Counter-Battery work

Used only in a most elementary form on the Somme in 1916, counter-battery work assumed an increasingly important role during 1917. By the time of the Battle of Amiens in August 1918, counter-battery work overwhelmed German artillery, partly by destroying guns and partly by rendering them unusable. Some 450 of 500 German guns taken were captured intact.[2] Excellent air reconnaissance, improved mapping and important scientific developments by William Bragg[3] in localising German gun positions by sophisticated sound ranging techniques all contributed to success, as well as improved artillery and ordnance design and manufacture.

The Somme was the catalyst for these developments, although existing artillery in 1916 could have been put to better use if the British high command had realised the importance of effective gun distribution over a broad front. This would have allowed the artillery to challenge enemy batteries firing in enfilade from the right and left flanks. Suppression of these guns and consequent reduction of losses in men and material might have increased the chance of success in the attack centre. Persistent small-scale attacks on narrow fronts ensured maximum casualties for minimum gain. Even the half success of 14 July, where supporting artillery was four times greater than 1 July, did not subsequently alter the wasteful pattern of piecemeal assaults.

THE GERMANS AND THE SOMME

German losses on the Somme are difficult to assess. Estimates of killed, wounded and missing vary considerably, but they probably sustained about

---

2   Prior, R. & T. Wilson, *Command on the Western Front* (Oxford: Blackwell, 1992), pp.320-321.
3   Griffith, P., *Battle Tactics of the Western Front* (New Haven: Yale University Press, 1996), p.153.

237,000 casualties.[4] Given that German strategy on the Somme was to remain on the defensive, it is no surprise they sustained fewer casualties. Prior and Wilson make the point that the arguments put forward by Edmonds in the British Official History "in a desperate attempt to establish some equivalence between British and German figures" have been effectively demolished.[5] They are of the opinion that Churchill's figures are an accurate representation of German losses.

On the face of it, the balance in terms of men lost favoured the Germans, but this was not the whole story. The Germans attacked the French at Verdun on 21 February 1916 with the aim of bleeding France white of manpower. The campaign lasted until the following December. German losses amounted to approximately 337,000; French 377,000. The latter's commitment meant that the BEF took on the primary role during the Somme offensive. The strategic aim would be relief of the pressure on Verdun. The strategy ultimately proved successful when operations against the Meuse fortress area were terminated the following August.

There is another important factor to consider. The Battle of the Somme had an extremely adverse effect on German morale despite the fact that they had sustained fewer casualties. Captain von Hentig, a staff officer with the Guard Reserve Division graphically described the Somme as 'the muddy grave of the German field army' on account of the unbelievable state of the ground:[6]

> Our positions were well built, but the ways up to them, and the positions themselves were filthy and muddy due to the autumn weather and continuous rain. The shell holes became ponds; the trenches kept falling in, and were transformed into swampy channels. The deep dugouts were often filled with water.[7]

GERMAN WITHDRAWAL TO THE HINDENBURG LINE

In late February 1917, British forces at Serre discovered that enemy positions opposite were very quiet. On 24 February, three patrols from the 21st Manchester Regiment reached the western outskirts of Serre without encountering the enemy. By the evening of 24 February, there was every indication of an enemy withdrawal along the entire front. Orders were issued for an advance

---

4   Churchill, W.S., *The World Crisis, 1911-1918* (London: Odhams Press Ltd., 1938), pp.961-968.
5   Prior, R. & I. Wilson, *The Somme* (New Haven: Yale University Press, 2005), p.301.
6   http://www.johndclare.net/wwi2_Simkins_Somme.htm
7   Duffy, C., *Through German Eyes: the British on the Somme in 1916* (London: Weidenfeld and Nicolson, 2006), p.325.

through Serre the following morning. The retirement was but a prelude to a general withdrawal (codenamed 'Alberich') from the salient between St Quentin and Arras during 9 February-20 March 1917.

Towards the end of October 1916, a Royal Flying Corps patrol reported the construction of new defence works east of the battlefield. This was the first glimpse the Allies had of the "Siegfried Stellung" or, as it became known to the British, the "Hindenburg Line". A defensive position of great strength and depth, its occupation shortened the German front by 40 to 45 kilometres and released 13 divisions into reserve.

Those killed on 1 July as well as subsequent actions could now be buried. Many of the remains were reduced to blackened skeletons picked clean by rats. This was a far cry from the far off days of 1914 when thousands of volunteers answered Kitchener's call, fearful they would be too late to participate in the great adventure.

A Dead Man

A dead man dead for weeks
Is sickening food for lover's eye
That seeks and ever seeks
A fair one's beauty ardently.

Did that thing live of late?
That sodden thing of ebony head
With empty holes that gape?
Good God! Will I be that, when dead?

Perhaps those blackened bones
Were subtly fashioned hand and wrist
That made sweet violin tones,
Or held a face till lips had kissed.

Perhaps-but no! It cannot be,
This thing is but a heap of slime-
A hideous mockery-
The man is safe from rotting time.

Then stick it underground!
It is a thing for spades, not tears;
And make no mourning sound,
And finished, have no fears.

For, glowing in some woman's heart,
He lives embalmed, unchanging, and apart!
Then come! Let's kill the memory of this place-
O friends! It has a hideous ebony face.

Roderick Watson Kerr MC 1893-1960
(With grateful thanks to Neil Kerr for permission to reproduce his
Father's poem)

The human cost of the Somme was great. Figure 17.3, taken at Y-Ravine Cemetery, is a poignant reminder of the heroism and sacrifice. A young Newfoundland soldier lies buried next to a Gordon Highlander. The former was killed on 1 July. His immediate neighbour, hailing from the tiny fishing village of Buckie in Scotland, died on 13 November. Seaside dwellers in life, they are united forever by death and a shared resting place.

Figure 17.2 Queen's Cemetery Serre.

Figure 17.3
Y-Ravine Cemetery:
Newfoundlander and
Gordon Highlander in
the same grave.

Selected Bibliography

Adams, B., *Nothing of Importance: A Record of Eight Months at the Front with a Welsh Battalion October 1915 to June 1916*. London: Methuen, 1917.

Alexander, J., *McCrae's Battalion. The Story of the 16th Royal Scots*. Edinburgh: Mainstream Publishing, 2003.

Arthur, M., *Symbol of Courage: A History of the Victoria Cross*. London: Pan MacMillan, 2005.

Arthur, W.J. & I.S. Munro, *The Seventeenth Highland Light Infantry, Record of War Service 1914-1918*. Glasgow: David J. Clark, 1920.

Ashurst, G., *My Bit: A Lancashire Fusilier at War, 1914-18*. Marlborough: Crowood Press, 1987.

Bean, C.E.W., *Anzac to Amiens: A Shorter History of the Australian Fighting Services in the First World War*. Canberra: Australian War Memorial, 1946.

Bewsher, F.W., *The History of the Fifty First (Highland) Division*. Edinburgh: William Blackwood and Sons, 1921.

Blunden, E., *Undertones of War*. London: Richard Cobden-Sanderson, 1928.

Chalmers, T., *History of the 16th Battalion The Highland Light Infantry*. Glasgow: John McCallum & Co., 1930.

Christie, N., *The Canadians on the Somme*. Winnipeg: Bunker to Bunker Books, 1996.

Churchill, W.S., *The World Crisis, 1911-1918*. London: Odhams Press, 1938.

Conan-Doyle, A., *The British Campaign in France and Flanders, 1916*. London: Hodder and Stoughton, 1918.

Crozier, F.P., *A Brass Hat in No Man's Land*. London: Jonathan Cape, 1930.

Cuttel, B., *One Day on the Somme*. Peterborough: GMS Enterprises, 1998.

Dyer, G., *The Missing of the Somme*. London: Hamish Hamilton, 1994.

Duffy, C., *Through German Eyes: The British and the Somme, 1916*. London: Weidenfeld & Nicolson, 2006.

Edmonds, J.E., *Military Operations France and Belgium 1914 Volume I* London: Imperial War Museum Department of Printed Books, in association with Battery Press, Nashville, 1996 (reprint).

Ewing, J., *The History of the Ninth (Scottish) Division*. London: John Murray, 1921.

Gough, H., *The Fifth Army*. London: Hodder & Stoughton, 1931.

Graves, R., *Goodbye to all that*. London: Jonathan Cape, 1929.

Griffith, P., *Battle Tactics of the Western Front*. New Haven: Yale University Press, 1996.

Jones, S., *Underground Warfare 1914-1918*. Barnsley: Pen & Sword, 2010.

Lewis, C., *Sagittarius Rising*. London: Peter Davies, 1936.

Malins, G.H., *How I Filmed the War*. London: Herbert Jenkins, 1920.

Masefield, J., *The Old Front Line*. London: William Heinemann, 1917.

Nicholson, G.L.W., *The Fighting Newfoundlander*. Montreal: McGill-Queen's University Press, 2006.

Prior, R. & T. Wilson, *Command on the Western Front*. Oxford: Blackwell, 1992.

Prior, R. & T. Wilson, *The Somme*. New Haven: Yale University Press, 2005.

Sassoon, S., *The Complete Memoirs of George Sherston*. London: Faber & Faber, 1937.

Scotland, T. & S. Heys, *War Surgery, 1914-18*. Solihull: Helion and Company, 2012.

Seton, B., & J. Grant, *The Pipes of War*. Glasgow: Maclehose, Jackson & Co., 1920.

Shakspear, J., *The Thirty-fourth Division 1915-1919*. London: H.F. & G. Witherby, 1921.

Sheffield, G. & J. Bourne, *Douglas Haig: War Diaries and Letters 1914-1918*. London: Weidenfeld & Nicolson, 2005.

Sparrow G. & J.N. MacBean Ross, *On Four Fronts with the Royal Naval Division*. London: Hodder & Stoughton, 1918.

Stewart, J., & J. Buchan, *The Fifteenth (Scottish) Division*. Edinburgh: William Blackwood and Sons, 1926.

Index

INDEX OF MILITARY FORMATIONS/UNITS

INDEX OF PEOPLE

INDEX OF PLACES

INDEX OF MISCELLANEOUS TERMS

Related titles published by Helion & Company

Stemming the Tide: Officers and Leadership in the British Expeditionary Force 1914
Spencer Jones (ed.)
ISBN 978-1-909384-45-3
(hardback)

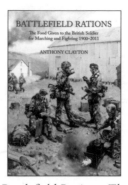

Battlefield Rations: The Food given to the British Soldier for Marching and Fighting 1900-2011
Anthony Clayton
ISBN 978-1-909384-18-7
(paperback)

Wars, Pestilence & the Surgeon's Blade: The Evolution of British Military Medicine and Surgery during the Nineteenth Century
Thomas Scotland & Steven Heys
ISBN 978-1-909384-09-5
(hardback)

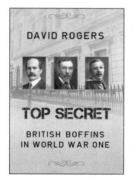

Top Secret: British Boffins in World War One
David Rogers
ISBN 978-1-909384-21-7
(paperback)

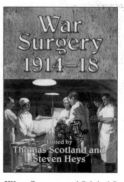

War Surgery 1914-18
Thomas Scotland & Steven Heys (eds.)
ISBN 978-1-909384-40-8
(paperback)
ISBN 978-1-909384-37-8
(eBook)

HELION & COMPANY
26 Willow Road, Solihull, West Midlands B91 1UE, England
Telephone 0121 705 3393 Fax 0121 711 4075
Website: http://www.helion.co.uk